Grandpa,

Enjoy the "Great Ones"

Merry Christmas - 1994

Love, Chris & Geoff

Great Ones

NFL Quarterbacks from Baugh to Montana

Beau Riffenburgh
and David Boss

Designed by
David Johnston

VIKING

VIKING
Published by the Penguin Group
Viking Penguin, a division of
Penguin Books USA Inc.,
40 West 23rd Street
New York, New York 10010, U.S.A.
Penguin Books Ltd.,
27 Wrights Lane,
London W8 5TZ, England
Penguin Books Australia Ltd.,
Ringwood
Victoria, Australia
Penguin Books Canada Ltd.,
2801 John Street,
Markham, Ontario, Canada L3R 1B4
Penguin Books (N.Z.) Ltd.,
182-190 Wairau Road,
Auckland 10, New Zealand

Penguin Books Ltd.,
Registered Offices:
Harmondsworth, Middlesex,
England

First published in 1989 by
Viking Penguin, a division of
Penguin Books USA Inc.
Published simultaneously in Canada

10 9 8 7 6 5 4 3 2 1

Copyright © 1989 National Football
League Properties, Inc.
All rights reserved

Library of Congress
Cataloging in Publication Data
Riffenburgh, Beau
Boss, David
   Great Ones: NFL Quarterbacks
From Baugh to Montana / Beau
Riffenburgh and David Boss
     p.   cm.
   ISBN 0-670-82979-X
   1. Football players—United
States—Biography. 2. Quarterbacks
(Football). 3. National Football
League. I. Title.
GV939.A1R52   1989
796.332'092'2—dc20
[B]

Edited by John Wiebusch
Designed by David Johnston
Type set in Helvetica

Printed in Japan by Dai Nippon

Dedicated to Pete Rozelle

Contents

"I don't think the job has ever been created that is more difficult than being a quarterback in the NFL. It requires more time, work, and dedication than any other profession I know. Its demands are both physical and mental. If there's a weakness anywhere in the quarterback's preparations, he lets down not only himself but his teammates, coaches, and fans. The pressures are simply overwhelming, especially today when the entire NFL schedule is televised and with the possible financial implications of every game. It takes a special kind of person to really make it as a successful NFL quarterback."

Quarterback Sonny Jurgensen
Pro Football Hall of Fame

Pro Football's Field Generals

The special people who have played quarter-back in the NFL have come in all shapes, sizes, and appearances—from Roman Gabriel, a big man who once was given a shot to make the Los Angeles Rams as a defensive end, to Eddie LeBaron, who could have been a dwarf at Disneyland; from Joe Namath, whose shoulders sloped down, to Sonny Jurgensen and Bill Kilmer, whose midsections sloped out; from Earl Morrall, who would have done the U.S. Marines proud, to Kenny Stabler, who might have come from a flower child's commune.

They have performed as disparately as they have looked. There was Johnny Unitas, whose composure and play-calling gave an operational definition to the terms poise and cool, and Norm Van Brocklin, whose fiery behavior belied his controlled approach to the game. Fran Tarkenton made mobility part of his game, but Dan Marino enjoys running with the ball about as much as he does losing. John Elway, who has a rocket launcher for a right arm, can throw a tight spiral more than 70 yards while backpedaling; Jim McMahon, who has only the remains of a once-healthy right shoulder, throws wounded ducks …and frequently no one knows where they'll fly.

Freewheeling, hell-raising Bobby Layne, who was known to draw game-winning plays in the dirt on the field, was an explosive, butt-kicking leader about whom teammate Yale Lary once commented, "When Bobby said block, you blocked. When Bobby said drink, you drank." On the other side of the ball in many of those 1950s championship games was Otto Graham, the stoic automaton who never would have dreamed of interfering with head coach Paul Brown's play-calling or of breaking training rules the night before a game, and who, when he became a coach himself, carried on most of his mentor's strict rules and regulations.

Quarterbacks are like fingerprints—no two have been alike. Some have been magnificent physical specimens, such as Randall Cunningham; some marvelously gifted in every facet of the game, such as Sammy Baugh; some supremely cerebral, such as Frank Ryan; some intensely dedicated, such as Bart Starr; and some simply unwilling to take "no" for an answer, in a game, such as Roger Staubach, or in a career, such as Len Dawson.

There are many differences but one thing is common: Above and beyond all else, the quarterback must be the leader of the pack.

It has been said the quarterback is the most important player on a football team. But such a statement is much the same as simply pointing out that Texas is a large state or that the weather can have an effect on the economic life of America's farms. It doesn't begin to tell the whole story.

Quarterback certainly is the most demanding position in pro football. As Paul Brown succinctly summed it up, "Playing quarterback in the NFL is so tough it is almost impossible. The basic reason is that there is a degree of excellence required that is so high it is virtually unimaginable to outsiders."

So who is this quarterback, and what is it he actually does? Why does it seem that a quarterback is so many different things to so many different people?

A quarterback is more than the person who runs the offensive show. He is more than a passer, more than a runner, and more than a man who has the stamina to take hits on play after play in every football game. What the quarterback achieves goes beyond simple physical and athletic ability.

The mental parts of the game—intelligence and perception—are important, but they aren't the most important things. The key qualities are the intangibles that coaches like to talk about, the undefined parts of a quarterback that place him a cut above other athletes.

Typically American in concept, winning is the bottom line, the one thing that coaches keep coming back to when they talk about the classic quarterbacks. The good ones can be the best passers or the most outstanding athletes, but the great ones are the winners.

"People ask me about the great quarterbacks, and I'll start with Otto Graham," says Howard (Red) Hickey, the former head coach of the San Francisco 49ers and one of the most innovative thinkers in NFL history. "He won a lot of championships. Then I mention Layne and (Bob) Waterfield and Van Brocklin, and, before I can get to Unitas or Starr, they'll say, 'But you left out Y.A. Tittle.' And I'll say, 'But Tittle never won a championship.' That's what a championship quarterback does—wins championships. Now Layne, as bad as he looked throwing the ball, was a winner. You'd work him out and you wouldn't want him. But you'd want him in your huddle. Players feel that way about a quarterback. When a leader is in there, they'll perform, they'll go."

The players, especially the quarterbacks, agree. Or, as writer Mickey Herskowitz once put it, "Winning is a quarterback's excuse for living."

When talking about quarterbacks, start with Otto Graham.

Bobby Layne, perhaps the greatest leader of them all, put it simply:

"There's something about being a winner. It's the greatest thing in the world. You can spot a winner by the way he walks down the street. When you're a winner, you don't have to park the car yourself; somebody parks it for you."

The biggest winners frequently haven't been the best at anything else, and the critics—usually coaches or writers from other cities—have enjoyed pointing out their supposed deficiencies. Layne certainly wasn't a classic passer. Van Brocklin received a knock in the opposite direction.

"Van Brocklin can throw—period," Chicago Bears owner and head coach George Halas once said. "In the full sense of the word, he is not a professional football player."

Even Terry Bradshaw, who was elected to the Pro Football Hall of Fame in 1989, wasn't safe from criticism. There was a supposition that he wasn't smart enough to be a big-time quarterback. "Bradshaw couldn't spell 'cat' if you spotted him the 'C' and the 'T'," Dallas linebacker Thomas (Hollywood) Henderson said before the Cowboys played the Steelers in Super Bowl XIII. So Bradshaw went out and spelled D-O-O-M for the Dallas defense, passing for 318 yards and winning the game's most valuable player award.

Of course, every team can't win a championship, so every quarterback—no matter how talented—isn't the ultimate winner. But there are other attributes that every successful quarterback must have and a number of things that each must be able to do.

"Being a leader, that is, having total control of your team, is above all the one asset a quarterback must have," Vince Lombardi, the late Hall of Fame coach of the Green Bay Packers and Washington Redskins, once said. "A coach would like a skilled play-caller, a slick ball-handler, and an accurate passer, but the one thing that is a must is having a person who can control any situation he is presented with. This requires a player with confidence, a forceful personality, and the ability to make his teammates believe in him as much as he does himself.

"If you look at the great quarterbacks through the years—Graham, Layne, Unitas, Starr—they have all had that in common. In the final moments of a close game, they could take total control of their own team, which usually meant taking control of—and winning—the game."

Today's coaches agree that leadership is the key to any quarterback.

"Leadership comes from the man himself," says Dallas quarterbacks coach Jerry Rhome, himself a former great college quarterback at Tulsa. "He has to be tough-minded. Just how he talks in the huddle can make a difference. It's going to show if he doubts himself. Players around him will feel it. He has to let it be known that he intends to keep plugging away right to the bitter end of the

game, regardless of the situation. You can't expect the others to live and die out there with you if you don't project that."

As Rhome says, a quarterback has to control the situation, whether it's firing a team up or keeping it in line. Once, when Johnny Unitas was a youngster with the Baltimore Colts, the team's star fullback came into the huddle and said, "We need two yards for a first. I'll carry the ball through the left side of the line and we'll get it." Unitas replied coldly, "You'll carry the ball when I tell you to. *I'm* the boss out here."

That kind of force and control requires an unfaltering confidence, something that can be inborn or hard-earned. Few have had more natural confidence than Norm Van Brocklin, who joined the Rams at the height of Bob Waterfield's career. Finding himself on the bench behind one of the best quarterbacks of all time, Van Brocklin chafed at his initial inactivity. Finally he approached Rams head coach Clark Shaughnessy and demanded a chance to play, arguing he was the best passer the Rams had. When he did get in, he backed up his words.

It took years for Bart Starr to build that kind of confidence.

"Confidence comes from success, and when I went to Green Bay, I had come off a year in which I had no success at all, my senior year at Alabama when I sat on the bench," Starr says. Indeed, his entire college career had been up-and-down. He was selected by the Packers in the seventeenth round of the 1956 draft.

"My first couple of years I knew I wasn't playing well, and I began to wonder if I was able to," Starr says. "I didn't often consider getting out of football, but I frequently wondered why I was wasting my time in it. That changed under Lombardi."

Midway through the 1959 season, Lombardi's first in Green Bay, the coach made it clear that Starr was his starting quarterback. He slowly built the young man's confidence while he tutored him in quarterbacking skills. The result was a new Starr, who led the Packers to the NFL Championship Game in his second season as a starter. He went on to take the Packers to five NFL titles, and led the NFL in passing three times.

Nowhere was the confidence Lombardi valued—and helped build—better shown than in Starr's performance in the 1967 NFL title game, the Ice Bowl. Battling a powerful Dallas defense and Arctic conditions with a backfield full of substitutes, Starr led the Packers 68 yards to the winning touchdown, which he scored with only 13 seconds left.

"Bart was at his peak today," flanker Carroll Dale said after the game. "When we went into the huddle to start that final drive, there was never any doubt about what was going to happen. Bart just let it be known that we were going to win that game. He didn't have to say anything. We just knew it from the way he acted."

Those words were echoed by Cincinnati wide receiver Cris Collinsworth 21 years later after the San Francisco 49ers drove 92 yards to score the game-winning touchdown with 34 seconds remaining in Super Bowl XXIII.

"We had them on their eight with three minutes to go," Collinsworth said, "and somebody came up to me and said, 'We got 'em now.' I said, 'Have you taken a look at who's quarterbacking the 49ers?' That's what it comes down to: Joe Montana is not human. I don't want to call him a god, but he's definitely somewhere in between. I'm sure he did it in peewee football, in high school, college, and now in professional football. Every time he's had the chips down and people were counting him out, he's come back."

Montana, like the other classic come-from-behind artist in NFL history—Roger Staubach—had confidence from the word go. They also had several other mental characteristics, including the desire to compete and win and an unfailing courage.

"One trait all the top quarterbacks have is competitiveness," says Tom Flores, former head coach of the Los Angeles Raiders as well as a former NFL quarterback. "They also are tenacious and brave. And they have a lot of pride in themselves and what they can accomplish. They always want one last chance at getting the ball, because they feel that they can win any game at the last moment if they need to."

Every fan is familiar with the physical courage that a quarterback must have. However, he must possess two kinds of mental courage.

First, he has to have the courage to pass from anywhere on the field in any situation. "A quarterback must be able to throw without fear," says Allie Sherman, the former head coach of the New York Giants. "I don't mean fear of being intercepted or incomplete. He must have absolute faith that each pass will connect, and he must transmit this faith to his teammates."

A quarterback also must have mental courage in adversity. Every time a game is lost, whether in the preseason, the regular season, or the playoffs, the quarterback gets the largest amount of the blame. After leading the Los Angeles Rams to the 1985 NFC Championship Game in his first year in the NFL, Dieter Brock virtually was chased back to Canada because of a poor performance against Chicago in the title match. The quarterback must have the courage to maintain confidence in himself despite the boos, the curses, the nasty signs at the stadium, the calls for his head by the media, and the lack of confidence in him that a coach or front office can show to the public.

Montana and Staubach both were key players in occasional quarterback controversies, but both men had the confidence and courage to come through, and eventually lead their teams to Super Bowl victories. Both also had a lot of other tools with which to work. That is not uncommon: In addition to their intangible qualities, all of the top quarterbacks have been blessed with a combination of outstanding mental and physical skills.

"There are certain measurable things the top quarterbacks all have," says Dick Steinberg, the director of player development for the New England Patriots. "The obvious ones are size, speed, native intelligence, and a quick release.

"There are also a number of other things that can't be measured but have to be there. The most important of these, to me, is arm strength. A quarterback has to have the ability to throw the fifteen-yard out pattern—that's a damn long pass, and it has to be on a line. For that pass he needs the ability to drive the ball into the zones and keep it away from the defenders who are reacting to it. It's also important to be able to get the ball downfield, because the farther you can get it down there, the more chance the receiver has of catching it.

"The top quarterbacks also should have leadership, poise, anticipation of the receiver, touch, mobility, and good overall athletic ability."

Of course, many quarterbacks don't possess all of Steinberg's ideal criteria. But they frequently can make up for it by excellence in one or more areas.

Jurgensen, for example, was not the most mobile quarterback, but no one has had a quicker release and few players have ever been calmer under pressure. In 1961, his first year as a regular with the Eagles, Jurgensen dropped back to pass, but one of the Redskins' defensive linemen grabbed his right arm before he could throw the ball. Jurgensen simply snatched the ball from his right hand with his left, and fired a left-handed pass to halfback Billy Ray Barnes for a 27-yard gain.

"Quarterbacks have to be composed at all times," Flores says. "If the quarterback panics, the whole team panics. The rest of the team must have confidence in him. Kenny Stabler didn't yell much. But when he did, they listened. On the other hand, Bert Jones was very demonstrative. He used to go around throwing up his arms and making all kinds of gestures. But it worked for him."

Jones, who played for the Colts and Rams, was one of those physically talented quarterbacks mentioned by Steinberg. Jones was like many of his colleagues at the position, the finest all-around athletes on their teams in their early years. They frequently will play running back, defensive back, and punter, as well as quarterback. They also might turn up on a basketball court, a baseball field, or a long-jump pit. In fact, one of the criteria most often mentioned about college quarterbacks scouted for the pros is their overall athletic ability. Jay Schroeder of the Raiders and John Elway of the Broncos both played professional baseball; John Brodie has gone on the seniors pro golf circuit; and when he was playing for the Kansas City Chiefs, the stories say that nobody, but nobody,

Sammy Baugh　　　　**Bobby Layne**　　　　**Otto Graham**　　　　**Johnny Unitas**

beat Len Dawson on the handball court.

"You usually find that every good quarterback is a good athlete at anything he tries," says Bill Walsh, the former head coach of the San Francisco 49ers. "If you are the parent of a young quarterback, I would recommend that you let him play as many sports as possible."

On the physical side of the game, quarterbacks always have had to be able to pass, fake, pivot, hand off, and run if necessary, but in recent years several other attributes have become increasingly important.

As offensive and defensive linemen have gotten bigger, quarterbacks have had to follow suit to be able to see over them when passing. Strength, speed, and mobility likewise have become more important. Mobile quarterbacks such as Elway or Cunningham keep pressure on a defense not only by rolling out or scrambling, but by being dangerous running threats themselves. In Super Bowl XIX, Joe Montana's running—59 yards on five carries— was a key to maintaining the scoring drives that gave San Francisco a 38-16 victory over Miami. Dan Marino of the Dolphins actually set Super Bowl passing records, but his lack of mobility gave a distinct advantage to the 49ers' defense.

On the other hand, few players have had a release as quick as Marino's. "Only Sonny Jurgensen and Joe Namath have been able to get rid of the ball as quickly as Marino," Miami head coach Don Shula says. "That quick release is important because you won't always have time to drop back, set up, find your receiver, and throw the ball with a perfect passing motion and follow-through. There simply are times when you have to put it in a certain spot before that defensive lineman grinds you into the ground. Marino can do that. He can find the open receiver—or the receiver who will shortly be getting open—and deliver the ball almost instantaneously. Usually his lack of mobility is not a big issue, because he can almost always get rid of the ball before he takes a sack."

The other part of that equation is having quick feet. Despite his bad knees, Namath had incredibly quick feet. He could drop back so quickly that he could get rid of the ball before the pass rush could reach him. He also could sidestep a fast rush.

Of course, how quickly a quarterback can get rid of the ball and how well he can avoid the rush still aren't the ultimate passing requirements.

"More important than anything else, the quarterback has to be able to throw the ball," says Hall of Fame coach Sid Gillman, one of the most innovative and progressive offensive minds in the history of football. "That isn't as easy as it sounds. A lot of people can drop back and hurl a football fifty or sixty yards, but the quarterback has to be able to put it in a precise spot; if it is six inches shorter, longer, or to either side, it will be intercepted. And he has to be able to do that while moving away from four monsters who are trying to dismember him.

"Passing takes not only strength but amazing accuracy. The keys to that accuracy are coordination, depth perception, the ability to project where players will be on the field before they have gotten there, and utter self-confidence. Some of that, of course, is trainable, but some isn't. It is a God-given talent, a natural, instinctive thing that you have or you don't. No coach can help you with it.

"As a matter of fact, coaches can sometimes hurt players by overcoaching them. There are certain fundamentals that every passer should have, but the most important issue is if he completes the pass. The classic passing form—delivering the ball straight over the top and releasing it near the ear—is fine...if it works. But Sammy Baugh dropped his arm to almost a three-quarters position, and today Bernie Kosar throws sidearm some of the time. But it worked for Baugh and it works for Kosar, so why would anyone ever want them to change?

"There was talk about having to work on Dan Marino's delivery when he first came into the NFL. He was perceived as forcing the ball too much, releasing the ball a little too early in his throw for maximum velocity and the best guidance, and waiting until the receiver got open rather than anticipating. But Don Shula didn't try to drastically change Marino, and his first year he led the AFC in passing, and the next he shattered all of the single-sea-

Sonny Jurgensen   **Dan Marino**   **John Elway**   **Bernie Kosar**

son passing marks. Can you imagine trying to change Marino?"

Many of the great passers have had totally different passing styles, all of which have worked.

Otto Graham used an overhand grip and a three-quarter motion. He threw a soft, floating pass that seemed to descend slowly and gently, but almost always to his receiver.

Bobby Layne threw the ball with his hands on or off the laces and with the ball coming behind the ear or in a three-quarters motion. He threw a hard pass that got to its target quickly but frequently was wobbly and difficult to handle.

Johnny Unitas had the classic throwing style, with his fingers on the laces, his arm coming through in a perfect behind-the-ear delivery, and a complete arm and body follow-through. His passing was arguably the best of them all.

Sonny Jurgensen dropped the ball from his ear a little, although not always to a three-quarters motion. His release was so quick that it seemed almost impossible to get it on film, and he could throw from either foot, while off-balance, or with an entire defensive line on him. If he had had the kind of offensive line and running backs that Unitas had, Jurgensen might be regarded as the best quarterback of all time and not just the best pure passer, as he frequently is described today.

Dan Marino relies on the aggressiveness of his receivers more than most quarterbacks. He fires an extremely fast pass with a release similar to Jurgensen's and with his fingers always on the laces. Marino still has a tendency to force the ball on occasion, but his wide receivers have been quick and strong enough to come back to get it.

John Elway throws a perfect spiral so hard that players talk about the Elway cross—the little mark made by the end of the football hitting a receiver's chest if he doesn't catch it with his hands. Elway has uncommon arm strength that allows him to throw a blazing pass even while backpedaling.

All of these quarterbacks—and the other great ones as

well—were different in passing style and athletic ability, but they all had one thing in common—intelligence. To be successful, a quarterback has to have a great deal of football sense. He must know his team's entire offense, including not only what he is supposed to do on every play and from every formation, but also what each man on his team is supposed to do.

He also must be able to judge both the talent and the desire of his teammates, because he must know how they will react in specific situations. And he needs to know each opposing team's defense and defensive personnel, so that he will know how to attack them in any given situation. Then, finally, he must have the ability to read the defense when he goes to the line of scrimmage and to change his play accordingly, if need be.

The quarterback must do all of this consistently and with a total disregard for the danger that always is facing him. NFL history is full of talented might-have-beens who looked like world-beaters one game and nobodies the next.

"The great ones are consistent, too," Starr says. "They aren't hot one Sunday and cold the next. You don't want the roller-coaster effect."

"The play that an NFL quarterback has to make consistently, the one that separates the real quarterback from the would-be, is the third-and-long play," Jurgensen says. "On third-and-long, you have to throw the ball and the defense knows it. In fact, everybody in the stands or watching on TV knows it. Your teammates know it, too, of course, and they are depending on you to make the call that will get the first down. If you can't make that call and come through under that pressure consistently, you'll be sitting with the other fans pretty soon."

The quarterback hasn't always had the same responsibilities. In fact, for years there wasn't even a position in football that corresponded to what we think of today as the quarterback. That is partly because in the early days of professional football—and the college game—not only was the

forward pass not legal, the entire concept of offensive football was different.

But football underwent a major change. Late in 1905, when President Theodore Roosevelt, horrified by a college sport that had recorded 18 deaths and 149 major injuries that year, stated, "Brutality and foul play should receive the same summary punishment given to a man who cheats at cards." He threatened to ban the sport by presidential decree if those in charge did not clean up the game.

In December, 1905, the Intercollegiate Athletic Association of the United States was organized to assist in the formation of sound requirements for intercollegiate athletics, particularly football. Five years later, on December 29, 1910, the organization changed its name to the National Collegiate Athletic Association.

At a meeting on January 12, 1906, the new rules committee for the IAAUS dramatically changed the focus of the game from a plodding, brutal, and unimaginative attack featuring popular but dangerous mass plays, such as the flying wedge, to one with more daring and offensive potential.

The changes included legalizing the forward pass, reducing the game from 70 to 60 minutes, establishing a neutral zone separating the teams by the length of the ball, increasing the distance to be gained for a first down from five to 10 yards, and requiring six (later seven) men to be on the line of scrimmage.

All of the 1906 changes were just as important for the pro game as for college football, because, at the time, the pros really had not developed any rules of their own. Although legalizing the forward pass eventually was to be the most important of the 1906 rules changes, the ones with the most immediate effect were those that required six men on the line, which helped eliminate mass plays, and the increase from five to 10 yards for a first down, which forced the development of outside running attacks, helped lead to the actual use of the forward pass, and increased the importance of the kicking game.

The new rules also led to the popularization of the first of the modern offensive formations—the T. Amos Alonzo Stagg used this formation in the early years of the century, and Bob Zuppke of Illinois used it the next decade when he served as the mentor to George Halas and Ralph Jones. Elsewhere, Glenn (Pop) Warner developed the Single Wing, which became the most popular formation in the first decades of the century.

Despite its legalization, the passing game didn't take off immediately and was used only in desperate situations or when one team could catch the other off guard. One reason was that a pass could not be thrown to a receiver within five yards of either side of where the ball was put in play—that is, the center. Also, it couldn't be thrown any closer than from five yards behind the line of scrimmage. Thus, the new attack was confined to simple

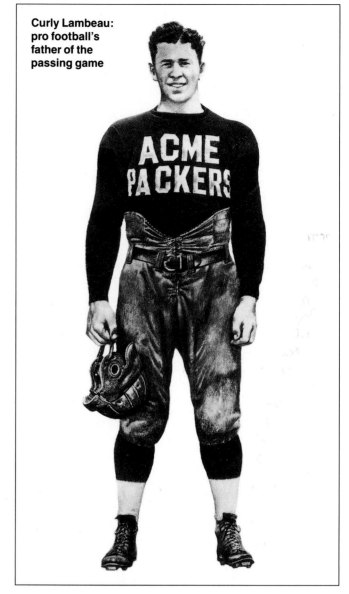

Curly Lambeau: pro football's father of the passing game

passes to the corners. Nevertheless, on October 27, 1906, against a combined team from Benwood and Moundsville, Ohio, George (Peggy) Parratt, the quarterback of the professional Massillon Tigers, completed a forward pass to end (Bullet) Dan Riley, the first authenticated pass completion in pro football history.

It was to be almost another decade, however, before anyone exploited the pass in a modern fashion. In 1913, Notre Dame shocked heavily favored Army 35-13 as quarterback Gus Dorais, throwing mainly to end Knute Rockne, completed 14 of 17 passes for 200 yards. The game focused national attention on the pass. Most coaches, then—as well as now—generally were conservative and concentrated on the running game.

Even though the potential of the T-formation quarterback gained national exposure in Notre Dame's upset of Army, the formation and position spread slowly. When Rockne became head coach at his alma mater, his teams ran the Notre Dame Box, which became popular throughout the country. Like the Single Wing, the Notre Dame

Box was primarily a running formation in which the center snapped the ball several feet back to a tailback rather than handing it directly to the quarterback. The formation differed from the Single Wing in that the line was balanced; in the Single Wing, both guards were on the same side of the center as the blocking back and wingback, and the wingback usually was in tight between the tackle and end, rather than flanking the end.

In the early days of the NFL, Green Bay, coached by Rockne pupil Earl (Curly) Lambeau (who also was the team's tailback), used the Notre Dame Box. The other teams ran the Single Wing or a variant of it, with the exception of the Chicago Bears, who stayed with coach George Halas's T-formation.

As well as being a Hall of Fame coach, and perhaps the NFL's first true advocate of the passing game, Lambeau also was a successful passer. A study of old newspaper accounts indicates that in 1924 he became the first professional to pass for more than 1,000 yards in a season (1,094). And sketchy records show that by the time he retired as a player, Lambeau had passed for more yards than anyone else in NFL history. Lambeau's offense also relied on other outstanding passers—halfback Verne Lewellen and tailback Red Dunn, who succeeded Lambeau as Green Bay's starter in the late 1920s.

In the first seven years of the NFL, no team emphasized throwing the ball like the Packers. But there were a number of other outstanding passers, the best of whom were Hall of Fame fullback Ernie Nevers, who played for the Duluth Eskimos and Chicago Cardinals, and Jack Ernst, who quarterbacked four teams in the 1920s. Other top passers included Hall of Fame tailback Jimmy Conzelman and tailback George (Wildcat) Wilson.

Jack Ernst, one of the first true quarterbacks, embarked on a six-year NFL odyssey that included stints with the Frankford Yellow Jackets, the Pottsville Maroons, the New York Yankees, and the Boston Bulldogs.

But it wasn't the varied success of Lambeau and the other aerial pioneers that eliminated the doubters and made the passing game respectable.

That honor belongs to tailback Benny Friedman, who entered the league in 1926 with the newly organized Cleveland Bulldogs. An All-America at Michigan the year before, Friedman shocked fans and players alike by frequently calling passes on first down, something rarely seen at the time. But Friedman's golden arm allowed him to get away with almost anything. His 12 touchdown passes and more than 1,700 passing yards as a rookie eclipsed Lambeau's single-season records.

The next year the passing game made another impor-

New York Giants owner Tim Mara bought the entire Detroit Wolverines team just to obtain the services of Benny Friedman (right), the best passer of the 1920s. Friedman poses with John (Shipwreck) Kelly, co-owner and primary receiver of the Brooklyn Dodgers. Friedman moved from the Giants to the Dodgers in 1932, and played until 1934.

tant stride forward when Pop Warner brought his Stanford University team to New York City to play Army. Warner occasionally had used a Double-Wing formation since 1911, when he created it at the Carlisle Indian School. But after Stanford easily beat Army with the Double Wing, the system was widely imitated. The Double Wing, with two backs spread out and close to the line of scrimmage, laid the foundation for the spread formations still in use today and was the basis of many of the first formations built around the passing game.

The development of the modern quarterback and today's passing game, however, also is connected with two other occurrences—the growing popularity of the T-formation and the appearance of pro football's first great receiver.

Although the T-formation had been used since the turn of the century, most people considered it a moribund offense in 1930. But the popular Single Wing never really was an offense designed for the passing game.

"I could pass well, but we didn't pass that often," Earl (Dutch) Clark, the Hall of Fame quarterback for the Portsmouth Spartans and Detroit Lions, once said. (The Lions were one of the few teams running the Single Wing that called the man who received the snap from center the quarterback rather than the tailback.) "Actually, passing was the one thing where my left eye, which was partially blind, would give me a little trouble. In the Single Wing, I'd

roll to the right, faking a run, and then drop back and throw quickly. My best vision was always to the right. So there would be times when a man would be open down the left side of the field, and I just couldn't see him. The T changed a lot of that, because a quarterback began to have to be a real passer."

That transition began in 1930, when Ralph Jones took over for George Halas as head coach of the Chicago Bears. Jones moved the Bears' ends wide, spaced the halfbacks wider, and made one of the halfbacks a man-in-motion. With his split ends and man-in-motion, Jones not only spread the game horizontally, but spread it up and down the field as well, because, once players were

Lambeau's passing fancy changed the face of football in the late 1930s when end Don Hutson (left) and quarterback Cecil Isbell joined the team.

out wide, they could get downfield for passes. Moreover, the man-in-motion initially gave tremendous problems to the defenses, which were not nearly as sophisticated as the offenses of the time. The back could turn in and make a crackback block on the defensive end, lure a linebacker out of position, opening up a running lane, or pull a defensive back out of position, opening up areas to pass.

Jones's innovations with the T helped make the Bears a powerhouse. In 1932, they beat the Portsmouth Spartans in the first NFL Championship Game. Because of a blizzard, the game was played indoors at Chicago Stadium, and helped spawn an entire set of new rules that would have a profound influence on professional football.

Before the 1933 season, the NFL, which long had followed the rules of college football, made its first significant changes from the college game. As a result of the successful use of inbounds lines (or hashmarks) in the 1932 NFL Championship Game, a new rule dictated that the ball would be moved in 10 yards to an inbounds line whenever it was in play within five yards of the sidelines. Also, passing from anywhere behind the line of scrimmage was permitted, and the ball was slimmed down a full two inches to facilitate the new emphasis on the pass. These rules changes removed strictures both real and imagined from the passing game. And the way was opened for rollout, sprint-out, bootleg, and halfback passing.

The rules had their desired effect. In 1933, there was a dramatic increase in passing and scoring.

The first team to take full advantage of the new rules was, once again, Lambeau's Packers. In the 1930s the key to the passing game was the tailback. In the mid-1930s a new name flashed on the scene. Don Hutson, a slim end with 9.7-second speed in the 100-yard dash, had moves that not only were light-years ahead of his contemporaries but still are models for study today. Hutson was the first modern wide receiver, and he dominated offensive action like perhaps no other player in history. When he entered the NFL in 1935, the record for receptions in a season was 26. He caught 34 in 1936, increased the record to 41 the next year, made 58 catches in 1941, and broke that mark with 74 in 1942. He also increased the yardage mark for a single season from 433 yards to 1,211.

The Packers had a pair of outstanding passers for Hutson—future Hall of Fame tailback Arnie Herber and his alternate and eventual successor, Cecil Isbell.

But they were only two of the first great set of NFL passers, which also included Harry Newman and Ed Danowski of the Giants, Ace Parker of the Brooklyn Dodgers, and Parker Hall of the Cleveland Rams.

In 1939-40, one of the NFL's first great little quarterbacks, Davey O'Brien, the Heisman Trophy winner from Texas Christian, set passing records for Philadelphia. He might have gone down as one of the great passers of all time, had he not retired after only two years to join the FBI.

But the head of the class in the 1930s—and through the 1940s—was the man many still consider the best quarterback—and maybe best overall player—in NFL history. What Don Hutson did for pass receiving, Slingin'

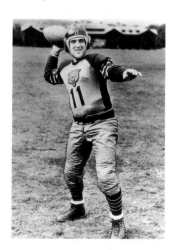

Harry Newman, pictured in the not-so-ferocious looking uniform of the Brooklyn Tigers of the American Football League in 1936, jumped to the rival league after quarterbacking the New York Giants for three years.

A MASTER AT "QUICK-KICKING" – HE IS FOREVER EMBARRASSING OPPOSING SAFETY MEN WITH LONG KICKS OVER THEIR HEADS.

HE COMPLETED 30 OF 62 FORWARDS ATTEMPTED THIS SEASON – AGAINST BROOKLYN LAST FALL HE TOSSED SEVEN BULL'S EYES IN A ROW.

ED -DANOWSKI- -THE N.Y. GIANTS GREAT FORWARD PASSER-

THE FORMER FORDHAM STAR CAN LUG THE BALL WITH ANY MAN IN THE NATIONAL LEAGUE

Sammy Baugh did for throwing the football. In his rookie year, 1937, he led the Washington Redskins to the NFL Championship Game, where he gunned down the Bears 28-21 with 358 yards and three touchdown passes. That year, he set an NFL record with 81 completions, a mark he eventually raised to 210 to go along with the record he later set for passing yards (2,938, breaking the previous record of 2,194).

Baugh helped make the forward pass an irreversible part of the pro game. He was one of the first advocates of the short passing game, and Washington became the first team to use a ball-control offense. With his ability to see the entire field, to instantly comprehend defensive reactions, and to fire the ball without hesitation, Baugh made the primitive three-deep defenses of his day obsolete.

"He would cock the ball," New York Giants head coach Steve Owen later wrote, "bring it down, and drift off as if about to run, cock again, make a mock throw to one side, and shoot a touchdown to the other. He was never committed until he was flat on the ground and the ball with him. I have seen him make bullet-like throws with his tremendous wrist action as he was nailed by a hard tackle and falling."

For the first half of his 16-year career, Baugh was a tailback in the Double Wing. In 1945, he made the transition to a T-formation quarterback and helped prove that that formation could be even more devastating for an accurate passer when he broke his own NFL completion percentage record of 62.7 by hitting 70.3 percent, a mark that lasted until 1982.

Baugh's move was symbolic of a shift to the T-formation in pro football in the 1940s. The two men most responsible for it were Clark Shaughnessy and Sid Luckman.

By 1939, the Bears' T again had fallen on difficult times. Other teams, principally the Lions and Packers, had solved it by rotating their defensive backs to the side of the motion. That year the Bears drafted Luckman, an All-America tailback at Columbia. After a year of learning under Halas, who was back again as head coach, and Shaughnessy, who was the head coach at the University of Chicago and a volunteer consultant for the Bears, Luckman suddenly helped make the Bears' T virtually unstoppable.

One of the smartest quarterbacks of all time, Luckman not only was a masterful ball-handler and an accurate passer but a master at the new system that Shaughnessy installed. Luckman spun from under the center and faked, handed off, or pitched on quick-opening plays unlike the slowly developing plays of the traditional Single Wing. Because of Luckman's speed, double blocking no longer was necessary and linemen could move out fast, brush block their opponents, and move downfield to throw a block at someone else.

Shaughnessy also instituted the same system at Stanford, where he became head coach in 1940, and his team went 10-0 behind another T quarterback wizard, Frankie Albert. But before taking his team to the Rose Bowl, Shaughnessy made a critical stop. Prior to the 1940 NFL Championship Game, he returned to Chicago to revamp the Bears' offense even further. His major change was to add a counter play in which the Bears split one man wide, motioned away from him, and then ran back to the side of the spread end. The counter was as old as football itself, but Shaughnessy realized that it would be devastatingly effective against the Washington defense, which predictably shifted its linebackers toward the man-in-motion.

"I drew up the entire offense," Shaughnessy said later. "I threw out all the junk that wasn't working. Then I looked at the pictures of the Redskins-Bears game of two weeks earlier [the Redskins had won 7-3]. It was obvious that Washington was going to use a certain defense and wasn't going to change it."

Shaughnessy's offense took full advantage. On the first play of the game, halfback George McAfee of the Bears went in motion. Washington's linebackers moved with him, just as Shaughnessy knew they would. The Bears ran the same motion on their next play, but fullback Bill Osmanski swept around end in the opposite direction and ran 68 yards for the touchdown that started a 73-0 rout, the biggest margin of victory in National Football League history.

A few weeks later, when Stanford defeated Nebraska in the Rose Bowl, the T was hailed as the offensive wave of the future. In the next eight years, all NFL teams except the Pittsburgh Steelers went to the T full-time. Modern football—and the modern quarterback—had arrived.

Shaughnessy wasn't done refining the pro offense, however. In 1948, he became the head coach of the Los

Angeles Rams. The next year, he decided he wanted to get newly acquired halfback Elroy (Crazylegs) Hirsch into the offense. But he was concerned about whether Hirsch, who had suffered a fractured skull the year before with the Chicago Rockets of the All-America Football Conference, could take the pounding a halfback normally received. So, despite having two outstanding ends in league receiving leader Tom Fears and Bob Shaw, Shaughnessy split Hirsch out wide as a flanker, creating the first full-time player at that position.

The result was devastating. When combined with star quarterback Bob Waterfield and rookie Norm Van Brocklin, the Rams roared to the Western Conference title. Los Angeles, however, lost to Philadelphia in the NFL Championship Game on a rain-soaked, muddy field that nullified the Rams' speed. Shaughnessy became the fall guy for the loss and eventually was fired.

Shaughnessy's replacement was Chicago Bears Hall of Fame tackle Joe Stydahar, whose greatest move was hiring former teammate Hamp Pool as his offensive coach. Pool further refined Shaughnessy's offense and constantly found new ways to get Fears and Hirsch open to grab strikes from Waterfield and Van Brocklin. Incredibly, all four men ended up in the Hall of Fame.

"We had all kinds of formations," Pool says. "We used quite a lot of the slot formation—with the halfback just outside the linemen and off the line of scrimmage. Then we'd put the other halfback in motion the other way. This would leave us with only one setback, the fullback, to block on pass protection. But we would get four men into deep patterns in a hurry, and we would just eat them up. The defenses we were facing were exclusively man-to-man, and no person could stay with Hirsch or Fears."

With perhaps the most electrifying offense the NFL has ever seen, Los Angeles scored an unbelievable 38.8 points per game in 1950. "The plan was, Van Brocklin would tell us, 'You guys hold 'em to three touchdowns and we'll win by two,'" says Don Paul, a linebacker who was defensive captain for the Rams. "We spent most of our practices working on the home-run offense. We were more dangerous inside *our* fifteen-yard line than inside theirs. The record that still amazes me from 1950 was the forty-one points we scored in one quarter against a Detroit team with Bobby Layne."

But when the Rams ran into Cleveland in the 1950 NFL Championship Game, the Browns came out on top, winning on a last-minute field goal. In 1951, however, the Rams' big-play attack was successful, and they beat the Browns 24-17 in the NFL Championship Game when Fears scored on a 73-yard pass from Van Brocklin in the fourth quarter.

The Browns might not have been as exciting as the Rams, but they were the greatest winners of their time, perhaps of *any* time. In their first 10 years of existence— four in the AAFC and six in the NFL—the Browns won

Clark Shaughnessy imparts some wisdom to Bob Waterfield.

seven titles and played in the championship game the other three years.

There were two keys to their success—head coach Paul Brown and quarterback Otto Graham. Brown was the first coach to bring a true sense of science to professional football. Many of the things that are a routine part of the pro game today—full-time coaching staffs, the study of game films, calling plays via messengers, classroom study, intelligence testing, using playbooks, and extensive college scouting—were either Paul Brown innovations or were raised to a higher level of efficiency by him.

"I don't think it's stretching the truth to say Paul Brown redesigned the game," says Graham, who adopted most of Brown's methods when he later became head coach of the Washington Redskins in the 1960s. "He was the first to make football a year-round job for his coaches and players. He was the first to take his players to a hotel the night before a game in their hometown, to get them away from the kids and the noise and neighbors and distractions.

"We were the first team to carry notebooks. We'd start off each year talking about the most basic of fundamentals. He'd dictate to us, and we'd write it down, things like how to do your calisthenics, the right way to touch your toes, how to form a huddle. After ten years I was still writing it all down. It was like being in the navy and hearing the same lecture on how to make hospital corners on your bedsheets. But you remembered.

"And Paul was an innovator on the field. He took advantage of the fact that the defenses of the time were pretty basic and non-mobile. There were no blitzes, no stunts, no zones. So he took advantage of the defenses by de-

veloping the draw play for Marion Motley and the sideline pass—break to the side and come back for the ball—for [Mac] Speedie, [Dante] Lavelli, and myself."

One of Brown's major additions to the passing game was his insistence on running precise pass routes rather than the general, and what would be thought of today as somewhat sloppy, pass routes of the time.

"We had never seen such a spot-passing program as they had," Philadelphia defensive back Russ Craft once said, recalling how the Browns dismantled the 1949 NFL-champion Eagles in their first game in the NFL in 1950. "We would be on top of the receivers, but they caught the ball anyway because the pass was so well-timed."

It helped that the Browns had two all-time greats, Lavelli and Speedie, catching those passes, but even more important was "Mr. Automatic," quarterback Otto Graham, the finest mechanic of his time. Graham led his league in passing six times and finished second three times more in his 10-year career.

"Otto Graham was the key to the whole team," Brown says. "He had the finest peripheral vision I've ever witnessed, and that is a very big factor in a quarterback. He had total composure on the field, the ability to find whatever receiver was going to come open, and the arm and athletic ability to get the ball to him. His hand-eye coordination was most unusual, and he was bigger than you'd think and faster than you'd think.

Cleveland head coach Paul Brown had a lot to thank quarterback Otto Graham for. "Mr. Automatic" piloted Brown's Browns to six consecutive NFL Championship Games between 1950 and 1955.

"Otto was my greatest player because he played the most important position, and he played it to perfection. He was the crux of how we got things done. I don't discount Marion Motley, Dante Lavelli, or Jim Brown. But the guy who was the engineer, the guy with the touch that pulled us out of so many situations, was Otto Graham. To put it simply, find me another quarterback who took his team to as many championships."

If there was one area where the Brown and Graham mutual-admiration society fell down, it was over another of Brown's contributions to quarterbacking—calling the plays from the sideline.

"When Paul began calling the plays from the bench, I

disagreed, but the whole thing was exaggerated over the years," Graham says. "I didn't like it, but I didn't resent it. Calling a play is nothing more than a guess. You see those movies where the quarterback raises up from the huddle, looks at the defense, then ducks down and calls the play. Well, that's baloney. Paul could see as much or more from the sideline than I could from the huddle. My complaint was that he didn't want me to audible. He did let me check off now and then, but I had to be right. The rest of the time, Paul called the plays, and the record shows he called 'em pretty good."

Brown never had any doubt about the issue. "Otto was one of the brightest players you could imagine," he says. "But nobody under pressure of performing can give as much thought to play selection as he should. We were feeding in information from all our coaches in the press box—and we always had a coach sitting in the end zone. I was a quarterback myself—not a very good one—and in those days when you couldn't think of anything else, you'd run off tackle. What does a quarterback see when he makes a handoff? What part of the defense does he see? He doesn't see much. Field level is the worst vantage point in the stadium.

"Besides, a coach calling the plays takes a lot of heat off the quarterback—and a lot of coaches don't want this responsibility. I didn't care. The players perform and get the credit. If people wanted to blast me for a dumb call, I could take it."

At the same time Brown and Graham were having their greatest success, another man was helping to open up the passing game across the country in a different way. Chuck Taylor had been a little-known offensive lineman for Shaughnessy's 1940 Stanford team before serving as the Indians' freshman coach for several years. He then joined Buck Shaw's 49ers staff before returning to Stanford as head coach in 1951. Like Shaughnessy, he led Stanford into the Rose Bowl in his first year.

"I learned fast that Stanford wasn't going to run over anybody," Taylor says. "But passing could keep us in almost every game, and could allow us to upset a team that was physically stronger than we were. So we made the decision to go to a style of passing that was unique at the time. We would establish the passing game first. We wouldn't run to establish the pass, but the other way around. It was the real start of that strategy in football."

Taylor's shift of emphasis was the forerunner of the style of attack that became popular both at Stanford and

in the NFL. In the larger picture, he also broke the ground that helped make football the pass-oriented game it is today.

Taylor didn't simply use the pass more. He added sophistication to what had been rather primitive concepts.

"The traditional passing game had had the receiver run down ten yards and turn around," Taylor says. "There never was any deviation from the pattern. But we changed that. We divided the field up into nine zones and called zone patterns instead of specific routes. That way, it was up to the receivers to get open, and it was the quarterback's responsibility to be able to read the defense and his own receiver."

Quarterback John Hadl (21) and wide receiver Lance Alworth (19) prospered in the high-octane offense of Sid Gillman's San Diego Chargers in the 1960s.

Taylor not only allowed for deviation *on* a play, but *before* the play. He allowed his quarterbacks to call audibles, helping to popularize the changing of plays at the line of scrimmage.

The argument over play-calling—of which audibles are simply a part—has continued for more than four decades. Through the 1960s, most quarterbacks called their own plays, but that began to change in the 1970s when Tom Landry of the Dallas Cowboys started calling the plays for his new quarterback, Roger Staubach. The Cowboys made five Super Bowl appearances in the decade and won twice, leading coaches around the league once again to start calling plays. At this point, coaches have taken over nearly entirely. Virtually all NFL teams today send the play in from the sideline by one manner or another, although the quarterback generally is able to change it at the line of scrimmage if he deems it necessary.

Nowhere was the argument over play-calling more acrimonious than in Los Angeles, where one of the great offensive minds of all time, Sid Gillman, got together with one of the great passers, Norm Van Brocklin. When Gillman joined the Rams in 1955, he brought with him experience obtained at Miami of Ohio and the University of Cincinnati. But he had not yet developed all of the theories and nuances of pro football that earned him selection to

the Pro Football Hall of Fame. His intermittent calling of the plays soured his relationship with Van Brocklin.

"The coach really shouldn't call the plays," Van Brocklin said later. "It is not good for the quarterback, because he becomes an automaton. He stops thinking. He comes to depend upon the coach and can't depend upon himself. Then, when a coach who has been calling all the plays starts doing it in fits and starts, it makes the whole situation difficult. I never objected to taking a suggestion from the bench, but I did object to play-calling becoming a divisive force on the team."

Nevertheless, the Rams won the Western Conference title in 1955. Gillman, who would be a leader in the use of the modern short-passing game, had the chance to learn some lessons of his own.

"At that point, it wasn't a question of innovations," Gillman says. "We simply had great talent—we had Dutch Van Brocklin and Tom Fears and Elroy Hirsch and Ron Waller.

"The main thing was Fears. We were just beginning to understand how moves are made by a receiver. Fears was one of the greatest 'move' men in the history of the game. He didn't have much speed, but he could turn 'em on their heads. We studied Fears and we began coaching what he was doing."

The result for Gillman was that when he later got truly talented receivers with great speed (at San Diego in the AFL)—such as Lance Alworth and Gary Garrison—he turned them into all-pros, or, in Alworth's case, Hall of Fame members.

Gillman also benefited from his association with Van Brocklin. "Just watching what Van Brocklin did in practice was a learning experience," Gillman says. "How he played and how he thought helped contribute enormously to the development of the passing game.

"Every time Dutch threw the ball, you could hear a little *'zzt!'* as it left his fingertips. We commented about it in practice. *Zzt! Zzt!*. Well, one week Van Brocklin hurt his hand, and he could hardly throw in practice. You no longer heard that *'zzt!'* And then one day, he started throwing better and better, and suddenly we could hear it again. Everybody started laughing and yelling, 'The *zzt* is back.'"

In later years, Gillman helped develop an enormous number of successful quarterbacks—Billy Wade, Zeke Bratkowski, Frank Ryan, Jack Kemp, John Hadl, and Ron Jaworski—with theories gleaned at least in part from his association with Van Brocklin.

In 1960, Gillman became the head coach of the Los

Angeles Chargers of the new American Football League. Not only did he lend the league a certain amount of immediate credibility, but he developed one of pro football's most explosive offenses of all time and was the leader of what could be termed "AFL-style" football, which emphasized a mixture of the deep-passing game to speedy wide receivers with short, safe passes to ends over the middle and flares to quick backs in the flats. Gillman also started training other football minds, including Jack Faulkner, Chuck Noll, and Don Klosterman.

None of Gillman's assistants added more to the passing game than Al·Davis, who became head coach of the Oakland Raiders in 1963. Davis became a major influence in the passing game of the 1960s and early 1970s. His "vertical passing game" emphasized huge offensive lines that could protect the quarterback a long time, and deep passing to speedy wide receivers, such as Warren Wells and Cliff Branch. Having Fred Biletnikoff constantly open short helped the Raiders' deep game, but Davis's scheme was what made Daryle Lamonica and Kenny Stabler among the most feared passers in pro football.

Meanwhile, Van Brocklin, the head coach of the new Minnesota Vikings, found out what a coach-quarterback disagreement was like—from the *other* side. Van Brocklin once stated that a quarterback should run the ball only if his life were in immediate danger. Therefore, it was with some distaste that he saw his quarterback, young Fran Tarkenton, reshape the future of pro quarterbacks throughout the 1960s.

Tarkenton went on to play in the NFL for 18 years. He threw and completed more passes for more yards and more touchdowns than any player in the history of pro football. Late in his career, he became a master of the short passing game and used dump passes to running backs as effectively as anyone ever has. Tarkenton's greatest contribution, however, was his use of—and the subsequent popularization of—the scramble.

Until Tarkenton, quarterbacks slowly had been doing less and less. They had gone through an evolution from Single-Wing tailbacks who ran, passed, kicked, and played defense, to T-formation quarterbacks who were primarily passers. Before Tarkenton entered the league in 1961, quarterbacks generally ran the ball because the play had broken down. Tarkenton started the swing in the other direction.

"It used to drive you crazy," says Don Shula, who was the coach of the Baltimore Colts when Tarkenton was in his first of two stints with the Vikings. "Tarkenton would scramble all around the backfield, giving ground and going farther and farther back toward his own goal line. Then, just when you thought your defensive lineman had him, he'd duck away and start going back to the line of scrimmage. He'd wander all over the field, just waiting for

a receiver to come open. Then he'd complete the pass."

Van Brocklin was distressed by Tarkenton's scrambling. "With Tarkenton," he said in 1964, "you need to have an exceptionally good third-and-forty offense." However, Van Brocklin did build his offense around his young quarterback's remarkable talents.

The Vikings' receivers had two sets of routes to run. First was their normal pattern—if Tarkenton dropped back and threw from the pocket like other quarterbacks. But if he started weaving around, dodging defensive players, and generally looking like a jackrabbit on the loose, the receivers would go to another set of patterns that emphasized hooks and comebacks.

Throughout the early 1970s, scrambling quarterbacks —even running quarterbacks—became popular. Unlike the 1960s, when players such as Johnny Unitas, Charley Johnson, Frank Ryan, Don Meredith, Norm Snead, and Sonny Jurgensen almost never ran the ball, mobility became a requirement in the seventies. Staubach was the ultimate in mobility—both scrambling and running— much like Joe Montana in the 1980s.

Some quarterbacks actually were more efficient as runners than scramblers. The runners and gunners who combined planned runs with the passing game most efficiently in the 1970s were Greg Landry of Detroit and Steve Grogan of New England. In 1971, Landry set an NFL record for quarterbacks by rushing for 530 yards for

Bobby Douglass—a running back in quarterback's clothing—did little to expand the art of passing, but he found other ways to pick up yardage for the Chicago Bears.

a 7.0-yard average, breaking the record set 20 years before by Tobin Rote of Green Bay. The next year, Landry added 524 more yards and an NFC-leading nine rushing touchdowns.

Grogan, who took over for Jim Plunkett as a rookie in 1975, scored 12 touchdowns in 1976 and gained 539 yards in 1978, when the Patriots became the first team ever to have four backs each gain more than 500 yards.

But it was the Bears who took running to its extreme when they installed Bobby Douglass at quarterback. An All-America in a ground-oriented attack at Kansas, Douglass was not an NFL-caliber passer. But at 6 feet 3 inches and 225 pounds and blessed with outstanding speed, he

was a standout runner. In 1972, Douglass shattered Landry's NFL rushing mark by running for 968 yards. His 6.9-yard average remains the second-best in NFL history. He completed just 38 percent of his passes, however. Within two years, Douglass had lost his starting job.

While Douglass was in Chicago, the magician most responsible for the popularity of the ball-control passing game entered the NFL. At San Diego State, Don Coryell had developed quarterbacks Rod Dowhower, Don Horn, Dennis Shaw, Brian Sipe, and Jesse Freitas. When he joined the St. Louis Cardinals they were perpetual losers, but he immediately turned the team around with his system and the arm of Jim Hart. After winning two division championships, Coryell moved to San Diego, where he joined with Dan Fouts in an era of aerial success unprecedented in NFL history.

"It was the system," Fouts says today. "If you check back through Don Coryell's history as a coach you'll find he had success throwing the ball wherever he went. We believed in his system, and that's what was most important. From the head man on down to the waterboys, everybody knew we were going to throw the ball and be successful doing it."

Coryell's system relied to a great extent on spot passes and mismatches. Fouts, like Hart before him, didn't throw the ball to where the receiver was, but rather to where the receiver figured to end up. He threw to *spots*. That al-

Head coach Don Coryell was the wizard of razzle-dazzle offenses in the 1970s and '80s. The Cardinals' Jim Hart was one of the beneficiaries of Coryell's advanced system.

lowed him to deliver the ball quickly, using two- and three-step drops instead of the traditional seven-yard drop into the pocket. Because the ball was in the air so fast, the defense had less time to react, which cut down on interceptions, increased the number of short passes, and fashioned a new offensive dimension—the ball-control passing game.

Under Coryell, the Chargers also became the first team to extensively use a one-back offense with two tight ends —a formation that became popular after Washington won Super Bowl XVII using it. That forced the defense to give single coverage to either a wide receiver or to Coryell's super weapon, tight end Kellen Winslow, who had tight

end size but possessed the speed of a wide receiver.

"We like to line up two tight ends and work over the middle," Fouts said while still playing for Coryell. "That forces teams to cover a tight end with a safety or linebacker. Our tight ends should have a speed advantage against linebackers and a size advantage against safeties, so we should get a completion. We can also get an advantage in numbers. We'll flood zones or overload zones. We'll put two guys in an area where there is one defender or three guys in an area where there are two defenders.

"We're tough to defend. If you play us zone, you can't blitz and the quarterback has time to throw. If you play us man, you might get beat long. There's always the threat that someone's going deep in our offense. We look to him first."

One reason Coryell's offense was so successful was the man pulling the trigger. Fouts was virtually a machine, making three, four, even five reads before deciding on his target. That choice also had to take into account decisions by the receivers, a concept initiated by Chuck Taylor but perfected by Coryell.

"Not only is a receiver at liberty to make adjustments in his route, he is expected to," Fouts said. "I have my reads and the receiver has his—and we're both reading the same thing. I'm expecting the adjustment to come. If the defense is in a zone coverage, I know what's coming from my receiver. Guys like Charlie Joiner, Wes Chandler, and Kellen Winslow have instant recognition. That's what separates the great ones from the guys selling cars."

One thing that helped Coryell and all other recent offensive coaches has been the rules changes that were adopted to open up the passing game and make pro football more exciting. In 1974, defensive players were limited to bumping or chucking a pass receiver only twice, and rolling blocks on wide receivers were made illegal. Four years later, rules changes permitted a defender to maintain contact with a receiver within five yards of the line of scrimmage, but outlawed contact beyond that point. The pass-blocking rule also was interpreted to permit the extending of arms and open hands, which allowed the offensive line to protect the quarterback more effectively.

No one—not even Coryell—adapted to the new rules for the passing game with more success than Bill Walsh

did in his 10 years as head coach of San Francisco. Walsh, a disciple of both Paul Brown and Coryell, established a brilliantly conceived ball-control passing offense after taking over the 49ers in 1979.

In Walsh's first year, Steve DeBerg set NFL records for pass attempts and completions. But the next year, DeBerg lost his job to Joe Montana, who was the perfect operative for Walsh. Montana's pinpoint passing, timely running, and ability to pull out games apparently lost helped make the 49ers the team of the decade in the 1980s as they earned victories in Super Bowls XVI, XIX, and XXIII.

Despite Montana's success—and he certainly is one of the most efficient passers and most talented quarterbacks in the history of the game—some people called for his removal in 1988 in favor of Steve Young, who might have more natural physical ability than even Montana. Montana's performance through the 1988 season—and especially in Super Bowl XXIII, when he led the 49ers 92 yards in the final three minutes for the winning touchdown—show that there are still a lot more dimensions to quarterbacking than just physical talent. Young's future still is ahead of him.

Shaughnessy and Waterfield have nothing on pass masters Bill Walsh and Joe Montana, the brains and the arm, respectively, behind three San Francisco Super Bowl triumphs in the 1980s.

If Tarkenton started the trend back to the multi-talented athlete who originally played Single-Wing tailback, Young is one of three quarterbacks today—along with Philadelphia's Randall Cunningham and Denver's John Elway—who epitomize that kind of player.

"Ultimately, all NFL teams will be trying to get a quarterback like Randall Cunningham," says Eagles head coach Buddy Ryan. "He is the best athlete among NFL quarterbacks. He can pass, run, scramble, anything. He's big [6-4, 203], strong, tough, and smart. He's going to be a classic before he's through."

The same things have been said about Elway, a man who carried two average Denver teams to the Super Bowl upon his shoulders. In certain ways, Elway more closely personifies the continuing reversion of the quarterback to the Single-Wing tailback. Like Cunningham, he is a superb athlete who is a threat as a short passer, a long passer, a runner, or a scrambler. He also is an outstanding punter who is especially adept at punting from the Shotgun formation.

The Broncos use the Shotgun as a formation from which to run their entire offense (not just the passing game, as many teams do), making Elway's role even closer to that of the Single-Wing tailback. Elway frequently takes a long snap and has many options.

"I like it," Elway says of the Shotgun. "It gives me extra time to see the receivers, plus, if we're getting a heavy rush, I can see it and avoid it more easily."

The Shotgun gives the offense a split-second more. The quarterback has more time to read the pass coverage before he has to throw the ball. The receivers have more time to get open and more time to go deep. And the quarterback has more time to stay with a deep receiver before dumping a pass off to a running back serving as a safety valve. The passer also has more space to move away from pass rushers, who have to be aware that a quarterback like Elway can turn a scramble into a big gain.

But the Shotgun is not just for quarterbacks such as Elway or Cunningham or Young. "I think the Shotgun helps a quarterback who can't move as much as it helps a mobile quarterback," says Mike Shanahan, the head coach of the Los Angeles Raiders and, when he was offensive coordinator of the Broncos, one of the men responsible for Denver's adoption of the formation. Shanahan believes that a quarterback who is less mobile—such as Marino or Ken O'Brien of the Jets—actually can benefit just as much by the separation from the pass rushers.

"I would have no problem putting players like Elway or Cunningham or Steve Young in a Single Wing and letting them just control the entire offense," says Sammy Baugh. "They are the kind of players who could really make the whole thing go. At the same time, they also are guys who could go ahead and play defense. They are real throwbacks. Either that, or in certain ways the game—or at least the quarterback position—is going back to what it was when I came in. Actually they might not be throwbacks as much as they are previews of the future.

"Those three guys have a lot in common. They all have great arms. They all are ferocious competitors. They all are fabulous athletes with a real drive to succeed. They all are tough. And they all are leaders. More than that, you can tell from what they've accomplished—sometimes totally on their own efforts—that they are the walking, talking personification of what any quarterback is really all about: They're winners."

Champions

Joe Theismann, the former Washington quarterback who led the Redskins to Super Bowls XVII and XVIII, had this theory of motivation: "A lot of people think that football players are mainly in the game because of the money. But I don't think that is true at all. These guys are out there because they want to win. That's what drives them. Each of them wants to get to the Super Bowl and get that ring. Sure, you get a lot of cash out of winning a title, but a lot of people have money. Not many have a Super Bowl ring. Winning the championship...that's what pro football is all about."

And when that ultimate goal has been reached—when a team has won the championship—the man the fans usually remember the most is the quarterback. Everybody knows Joe Namath led the Jets to a major upset victory in Super Bowl III. But who was the running back who set the Super Bowl record for yards rushing that day? Who was the cornerback who made two interceptions? Who was the kicker who scored 10 of the Jets' 16 points?

In so many ways, it is a quarterback's game to win or lose—and not just in the playoffs. It is up to the quarterback to keep the offense moving, to keep the defense off the field, to score enough points to win the game.

The most desirable quarterback to coaches, fellow players, and fans is a quarterback who can win. More than that, who can win *championships.*

"You can't win championships without a great quarterback," said Buddy Parker, the head coach of Detroit's three NFL championship teams of the 1950s. "You may win five or six games with an ordinary player at the position, but as far as a title is concerned you might just as well stay at home if you don't have a real big guy at the spot....That quarterback who can win championships is the most precious commodity in pro football."

The first great championship quarterback was George Parratt, whose celebrity status pre-dated his entry into pro football in 1905. Parratt was perhaps the best athlete in Ohio when he attended Case University. He was the captain of the baseball team, the star of the basketball team, and an outstanding quarterback. Parratt eventually played all three sports professionally.

In late 1905, Parratt was accused of playing professionally for Shelby (Ohio) under the name of Jimmy Murphy. When Case officials called him in to answer the charges, they were shocked. Instead of the denial to get both the player and the university off the hook, Parratt responded differently when asked if he were playing pro

football. "Sure," he said. "And I intend to keep doing it."

In 1906, Parratt led Massillon to the unofficial national championship of pro football. He also completed the first authenticated forward pass in pro football history.

He then turned promoter and coach as well as quarterback. In 1910 and again in 1911, his Shelby team won the unofficial Ohio League title, which generally meant the team was the best in the United States. Parratt moved on to Akron, where his team won the title in 1913 and 1914.

The first great championship quarterback in the NFL actually was a tailback in Green Bay's Notre Dame Box offense. The Packers won three consecutive titles from 1929-1931 under Verne Lewellen.

The late 1930s through the 1940s virtually were owned by the Chicago Bears and quarterback Sid Luckman. Still, Luckman had to share the NFL quarterback spotlight with some other great leaders during those years.

Sammy Baugh led the Washington Redskins to the NFL title as a rookie in 1937. After leading the NFL in passing that year, Baugh dominated the championship game. He passed for 354 yards, including touchdown passes of 55, 78, and 35 yards in the third quarter, as Washington came from behind to defeat the Bears 28-21. Baugh's Redskins won another title in 1942, and also played in the NFL Championship Game in 1940, 1943, and 1945.

"A lot of people think of Luckman as the great winner and of Baugh as the great player who could do everything on a football field but win," said Hall of Fame member Ray Flaherty, who coached the Redskins from 1936-1942. "But that is unfair to Sammy. The Bears won four titles during Baugh's career, but they didn't dominate the league. We won two, the Eagles won two, the Rams won two, and the Packers won two. So give Luckman his due, but don't forget Baugh, [Tommy] Thompson, and [Bob] Waterfield. They were splendid quarterbacks. So was Arnie Herber, who led the Packers to titles in 1936 and 1939."

Herber, like Baugh, was one of the first great NFL passers, and in 1966 was selected to the Pro Football Hall of Fame. He actually joined the Packers in 1930, in the middle of their three-year title streak. But he didn't take over as a regular until 1932.

Thompson was one of the great success stories of the NFL. He initially was a backup with Pittsburgh, but head coach Earle (Greasy) Neale traded for him in 1941 when Neale began his career in Philadelphia. Although he was officially blind in one eye, Thompson was an amazing deep passer and a strong leader on a young team. However, his career was put on hold temporarily when

Thompson—and many other pro football players—went into the armed forces in 1943 during World War II.

When Thompson returned midway through the 1945 season, Neale had begun to put together pieces of his title teams, the most important of which—halfbacks Steve Van Buren and Bosh Pritchard, center Alex Wojciechowicz, and end Pete Pihos—were assembled by 1947. For the next three years, Thompson and Van Buren led the most powerful attack in the NFL. With Van Buren leading the league in rushing each season, and Thompson finishing second, first, and third in passing, the Eagles played in the NFL Championship Game each year. They lost to the Cardinals 28-21 in 1947, but rebounded to beat the Cardinals 7-0 in 1948 and the Rams 14-0 in 1949.

"It would be hard to say that Steve Van Buren wasn't the star of those teams as well as of the entire NFL," said Al Wistert, an all-pro tackle on those Eagles teams. "You could always count on the yards that Steve was going to get you. But I think the real key to the titles was Tommy Thompson. He wasn't just a leader or a passer, although he was outstanding as both. He was much more. He had those indefinable qualities that make a player a winner. And he could transfer those to the rest of the team to make it a championship team. Without Tommy, we still would have been a team of stars. But I don't know if we would have been a great team—a championship team."

The 1950s were boom years for legendary quarterbacks. There was the greatest winner of them all—Otto Graham. There was the greatest leader—Bobby Layne. There was the greatest duo ever—Bob Waterfield and Norm Van Brocklin. And there was the most composed and perhaps proficient of them all—Johnny Unitas.

No one exemplified the spirit of winning then—or ever —as much as Layne, the rugged, free-wheeling, independent-thinking Texan who won not only because *he* wanted to, but because he could make everybody around him want to just as much.

"On the field, I can get a little irritated," he once said, "because I want to win. One year at Detroit, I quit getting on the ball players and they went to the coach and asked him to make me get on them. They said it made them play better. I was trying to be a good guy that year—the guy with the white horse and the white hat. But it's more fun being on the black horse and wearing the black hat."

Part of Layne's mystique, of course, was that he had almost as big a reputation for his antics off the field as on. He was the only man to beat Graham and the Browns twice in a row in championship games. But he also was one of the first to make the hazing of rookies a regular part of training camp. He probably also was the first to call weekly player meetings at a local bar.

"I'm the kind of guy who can't go to bed early," he said. "I don't need more than five hours sleep. If I go to bed early, I wake up early, maybe five o'clock, and if there's a game to play that day I play it over in my mind maybe a dozen times before I even get out on the field. When the Lions played the Browns for the title in 1954, we were all concerned with being the first team to win three championship games in a row. So we all went to bed at ten o'clock and we got beat 56-10. That's no excuse for losing, but I think it shows it takes more than an early bedtime to win a ball game."

Indeed, it took a devotion to hard work, winning, and to the other members of the team. Layne had them as much as any other quarterback. The Lions—the team and the players—were his greatest love.

"We had a team of leaders," he said. "The fellowship between our players was practically legendary. We all thought the same way. You could have all the fun you wanted to, but when you went out to play, you had to win. We looked forward to practice, we looked forward to games. We even looked forward to training camp. Damn, it was like going on a vacation when we went to training camp. Guys got there early, just to get up there and get their hands on the football."

That kind of team spirit is gone today. Most veterans don't come to camp early. But they still want to win.

"The highlight of my career, of the career of anyone on the Chiefs obviously was Super Bowl IV," said Hall of Fame quarterback Len Dawson, the most valuable player in that game. "We had been AFL champs twice, in 1962 and again in 1966. But we wanted to be champs of everything. The mental and physical preparation we went through for that game was unbelievable. We had been close, but it wasn't enough. We all wanted to know what it was like to be the best team in the *entire world*. The feeling proved to be worth all the work."

That emotion, that feeling about winning, runs deep in all of those players who have made themselves champions. It has to because winning titles doesn't come easily in the NFL. Be it Terry Bradshaw, who quarterbacked the Steelers to four Super Bowl titles in the 1970s; or Roger Staubach, who never knew what it meant to surrender; or Jim Plunkett, who overcame tremendous adversity to lead the Raiders to two Super Bowl titles; or Joe Montana, whose desire and belief in himself and his team made him the quarterback of the 1980s, the championship quarterback must above all have one goal: to win.

"We have done well the past several years," said Jim McMahon, who quarterbacked the Chicago Bears to the playoffs five consecutive seasons. "But having the best record in the league during the regular season isn't much of a consolation when you lose in the playoffs.

"When we won Super Bowl XX, we seemed to feel that nothing would ever change, that we would keep on winning Super Bowls forever. So the past several years have been real downers. I know now that once is not enough. I want to be the quarterback of the world champs again. Being a winning quarterback, and even more, being a championship quarterback, is what life is all about."

Sammy Baugh

Sammy Baugh just might have been the greatest player ever to have played football. In an informal vote at an executive meeting of the Pro Football Researchers Association in 1987, Baugh was one of only three people to be named when the question, "Who was the best football player ever?" was posed. Votes for Baugh handily outnumbered those for the other two players—Jim Thorpe and Jim Brown. The numbers support that conclusion: Baugh, who played his college football at TCU, was a member of the initial class of the Pro Football Hall of Fame in 1963, after helping the Redskins to two championships and leading the NFL in passing a record six times and in punting four consecutive years. He not only retired as the league record holder in most season and career passing records, but as the all-time single-season and career punter (51.3- and 45.1-yard averages). He still holds both records. Baugh also made 28 interceptions while playing safety, even though the statistic wasn't kept by the league in his first three seasons, and the Redskins let him play only on offense most of his final seven years. In 1943, he led the league in passing, punting, and interceptions. Baugh's consistency is best shown by his five Pro Bowl appearances—he was selected to four of the first five games between 1939 and 1943. When the game resumed after a decade, he was selected to play in the 1952 game. Baugh truly loved playing the game. When he was asked why he stopped punting late in his career, he said, "In those days because we used a short-punt formation, the punter was usually one of the first two players downfield

making the tackle. On several occasions I hurt my shoulders making tackles, and finally Mr. Marshall [Redskins owner George Preston Marshall] said he didn't want me to go down to make tackles any more. Well, I figured that if I couldn't try to make the tackle—if I couldn't play as hard as I could on the field—I shouldn't be in the game. So I quit punting. There is no point in playing if you can't try to do your absolute best to be the best you can."

When George Halas of the Bears drafted Sid Luckman on the first round of the 1939 draft, he got a rare combination of mental and athletic abilities. Although Luckman had been a Single-Wing tailback at Columbia, he quickly mastered Chicago's highly complex T-formation offense and executed it flawlessly. Luckman's ball-handling, running, passing, and leadership helped the Bears win four NFL titles. The near-perfect performance of Luckman and the Bears in a 73-0 victory over the Washington Redskins in the 1940 NFL Championship Game—the largest margin of victory in NFL history—caused a mass switch to the T-formation with a man-in-motion at all levels of football. Luckman was an all-pro six times. He was the NFL's most valuable player in 1943, when he set league records with 2,194 yards passing and 28 touchdown passes. Luckman was inducted into the Pro Football Hall of Fame in 1965. He still is the Bears' career passing leader, with 14,683 yards and 137 touchdown passes.

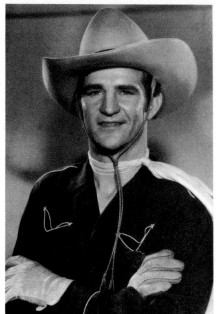

Sammy Baugh in action, and as "King of the Texas Rangers" in a 1940 serial.

Sid Luckman

Norm Van Brocklin

Bob Waterfield

It is virtually impossible to think of Bob Waterfield without also imagining Norm Van Brocklin...and vice-versa. "Buckets" and "Dutch," as the two were nicknamed, were the greatest quarterbacks ever to play together on the same team.

Waterfield, the last player to be named the NFL's most valuable player *and* to lead his team to the league title in his rookie year (1945), was one of the two or three best players in league history. A cool, gifted performer in all phases of football, he led the NFL in passing in 1946 and 1951 and in field goals in 1947, 1949, and 1951. His 315 points is a long-standing Rams record, and his career punting average of 42.4 yards remains one of the best career averages in league history.

Van Brocklin was such a faultless passer that opponents had to find other facets of his game to criticize, to which the Dutchman responded, "That's like saying a pitcher who wins twenty games is a bum because he didn't hit three hundred. And Joe Louis wasn't a great fighter...all he could do was punch." Van Brocklin, who went to college at Oregon, led the NFL in passing three times and in punting twice. In 1951, the same year he threw the winning touchdown pass in the NFL Championship Game, he passed for a single-game record 554 yards against the New York Yanks. Van Brocklin was selected to nine Pro Bowls. At age 34, he was the most valuable player of the NFL in 1960, when, by the sheer dominance of his will and athletic ability, he led the Philadelphia Eagles to the NFL title. He was named to the Pro Football Hall of Fame in 1971, six years after Waterfield.

CHAMPIONS

Otto Graham

I f winning is the measure of a quarterback, then no NFL quarterback ever stood taller than Otto Graham of the Cleveland Browns. Graham, who was a Single-Wing tailback (as well as an All-America in basketball) at Northwestern, was converted to a T-formation quarterback in his first year (1946) with the Browns. In the next 10 seasons, he led Cleveland to 10 title games. Graham and the Browns won seven of them. Graham led the All-America Football Conference in passing

three times and the NFL twice. He was named the most valuable player twice in each league. But he saved many of his best performances for the biggest games: In the 1954 NFL Championship Game, he passed for three touchdowns and ran for three; and in his final game, for the 1955 title, he passed for two scores and ran for two more. But Graham was more than an athlete—he personified everything that head coach Paul Brown considered perfect about a football player, both on and off the field. Graham was selected to the Pro Football Hall of Fame in 1965, the same year as Sid Luckman and Bob Waterfield.

Bobby Layne

Tobin Rote

Bobby Layne began his NFL career at the top, finished it at the top, and was an undisputed master of the game all the time in between. He was the first-round draft choice of the Chicago Bears in 1948 after being a two-time All-America at Texas (where he also was an All-America baseball pitcher). When he retired following the 1962 season, he had completed 1,814 passes in 3,700 attempts for 26,768 yards and 196 touchdowns, all NFL records at the

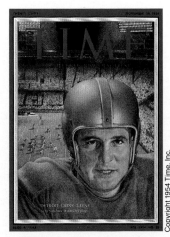

time. Still, numbers never were Layne's strong suit—leadership and winning were. Layne helped lead the Detroit Lions to three NFL titles in the 1950s, and when he was traded to the Pittsburgh Steelers, he led that team to the best record it ever had. Layne drove, pushed, threatened, and shamed in order to win. At times he used a needle; at times he wielded a machete. "Beatty," he once castigated the Steelers' center Ed Beatty, "once, just once, take out your man, and we'll all de-

clare a damned holiday." "Bobby never lost a game," said halfback Doak Walker, his high school teammate in Dallas and with the Lions. "Time just ran out on him." Layne was selected to the Pro Football Hall of Fame in 1967.

Tobin Rote was an anomaly—a man out of sync with his own game. He was a T-formation quarterback for 10 years in the NFL, three in the Canadian Football League, and three more in the AFL. But he always played as if he were the last of the Single-Wing tailbacks. Rote was the second-round draft choice of Green Bay in 1950 out of Rice. He became an immediate starter. In his second year, he set an NFL record for rushing yards by a quarterback with 523. He led the Packers in passing seven consecutive years and in rushing three times, before being traded to Detroit in 1957. That year, he shared the quarterback job until Bobby Layne broke his leg with two games remaining in the season. Rote led the Lions to four consecutive victories, including a 59-14 rout of Cleveland in the NFL Championship Game, in which he passed for four touchdowns and ran for a fifth. Rote left for Canada in 1960, but he joined the San Diego Chargers in 1963. He led the AFL in passing that year, and led the Chargers to their only championship, a 51-10 victory over Boston in which he passed for two scores and ran for another. When Rote retired at Denver following the 1966 season, he had not only passed for 18,850 yards, but had run for 3,128, more than any previous quarterback.

Johnny Unitas

Unitas with Pittsburgh in 1955

I t wasn't until the late 1950s that it became obvious Cinderella never wore glass slippers, but black high-top football shoes. Johnny Unitas, with his golden arm and flat-top crewcut, was a legend in his time. He was selected by Pittsburgh in the ninth round of the 1955 draft after playing at the University of Louisville. Cut by the Steelers, he earned $6 per game with the semipro Bloomfield, Pennsylvania, Rams, before receiving an offer to try out with the Baltimore Colts in 1956. Unitas took over as a rookie when starter George Shaw was injured, and he quickly became what many consider the premier quarterback in the history of the NFL. Unitas was the most valuable player of the NFL three times—in 1959, 1964, and 1967. He played in 10 Pro Bowls, and was selected to the Pro Football Hall of Fame in 1979, his first year of eligibility. When he retired in 1973, he held virtually every meaningful career passing record, including most attempts, completions, yards, touchdowns, and 300-yard games. From 1956 to 1960, he set a monumental pro football record by throwing at least one touchdown pass in 47 consecutive games. What do not show in Unitas's statistics, however, are his poise and leadership. His tying and winning drives in the 1958 NFL Championship Game (*above*) were textbook examples of how to direct a team under pressure.

Bart Starr is the perfect example of how a solid but unremarkable player can flourish when given a chance by the right coach. Starr finished his college career on the bench at Alabama and then was drafted by Green Bay as an afterthought in the seventeenth round in 1956. He played on and off, but never too successfully, his first several years in the NFL, and appeared headed for a career as a journeyman. But when Vince Lombardi became the head coach in Green Bay in 1959, he decided Starr would be his quarterback. The next year the Packers were in the NFL title game. In the seven years following that, they won five NFL titles and the first two Super Bowls. Starr was one of the major catalysts in that success. He was a heady quarterback who took full advantage of all parts of the Packers' epic machine. He was a superb technician who led the NFL in passing three times—in 1962, 1964, and 1966, and was named NFL player of the year in 1966. He was selected to the Pro Football Hall of Fame in 1977, his first year of eligibility. But it was his brilliance in postseason play that set Starr apart. In six NFL title games, he completed 84 of 145 passes for 1,090 yards and 11 touchdowns, with only one interception. In the two Super Bowl victories, he was even better, being named most valuable player both times.

Bart Starr

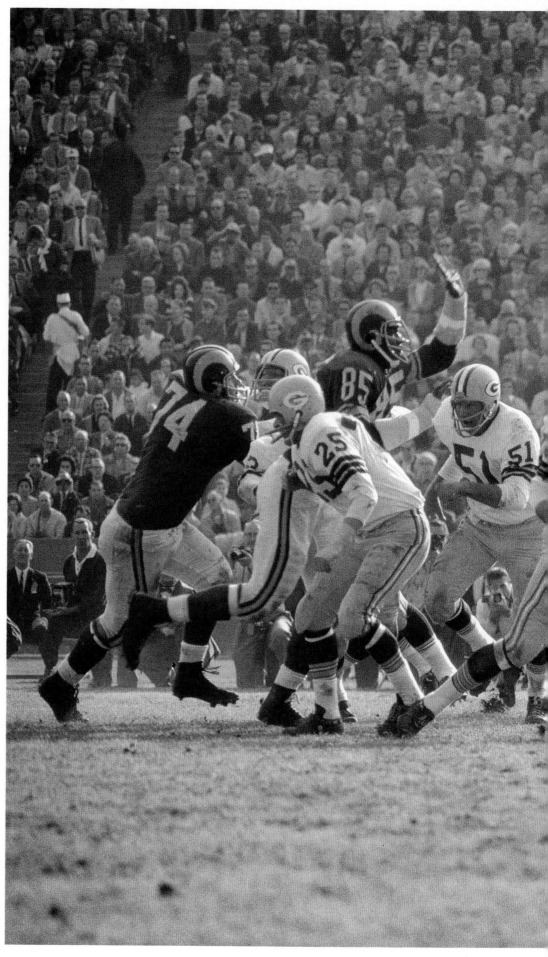

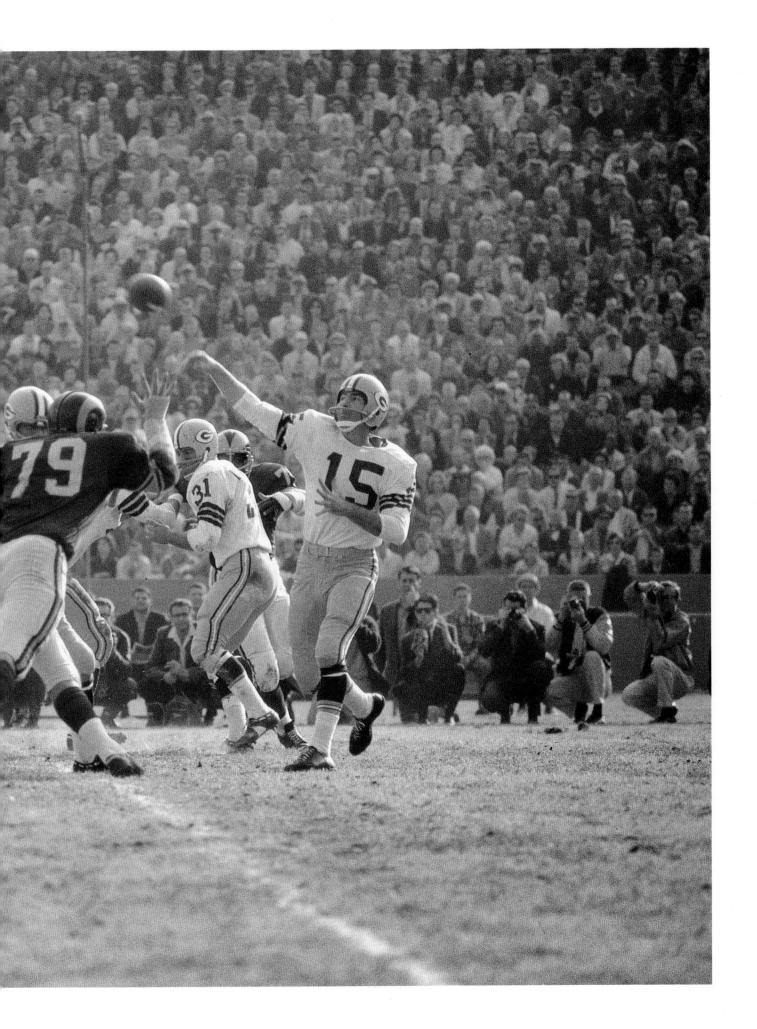

Jack Kemp

Len Dawson

Jack Kemp and Len Dawson had remarkably similar careers. Both had outstanding college careers, Dawson in the national limelight at Purdue, and Kemp at little-known Occidental College in Los Angeles. Both started their NFL careers with the Pittsburgh Steelers in 1957. And neither man promised to be much of a football player early in his pro career. But when given the right coaching, both went on to direct championship teams.

Kemp actually began his pro career as the backup to Earl Morrall. But after a year at Pittsburgh, Kemp played one season in Canada before getting out of football. He returned to the game with the Los Angeles Chargers of the new American Football League. Kemp led the AFL in passing in 1960 and took the Chargers to the title game each of the league's first two years. Picked up on waivers by Buffalo in 1962 (after San Diego head coach Sid Gillman tried to sneak the injured Kemp onto the reserve list), he became a multi-year starter there and led the Bills to AFL titles in 1964 and 1965 and to an Eastern Division championship in 1966 that saw the Bills end up just one game short of the first Super Bowl. Kemp retired following the 1969 season, having been selected to the AFL All-Star Game seven times. After nine terms as a U.S. Congressman from upstate New York, Kemp now is the U.S. Secretary of Housing and Urban Development.

Dawson's career took even longer to flower than Kemp's, although it was ultimately longer and more successful. Dawson spent five lackluster years on NFL benches with the Steelers and Cleveland Browns before joining the Dallas Texans of the AFL in 1962. That year, he led the Texans to the AFL title, was named the league's MVP, and led the AFL in passing for the first of four times. Four years later, Dawson's team, which moved to Kansas City in 1963 and renamed itself the Chiefs, won the AFL title and earned the right to play Green Bay in Super Bowl I, a game the Pack-

ers won 35-10. But in the final game between the AFL and the NFL—Super Bowl IV—Dawson and the Chiefs were back with a chance for redemption. Behind Dawson's brilliant play-calling, the Chiefs shocked Minnesota 23-7. For his play after a week in which he supposedly had been linked to a federal gambling investigation (he eventually was totally cleared), Dawson was named the game's most valuable player. He was selected to the Pro Football Hall of Fame in 1987 after having passed for 28,711 yards and being selected to seven postseason all-star games.

The 10-year AFL patch worn by the Chiefs in Super Bowl IV.

Joe Namath

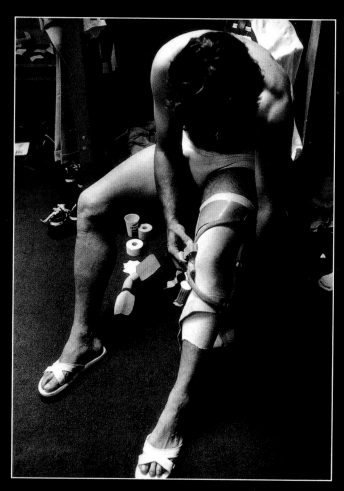

Few people believed that the level of play in the American Football League was anywhere near that of the NFL. In the first two Super Bowls, the Green Bay Packers added an exclamation point to this belief by destroying two AFL teams. But in one game, confident Joe Namath gave the AFL credibility. Namath joined the New York Jets of the AFL in 1965 out of Alabama as one of the most sought-after prospects ever to come from the college ranks. He immediately proved he was worth his record price tag of $400,000. Namath was named the rookie of the year, and two years later he became the first quarterback ever to pass for 4,000 yards in a season (4,007). In 1968, he led the Jets to the AFL title, and the seemingly dubious right to play what was considered one of the greatest football teams of all time, the Baltimore Colts, in Super Bowl III. Namath not only predicted that the Jets would defeat the Colts, he backed up his words. Calling a masterful game, Namath engineered a 16-7 victory, following which he was named most valuable player. Because Namath's great right arm was supported by two of the worst knees in football, his career never reached such heights again. Still, he was named the AFL's all-time quarterback, was selected to play in five AFL All-Star Games or AFC-NFC Pro Bowls, and was inducted into the Pro Football Hall of Fame in 1985.

Roger Staubach

Bob Griese

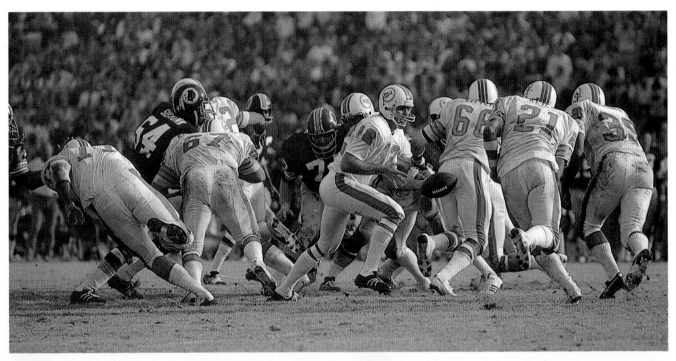

Former Dallas Cowboys head coach Tom Landry once said, "Roger Staubach might be the best combination of a passer, an athlete, and a leader ever to play in the NFL." That is incredible praise from someone who played or coached against Baugh, Graham, Layne, Waterfield, Van Brocklin, Unitas, and Jurgensen. Staubach had all the qualities that make a classic quarterback. He was an outstanding passer, leading the NFL in 1971, 1973, 1978, and 1979, and finishing his career as the all-time leader in passer ratings. He also was an outstanding scrambler and runner, netting 2,264 yards on a 5.5-yard average. Staubach's knack for coming up with the big play made him a great crowd pleaser. But the thing that set Staubach apart from other quarterbacks was his ability to bring his team back from the edge of defeat. In his 11-year career, he led the Cowboys to an unbelievable 23 come-from-behind victories, and almost pulled out both Super Bowl X and XIII. Staubach's exploits started at the U.S. Naval Academy, where he won the Heisman Trophy as a junior. After spending four years in the Navy, he joined Dallas as a 27-year-old rookie. In 1971, his third year, he led the Cowboys to a victory in Super Bowl VI, where he was the most valuable player. Staubach helped the Cowboys to five NFC titles and two Super Bowl victories. Selected to six Pro Bowls, he was inducted into the Pro Football Hall of Fame in 1985, his first year of eligibility.

At the beginning of his pro career, it looked as if Bob Griese was going to have to take a back seat to Steve Spurrier, just as he did in college. An All-America as a junior at Purdue, Griese was beaten out for the Heisman Trophy by Spurrier as a senior. Then he was the fourth player selected in the 1967 NFL draft, one place after Spurrier. But when Don Shula took over in Miami, he helped

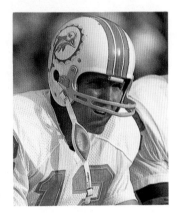

Griese become one of the most successful quarterbacks of all time. Behind Griese's leadership and timely passing, the Dolphins became the only team to play in three consecutive Super Bowls. After a loss to Dallas in Game VI, they came back to win Super Bowls VII and VIII, games in which Griese completed a combined 78 percent of his passes. When the Dolphins' running game declined later, Griese began to pass more, finishing his career with 25,092 yards and 192 touchdown passes. Griese quarterbacked Miami to the playoffs seven times, was selected to eight AFL All-Star Games or AFC-NFC Pro Bowls, and was named NFL player of the year in 1977.

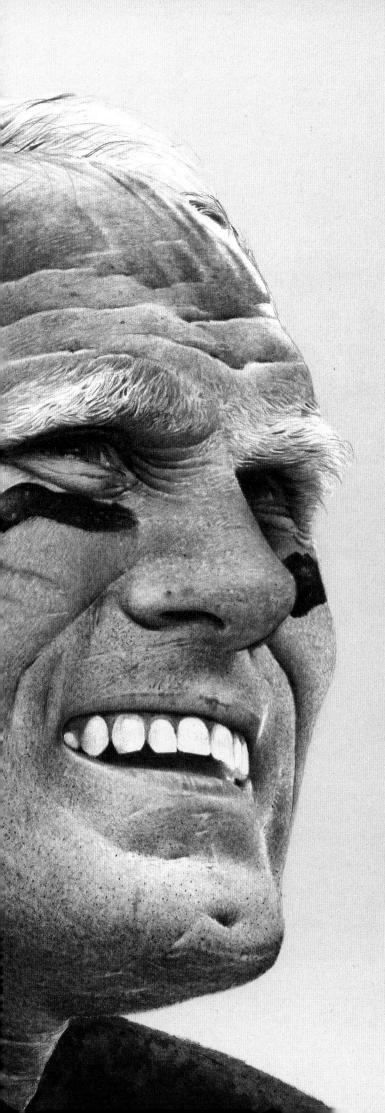

Terry Bradshaw

Terry Bradshaw has something no other quarterback in the history of pro football has—four Super Bowl rings. Bradshaw was considered the perfect prospect when Pittsburgh made him the first selection of the entire 1970 draft out of Louisiana Tech. His enthusiasm, leadership, and running ability made him an immediate starter, although his passing was erratic early in his career. With Bradshaw pulling the trigger, the Steelers won Super Bowls IX and X, the second when he threw a 64-yard touchdown pass to Lynn Swann with 3:02 remaining in the game. He was knocked unconscious on the play. In the Steelers' next two Super Bowl appearances, Bradshaw dominated. He threw for 318 yards and four touchdowns in Game XIII and for 309 yards and two touchdowns, including the winning 73-yard pass to John Stallworth, in Super Bowl XIV. He was named the most valuable player both times. Bradshaw also was chosen as the NFL's MVP in 1978, when he led the AFC in passing, and was named to the official NFL team of the 1970s. He was elected to the Pro Football Hall of Fame in 1989.

Ken Stabler

Jim Plunkett

There were times during their pro careers when fans—even coaches—gave up on both Kenny Stabler and Jim Plunkett. But neither gave up on himself, and both men became leaders of Raiders Super Bowl champions and constant challengers.

Stabler may have been the best of Alabama's long line of quarterbacks. Chosen by the Raiders in the second round of the 1968 draft, Stabler didn't actually join Oakland until 1970. After three years as an apprentice quarterback behind Daryle Lamonica, Stabler took over in 1973 and led the AFC in passing. The next year, he was the AFC's most valuable player, and his four touchdown passes in an AFC Divisional Playoff Game, including an off-balance throw

Plunkett was even more prolific in college, taking Stanford to its first Rose Bowl victory in 30 years, finishing his career as the NCAA's all-time total offense leader, winning the Heisman Trophy, and being the first player selected—by New England—in the 1971 draft. Although he was named rookie of the year in 1971, Plunkett's career began to go downhill from that point. Injuries and the lack of understanding of the pro passing game by Chuck Fairbanks, the Patriots' head coach,

to Clarence Davis with 26 seconds left, dethroned the two-time defending Super Bowl champion Dolphins 28-26. In 1976, Stabler had his greatest year, leading the NFL in passing with a 66.7 completion percentage (the second-best ever at the time). He helped the Raiders to a 16-1 record and a victory in

Super Bowl XI, and he was named the league's player of the year. In 1980, Stabler was traded to Houston, and he led the Oilers to the playoffs his first year there. He finished his career with New Orleans, having passed for 27,938 yards and a phenomenal 59.8 career completion percentage mark.

kept Plunkett from meeting the high expectations of others. He was traded to San Francisco in 1976, but the 49ers released Plunkett shortly before the 1978 season. He then joined the Raiders as a free agent. Two years later, when Dan Pastorini was injured, Plunkett got his chance to play again. He responded by taking Oakland to a victory in Super Bowl XV, where he was named the most valuable player after passing for three touchdowns. Three years later, he helped the Raiders to another Super Bowl ring in Game XVIII. Plunkett retired after the 1987 season with 25,882 career passing yards and a legacy as a player who kept getting up—and then winning—no matter how many times he was knocked down.

Joe Montana

Former San Francisco head coach Bill Walsh says, "When the game is on the line, and you need someone to go in there and win it right now, I would rather have Joe Montana as my quarterback than anybody else who ever played the game. No one has ever been able to win with all the chips down like Joe." Seemingly no one has ever been able to pull so many rabbits from so many helmets in front of so many fans in so many playoff games. Along with Roger Staubach, Montana has been the master of the come-from-behind victory. Earlier, Montana led Notre Dame to the national championship in 1977, and climaxed his career with a 35-34 win over Houston in the 1979 Cotton Bowl, a game in which Notre Dame trailed 34-12 with five minutes left. In his first year as an NFL starter—1980—there was the game against New Orleans when, trailing 35-7 at halftime, Montana threw for two touchdowns and ran for another to give the 49ers a stunning 38-35 triumph. There was the 1981 NFC Championship Game, when he capped an 89-yard drive with the winning touchdown pass to Dwight Clark with 51 seconds left as the 49ers beat the Cowboys 28-27 to go to their first Super Bowl. There were Super Bowls XVI and XIX, where he was named the most valuable player, the second after passing for a record 331 yards, rushing for 59 more, and accounting for four scores. And there was Super Bowl XXIII, where he directed a 92-yard march down the field, throwing a 10-yard touchdown pass to John Taylor with 34 seconds left for a 20-16 victory. Montana is the number-one ranked passer of all-time. He led the NFC in passing in 1981, 1984, and 1985, and the entire NFL in 1987. In his eight full seasons as a starter, Montana has taken the 49ers to six NFC West titles and seven playoff appearances. "If the 49ers are the team of the decade in the 1980s—and they are," says Walsh, "then Joe Montana is the NFL's player of the decade."

Masters of the Game

The man whose picture just might be next to the word "master" in the dictionary is Fran Tarkenton, who quarterbacked the Vikings for 13 years and the Giants for five more.

"I think Tarkenton has to be considered the finest quarterback ever to play the game," the late Tex Maule once wrote in *Sports Illustrated*. "His production was unmatched—he passed for 47,003 yards for goodness sakes—and he added whole new dimensions to the game. His scrambling changed the face of football forever...and late in his career he helped popularize the short-passing offense of which he was a master. Taking a team to three Super Bowls isn't a half-bad accomplishment at that."

Y.A. Tittle's career bridged the gap between the postwar era and the modern era. He twice broke the NFL record for most touchdown passes in a season. "The game was so different," said Tittle, who played with the Colts, 49ers, and Giants. "We did not study two sets of films before each game...We never studied automatics...we didn't even *have* automatics. There was none of the preparation we know today. We did not have to face the great defensive stars who now play in the NFL. In those days, the average life span of a pro was two or three years; today quarterbacks have to contend with defensive specialists who have seven, eight, or nine years experience."

Sonny Jurgensen was perhaps the finest pure passer of all time, although his teams were winners only when he was on the bench—the Eagles when Norm Van Brocklin took them to the 1960 NFL title, and the Redskins when Billy Kilmer took over in 1972.

Earl Morrall made his reputation in the seasons he began as a benchwarmer. Morrall replaced an injured Johnny Unitas in 1968 and took the Colts to Super Bowl III. He replaced Unitas in Super Bowl V and helped the Colts win 16-13. He replaced Bob Griese in week 5 in 1972 and led the Dolphins to a perfect season en route to a victory in Super Bowl VII. But Griese played in the Super Bowl.

Dan Fouts and Dan Marino are the king and the crown prince of the modern passing attack.

"Fouts is a machine," former Cleveland Browns head coach Sam Rutigliano once said. "I think he sees more on a football field than any other quarterback ever. He has the vision to spot any receiver that is open and the arm strength and quick release to get him the ball before he is covered again. He is the most proficient passer I have seen since I've been paying attention to pro football."

In 1979, Fouts became only the second player ever to pass for more than 4,000 yards in a season. The next year, he was the first to do it twice. In 1981, he was the first to do it three times.

It looked as if his marks would remain unchallenged until Dan Marino entered the league. From 1984 through 1988, Marino threw for 4,000 or more yards in a season four times, including a record 5,084 in 1984.

"Marino is not the same kind of passer as Fouts," said Miami head coach Don Shula. "Fouts was a much more controlled passer and as efficient as anyone at the short passing game. Fouts could see the entire field and then throw to the most open receiver.

"On the other hand, Marino likes the deep game more than Fouts, and he takes more chances with it than Fouts. He doesn't always go to the wide open receiver, but sometimes to the one with the potential to be the most dangerous. A lot of coaches wouldn't want a quarterback who forces the ball into seams like Marino does, but, no matter how dangerous his passes look, he always seems to complete them. So Marino has the green light to throw whatever kind of pass he wants at whatever time."

Another player at the top of his game—and his game is putting constant pressure on the defense due to sheer versatility—is Denver's John Elway.

"Elway is easily the most dangerous quarterback in the NFL," said Mike Shanahan, the head coach of the Los Angeles Raiders and the former quarterbacks coach for the Denver Broncos. "He can beat you in so many ways. He can kill you with one deep pass. He can get you by running or by scrambling for a long gain after you think you've got him for a loss. And he can beat you with a ball-possession offense that takes advantage of his own running, short passing, and leadership as well as the abilities of his running backs. All of Elway's skills were put together in that last drive he engineered against Cleveland to win the 1986 AFC title game."

The 98-yard drive actually ended with a tying field goal, putting the 1986 AFC Championship Game into overtime. Like Unitas in the 1958 NFL Championship Game, Elway then marched his team to the winning points.

"The Elway legend and mystique were already there," said Jack Faulkner, the director of football operations for the Los Angeles Rams. "That drive allowed everyone who already knew how great Elway was to say, 'See?' It also proved to all the doubters what the guy could do under pressure."

San Diego's Dan Fouts

Y.A. Tittle

Y.A. Tittle did everything a great quarterback could possibly do except win a title. A record-setting quarterback at LSU, Tittle signed with the Baltimore Colts of the All-America Football Conference in 1948 despite being the top draft choice of the NFL's Detroit Lions. In his professional debut, Tittle threw four touchdown passes in an upset of the New York Yankees. When the Colts folded after one year in the NFL (1950), and their players were made eligible to be drafted, Tittle was the first choice of the San Francisco 49ers. The balding, ungainly-looking Tittle spent 10 years with the 49ers, beating out Frankie Albert late in his first year and remaining the starter until his final year with the team. Traded to the New York Giants in 1961, Tittle found new life, and led the Giants to three consecutive NFL Championship Games. In 1962, when he was named the NFL player of the year for the second time in his career, he set an NFL record with 33 touchdown passes. He broke the mark the next year with 36. When he retired, Tittle had passed for 33,070 yards, the most in pro football history, and had been named to six Pro Bowls. He was voted into the Pro Football Hall of Fame in 1971.

It wasn't his finest hour, but who can forget this image of Y.A. Tittle in 1964?

Earl Morrall

George Blanda

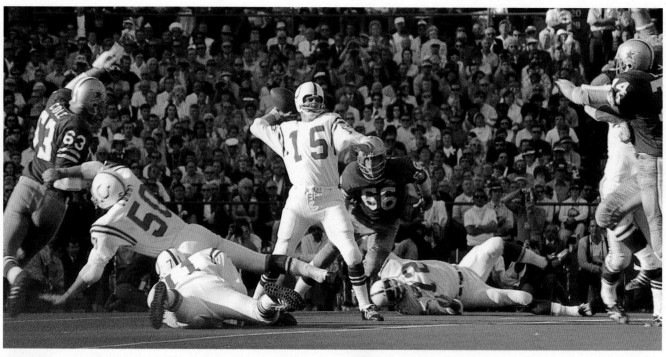

No quarterbacks in the history of pro football played more years than Earl Morrall and George Blanda.

Morrall had an undistinguished career for much of his 21 years, but when he was surrounded with a good supporting cast, he proved a solid pro quarterback. The first-round draft choice of San Francisco in 1956 (from Michigan State), Morrall played with the 49ers, the Steelers, the Lions, and the Giants before joining the Colts in 1968. When Johnny Unitas went out with an arm injury, Morrall took over as the starter and led the Colts to a 13-1 regular-season record—best in the NFL—and, following a 34-0 defeat of Cleveland for the NFL title, an appearance in Super Bowl III. The Colts, of course, lost that game to the AFL's Jets, but Morrall got a chance at vindication two years later. He re-

placed Unitas midway through Super Bowl V (*above*), completed 7 of 15 passes for 147 yards, and helped Baltimore to a last-second victory over Dallas. In 1972, his first year with Miami, Morrall took over when Bob Griese was injured early in the season. Morrall helped the Dolphins to a 17-0 record, that included a victory in Super Bowl VII, for the only perfect season in NFL history. Griese returned to play in the Super Bowl. Morrall was selected to two Pro Bowls—with Pittsburgh in 1957 and with the Colts more than a decade later in 1968. In the latter year, he also led the league in passing and was named the NFL's player of the year. He finished his career in 1976 with 20,809 yards and 161 touchdown passes.

After being drafted out of Kentucky in 1949, Blanda's pro career lasted 26 years, an NFL record for all players. His phenomenal success as a kicker helped him to become the NFL's career scoring leader, with 2,002 points. But Blanda was just as effective as a quarterback, leading the Chicago Bears in passing several times in the 1950s. Although he was out of football in 1959, Blanda returned with Houston of the newly formed American Football League in 1960 and led the Oilers to the first two AFL titles.

In 1961, he passed for a pro record 36 touchdowns, was named the AFL's player of the year, and was selected to the first of four AFL All-Star Games. In 1967, Blanda joined the Oakland Raiders as a kicker and

backup quarterback, a role he filled through the 1975 season. He was named the NFL's player of the year in 1970, becoming a folk hero at age 43 during a phenomenal five-week stretch in which he passed or kicked the Raiders to four victories and a tie in the last minute. Blanda was inducted into the Pro Football Hall of Fame in 1981.

Blanda wore these shoulder pads his entire college and pro career.

The Three Ages of George: 1951 (above left), 1964 (above right), and 1975 (right).

I f there is anything pro football observers of the 1960s and 1970s agreed on, it was that Sonny Jurgensen had the best arm they ever saw. "If I threw as much as Jurgensen, my arm would fall off," Johnny Unitas said. "And if I could throw as well, my head would swell up too big to get into a helmet." Dallas quarterback Don Meredith said, "We go into Washington every year with the best defense in the NFL, and Sonny still scares me to death. He's the one person who can pass a defense to death no matter who is rushing him and no matter who is in the secondary. He is an uncanny passer, simply the best the game has had." Jurgensen lived up to that praise year after year. In 1961, his first year as a starter in Philadelphia, Jurgensen, who had attended college at Duke, set NFL records for completions, yards, and touchdown passes. Six years later, with the Redskins, he set league records for attempts, completions, and yards, while leading the NFL in passing, something he did again in 1969, his one season under head coach Vince Lombardi (he led the NFC in 1974, his final season). What makes Jurgensen's passing accomplishments even more noteworthy is that he spent much of his career with non-contenders and continually seemed to be faced with playing catch-up. He was selected to the Pro Football Hall of Fame in 1983.

Sonny Jurgensen

MASTERS OF THE GAME

Fran Tarkenton

If statistics are the measure of a player, then Fran Tarkenton is in a class by himself. In his 18-year career, after being a third-round draft choice from Georgia, Tarkenton passed more times (6,467), for more completions (3,686), more yards (47,003), and more touchdowns (342) than any other quarterback in history. He also ran for 3,674 yards and an additional 32 touchdowns. But there was more to Tarkenton than just throwing and running a football. He was a true master, a player who could single-handedly dominate the tempo of a game and dictate its outcome by his

Super Tark, the quarterback-warrior, as colorfully depicted by Marvel Comics artist Jack Kirby.

ability to think ahead more clearly and react more quickly than other players. Early in his career, beginning in 1961, Tarkenton made the expansion Minnesota Vikings respectable with relatively little help from his teammates. After a stint with the New York Giants (1967-1971), he returned to a good Minnesota team and made it an outstanding one. In Tarkenton's final six years with the Vikings, they won six NFC Central titles and appeared in three Super Bowls. Tarkenton was selected to the Pro Bowl nine times, and in the 1965 game was named the outstanding back. He was named the NFL's player of the year in 1975, when he led the NFC in passing. Tarkenton was elected to the Pro Football Hall of Fame in 1986.

Ken Anderson

Not much was expected of Ken Anderson of Augustana College relative to most of the big quarterback names in the 1971 draft—including Jim Plunkett, Archie Manning, Dan Pastorini, Lynn Dickey, Joe Theismann, Scott Hunter, and Chuck Hixson. But Anderson became arguably the best of the bunch. In his second year at Cincinnati, he took over as the full-time regular. The next year he led the Bengals to a 10-4 record and the AFC Central title. He tied a record by leading the NFL in passing in consecutive years—1974-75—and then repeated the feat in 1981-82. In 1981, he was named the NFL's player of the year after leading the Bengals to their first Super Bowl appearance (Game XVI), where he completed a game record 25 passes in only 34 attempts for 300 yards. The next year, Anderson set an NFL record by completing 70.6 percent of his passes. For his career, Anderson completed 2,654 of 4,475 attempts for 32,838 yards, and 197 touchdowns. "Anderson never has received the credit he deserves," said former San Francisco head coach Bill Walsh, who once was Anderson's coach in Cincinnati. "He not only was an outstanding passer, but a great student of the game. Few players had the talent, the understanding of the game, and the intuitive feeling Ken did."

Jim McMahon might have been paid the ultimate compliment when it was said that he is the closest thing in modern football to Bobby Layne. Although his career has been plagued by injuries, McMahon still has been able to inspire the Chicago Bears to heights of emotion and performance. In 1985, with the Bears trailing Minnesota 17-9 in the third quarter of a Thursday night game, an injured McMahon came off the bench to throw touchdown bombs on his first two plays and three scoring passes in all, turning the game into a 33-24 Bears victory. Chicago went on to an 18-1 record that year, including a 46-10 victory over New England in Super Bowl XX, where McMahon passed for 256 yards and ran for two touchdowns. At Brigham Young, McMahon twice led the nation in total offense and passing, setting more than 80 NCAA records. He was the most productive single-season and career passer in college history. Selected by the Bears in the first round in 1982, McMahon has helped lead Chicago to five consecutive NFC Central titles.

Jim McMahon

Dan Fouts

The most exciting passing offense of all time might have been the one in San Diego that was known through the late 1970s and the early 1980s as Air Coryell. The man responsible for much of its success was quarterback Dan Fouts. "Dan likes to say that it's Don's [Coryell] system that makes him so effective," former San Diego assistant Tom Bass said. "And it certainly helps to have Don figuring things out. But Dan would be effective anywhere. He is so good that he could take any passing system and make his coach look like a genius." Fouts already was a success in 1973, his rookie year out of Oregon, when he took over the starting job in San Diego from an aging and injured Johnny Unitas. But Fouts really passed the rest of the pack in 1979. That year he directed the Chargers to their first divisional title in 14 years, led the AFC in passing, broke Joe Namath's record for a season's passing yards (with 4,082), earned the first of six Pro Bowl appearances, and was named the AFC player of the year. More of the same followed the next three years, and the Chargers played in two AFC Championship Games. In 1980, Fouts broke his own NFL season passing record with 4,715 yards as well as setting records for attempts (589) and completions (348). The next year he broke each of those again (4,802, 609, and 360). In 1982, he again was named the AFC player of the year after setting a still-existing record for the most yards passing per game in the strike-shortened season (320.3). Fouts retired in 1987 as the second most-prolific passer in NFL history.

Dan Marino

ost of the re-
cords that Dan
Fouts set in the
early 1980s al-
ready have
been erased by
Dan Marino, who is on his way
to becoming the most prolific
passer the NFL has ever known.
A star at Pittsburgh in a year of
stars, Marino was the sixth
quarterback selected in the
1983 draft. But he proved to be
the quickest—and perhaps the
best—study of them all. As a
rookie, he led the AFC in passing, the first rookie to do that

since the 1970 merger. He also
was selected as the starter in
the Pro Bowl. The next year, Marino unleashed the most devastating passing attack ever seen.
He led the NFL while completing a record 362 passes for a
record 5,084 yards and 48
touchdowns, a mark that shattered the long-standing record
of 36. Marino then set Super
Bowl records for attempts (50)
and completions (29), despite
the Dolphins' 38-16 loss to San
Francisco. Marino again led the
AFC in passing in 1986 when he
broke his own record with 378
completions and threw 44
touchdown passes, the second
best total ever. In his first six
years, he passed for 23,856
yards and 196 touchdowns and
was selected to five Pro Bowls.

John Elway

When the Baltimore Colts made Stanford All-America quarterback John Elway the first player selected in the 1983 draft, some scouts said he had the potential to be the best ever. Most of those personnel experts still feel the same way about the man who forced the Colts to trade him to Denver. "Elway doesn't quite have the numbers that some of the other quarterbacks in the league have," said Raiders head coach Mike Shanahan. "But he still is the best in the game. He can carry a team on his own phenomenal athletic ability and his intense desire to win. He was the key to the two consecutive Super Bowl appearances by the Broncos." In fact, while Elway doubters have pointed out that he hasn't yet led the league in passing like two players selected behind him (Dan Marino and Ken O'Brien), all one needs to appreciate his value is to look at what the Broncos have done with and without him. The year before he came to Denver, they won two games. But in Elway's six years, they have won two AFC titles, made the playoffs four times, and, in 1985, finished with the best record ever *not* to make the playoffs (11-5). Meanwhile Elway has become Denver's all-time passing leader, a two-time Pro Bowl selection, and perhaps the most feared quarterback in the NFL. "There is no way to prepare against Elway," Shanahan said. "He can do too many things. When you play the Broncos, all you can do is hope the offensive line doesn't play well, or that the receivers drop passes, or that your offense can control the ball. . . .It is basically impossible to really stop Elway. He is just too good a quarterback."

The Long Season

For quarterbacks, there is a great deal of truth to the maxim, "You are only as good as your last game." Win the Super Bowl and the fans love you. Lose it the next year and you are as popular as a used-car salesman. Likewise, go out on the top of your game and everybody misses you and wishes you still were playing. Retire after being replaced as the regular or after having a down season or two and you are just another loser.

"I saw a lot of my friends go through some really difficult times when they got out of football," said former New Orleans Saints great Archie Manning. "It wasn't just the change in their financial status, which certainly is enough to throw those who haven't prepared themselves properly for a loop. Nor was it the loss of the camaraderie, although the other team members played a significant role in a player's social life. No, even more it was the loss of celebrity status. A player who has been a personality every time he walks into a restaurant suddenly is a nobody. It can be a crushing experience."

Sadly, it is an experience that most football players must someday go through. It is especially true of quarterbacks, who generally have received the most attention

Jim Ninowski

**Bill Wade
with Chicago**

and adoration of anybody on the team.

If a quarterback hasn't been selected to the Pro Football Hall of Fame (and only 21 have been) or he didn't win at least one championship (again, a very limited number have), then his chances of being remembered by the public decrease even more significantly. For every 1960s player with the status enjoyed today by Bart Starr, there are several contemporaries—such as Jim Ninowski, Rudy Bukich, Randy Johnson, and Dick Shiner—who are mostly forgotten except in trivia contests.

Realizing that ex-quarterbacks, like all ex-football players, are consigned to out-of-sight, out-of-mind status, it shouldn't be surprising that the names of many former solid NFL quarterbacks no longer are household words with most football fans.

Some of those faintly remembered players might be—in fact, *should* be—in the Pro Football Hall of Fame.

John Brodie quarterbacked the 49ers for 17 years, led them to their first three divisional titles, was the NFC player of the year in 1970, and passed for more than 30,000 yards. But Brodie is not in the Hall of Fame, and the longer he is out of football, the less likely people are to remember what he did.

Brodie is only one example of many outstanding quarterbacks who toiled with great success for years, only to be forgotten when they finished playing.

There are a number of reasons for the disappearance of these former star quarterbacks.

The most obvious is that most of them went home at the end of each season without a league championship victory or, more recently, a Super Bowl ring—or, in the cases of Craig Morton and Danny White, with one earned while on the bench. Even some championship quarterbacks who made the mistake of predating the Super Bowl and all of its attendant hoopla have been forgotten. How many times do the names of Cecil Isbell, Charlie Conerly, Billy Wade, or Frank Ryan happen to come up?

Some quarterbacks get scant Hall of Fame consideration because their careers are tales of two—or three or more—cities. Eddie LeBaron split his career between Washington and Dallas; Norm Snead played for five teams; Charley Johnson started for three different clubs; and Billy Kilmer spent four years in San Francisco, four in New Orleans, and eight in Washington.

A quarterback's reputation also can be tarnished if he is traded to a new team late in his career, thus ending on a down-note for a club with which he has no history. Some players, such as Johnny Unitas and Joe Namath, had such superlative careers that they could overcome such finishes—Unitas spending his final season in San

Diego watching Dan Fouts begin his career, and Namath watching Pat Haden from the Los Angeles Rams' bench. However, other quarterbacks have been traded without the fanfare accorded a retiring hero, only to disappear unappreciated in a different part of the country.

John Hadl starred for 11 years in San Diego, then went to the Rams, where he was the NFC player of the year in 1973. But Hadl spent his last two years as a backup to Dan Pastorini in Houston. When he retired, it was no big deal, despite the fact he had passed for 33,503 yards, at the time the third-highest figure in pro football history.

A quarterback doesn't have to end up on another team's bench to be forgotten. Many players end up simply beaten out by someone on their own

Dick Shiner

team and sitting for their last couple of playing seasons.

"There is a tendency when a long-time starter is beaten out for his job to say that he just hung on too long and should have retired earlier," said Hall of Fame defensive tackle Merlin Olsen. "I don't think that is necessarily true. For one thing, the player might not have lost any skills at all, but a different player might appeal to the coach— who himself can be new—for whatever reason. If the player still has the skills that have made him a starter, why get out, unless he wants to?

"There are a lot of options for a player in that situation, especially for a quarterback, a position that every team desperately needs quality at. The player could get traded and become a starter. He can earn his job back, simply because he has a lot more mental preparation and experience than a young quarterback, even if the kid has more physical talent. Or he can be a backup and see if good things happen for him, because they frequently will.

"Earl Morrall went from being a backup to being the NFL's MVP because of an injury to Johnny Unitas. Steve Grogan went from being on the bench to regaining his starting job, simply because Raymond Berry realized that Grogan's experience and drive allowed him to move the team better than Tony Eason. And Roman Gabriel switched teams in midstream and earned selection to the Pro Bowl with the Eagles, just like he had with the Rams."

Many other players just fade away, however. After twice being most valuable player of the American Football League, Daryle Lamonica spent his last two years with the Oakland Raiders riding the bench behind Kenny Stabler. In 1974, his final season, Lamonica threw fewer passes than the other backup, Larry Lawrence.

Sonny Jurgensen spent the last several years of his career playing behind Billy Kilmer, although he did play enough to lead the NFC in passing his final year. Bill Nelsen, Jim Zorn, and Ken Anderson finished their careers watching Mike Phipps, Dave Krieg, and Boomer Esiason.

A final reason why some quarterbacks never get the long-term acclaim they deserve is that they are matched with an outstanding running back who receives most of the attention. Buffalo's Joe Ferguson was one of the most effective quarterbacks in the early 1970s. However, he never really received much notoriety because he played on the same team as Hall of Fame running back O.J. Simpson. For years, some people believed that all Ferguson did was hand the ball off to O.J., and that he didn't contribute in any other significant way to the Bills' attack. Disputing this notion are numbers such as these: Ferguson led the NFL with 25 touchdown passes in 1975; he set an NFL record by throwing only one interception in 151 attempts in 1976; and his 3,652 passing yards led the Bills to the playoffs in 1981, something they had accomplished only once during Simpson's tenure in Buffalo.

On the following pages are some NFL quarterbacks who have had careers in which they were—or are—at or near the top of their profession. Those who are retired

Seattle's Jim Zorn

should be remembered, even though many aren't. Maybe some of those still playing—Neil Lomax, Randall Cunningham, or Bernie Kosar, for example—will go down as all-time greats. Maybe they will be effective, even record-setting while they play, then immediately discarded from the collective memory when they retire.

THE LONG SEASON

Jim Finks

Frankie Albert

Most pro football fans know that Jim Finks helped build the Minnesota Vikings, Chicago Bears, and New Orleans Saints into Super Bowl contenders over the past two decades. But few remember that Finks once was one of the best passers in the NFL. A star quarterback at Tulsa, Finks joined the Pittsburgh Steelers in 1949, when they were the only NFL team still using the Single-Wing. In his first three years, he played primarily defense (combining that with a two-year career in pro baseball), but the Steelers switched to the T in 1952, and Finks became the starter. For four years, Finks was one of the most effective passers in the NFL, leading the league with 20 touchdown passes in 1952 and with 2,270 yards in 1955. He retired in 1956 to become an assistant coach at Notre Dame.

When he entered Stanford, Frankie Albert was considered too small (5-10, 160) to be an effective Single-Wing tailback. But in Albert's second year, head coach Clark Shaughnessy installed the T-formation. Shaughnessy put Albert —who was left-handed—in charge of making it work. A magician with a football, Albert became a two-time All-America leading Stanford's "Wow Boys" and was a first-round draft pick of the Chicago Bears in December, 1941. However, when he came back from the service following World War II, Albert chose to join San Francisco of the new All-America Football Conference. Albert shared the new league's most-valuable-player award in 1948 after throwing a record 29 touchdown passes, and he finished

as the AAFC's career leader with 88 touchdown passes (compared to 86 for Otto Graham). Albert then spent three more years with the 49ers after they moved to the NFL in 1950, finishing his career with 10,795 passing yards. In 1956, he became the popular head coach of the 49ers and in three seasons compiled a 19-17-1 record.

Albert was featured on a 1951 Bowman card.

Charlie Conerly   Ed Brown

After several years in the armed forces, Charlie Conerly led the nation in passing as a senior at Mississippi, setting an NCAA record with 133 completions, while earning All-America honors. In 1948, the Washington Redskins, who had drafted him when he became eligible in 1945, traded his rights to the New York Giants, who had just installed the T-formation. He became an immediate starter for New York. In the next 14 years, Conerly helped lead the Giants to one NFL title and three other appearances in the championship game. In the same period, he became the inspiration for the Marlboro Man cigaret campaign. He also led the NFL in passing in 1959 and was named to the Pro Bowl twice (1951 and 1957). New York fans often were tough on him, but those who really knew football knew how good he was. "Conerly got a lot of flak from the fans and press in the early part of his career," said Tom Landry, who played with Conerly and then coached the Giants' defense. "But the coaching staff was as content as it could be. [Giants offensive coach] Vince [Lombardi] always believed totally in Conerly. Vince always viewed him as the perfect pro."

Ed Brown spent most of his football career in the shadow of great running backs, but that didn't stop him from being one of the game's most efficient quarterbacks. In 1951, Brown quarterbacked one of the nation's top college teams—the University of San Francisco—but more credit went to All-America halfback Ollie Matson and star defensive lineman Gino Marchetti. After two years in the armed forces, Brown joined the Chicago Bears. He didn't wait long to take over. In his second year, he claimed the starting job from veterans George Blanda and Zeke Bratkowski, then finished second in the NFL in passing. The next season, he led the league in passing, helped the Bears to the NFL Championship Game, and was selected to his second consecutive Pro Bowl. But most of the team's offensive notoriety went to fullback Rick Casares, the league's leading rusher. Brown remained the Bears' starter for most of the next five years, be-fore he was traded to Pittsburgh in 1962. The next season, he succeeded Bobby Layne as the starter and passed for a personal high 2,982 yards. However, he again was overshadowed because of the play of fullback John Henry Johnson and end Buddy Dial. Brown retired after the 1965 season, following a brief stint with Baltimore, having passed for a total of 15,600 yards. He also averaged 40.5 yards as a punter.

Eddie LeBaron

The Dallas Cowboys' history of great quarterbacks includes Roger Staubach, Craig Morton, and Danny White. . .plus two men who go back to the beginning of the franchise, veteran Eddie LeBaron and rookie Don Meredith. LeBaron already was an established starter when Dallas traded its first selection in its first draft for him. He joined Washington from College of The Pacific in 1952 and became a starter as a rookie, succeeding Sammy Baugh and keeping the veteran on the bench much of his final season. In 1954, the 5-7, 165-pound LeBaron and defensive end Gene Brito jumped the Redskins' ship to play in Canada. But they returned a year later, and LeBaron made his first Pro Bowl, where he threw two touchdown passes, including the winning one. After that game in Los Angeles, LeBaron met his wife outside the locker room, just as Gene (Big Daddy) Lipscomb emerged from the losers' locker room. "My wife hadn't been around football much," LeBaron says. "Big Daddy walked over. He was six-seven, maybe three hundred pounds. He had a little beard and he wore a pork-pie hat. Sweat was dripping down his goatee. He loomed over me and said, 'You little s.o.b. I'll get you next year.' My wife wanted me to retire on the spot." But LeBaron's best years were ahead of him. In 1958, with Washington, he led the NFL in passing; in 1962, with Dallas, he finished third. He was selected to three more Pro Bowls, including one with Dallas.

While LeBaron was finishing his career, Meredith was beginning his. A two-time All-America at SMU, Meredith signed a personal services contract with Dallas founder Clint Murchison before the Cowboys officially had been awarded a franchise. He proved worth it. Meredith, a flamboyant leader who answered to the name "Dandy," shared the starting job with LeBaron for several years before assuming full-time duties in 1963. With Meredith throwing to Bob Hayes, Frank Clarke, and Lance Rentzel, Dallas had the most explosive offense in the NFL in the mid-1960s. Meredith led the Cowboys to the NFL Championship Game in both 1966 and 1967, but his best season was his last, 1968, when he finished second in the league in passing and took Dallas to its best-ever 12-2 record. He caught the football world off guard when he announced his retirement before the 1969 season, having passed for 17,199 yards and 135 touchdowns in his career.

Eddie LeBaron

In 1970, in his first year, Don Meredith won an Emmy for his work with the exceedingly verbose Howard Cosell on ABC's "Monday Night Football."

Don Meredith

Frank Ryan   Bill Nelsen

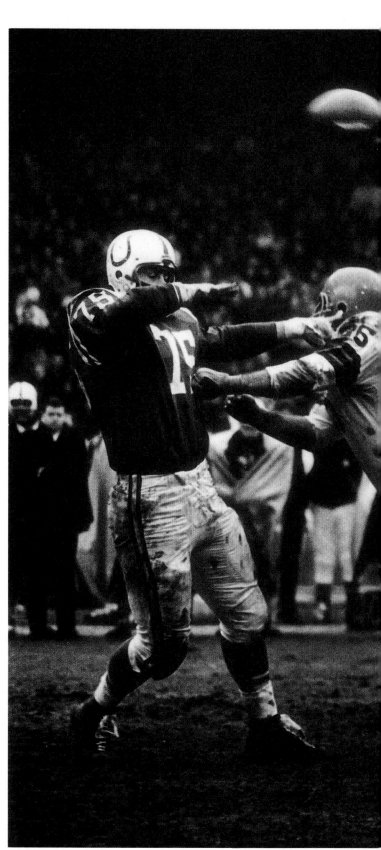

Through most of the 1960s and into the 1970s, Cleveland had one of the best running attacks in pro football, spearheaded first by Jim Brown and then by Leroy Kelly. The running backs weren't the whole story of the Browns, however. Two outstanding quarterbacks—Frank Ryan and Bill Nelsen—also were keys to the Browns' suc- ·cess. Ryan played for the Los Angeles Rams four years after graduating from Rice. He was traded to the Browns and immediately became the team's start-

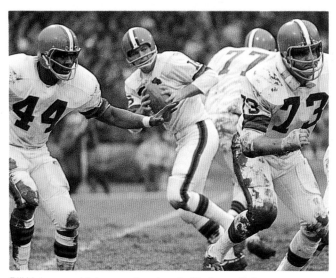

Cerebral Frank Ryan was one of Paul Brown's favorite players.

er. In 1963-65, he led the Browns to a three-year streak of 10 or more victories each season, matching the club's AAFC records in 1946-48. Ryan threw three touchdown passes to

Gary Collins in the 1964 NFL Championship Game as Cleveland surprised heavily favored Baltimore 27-0 (*right*). He led the team to the title game again in 1965, only to lose to Lombardi's Packers on a frozen, snowy field at Green Bay. Ryan remained the Browns' starter through the 1967 season, when he was replaced by Nelsen. Ryan finished his career as a reserve in Washington in 1970, having passed for a total of 16,042 yards and 149 touchdowns. He was named to the Pro Bowl three times.

After five years with the Steelers, Nelsen was obtained by Cleveland head coach Blanton Collier in 1968 as the eventual replacement for Ryan. But Nelsen immediately took over the job, and helped take the Browns to the playoffs four of the next five years, including 1968 and 1969, when they reached the NFL title game. Nelsen's deteriorating knees prompted Cleveland to trade Paul Warfield for the draft pick that was used to take Purdue quarterback Mike Phipps, but Nelsen's courage and desire allowed him to stay in pro football long enough to pass for 14,265 yards before retiring after the 1970 season.

Bill Nelsen could do more than hand off to Leroy Kelly.

John Hadl

Daryle Lamonica

Before Super Bowl III, Joe Namath horrified the pro football establishment by saying that at least four AFL quarterbacks were better than NFL most valuable player Earl Morrall. Two of the men he was referring to were John Hadl and Daryle Lamonica.

Hadl was one of pro football's most successful passers after a college career at Kansas in which he was as well known for his running and punting as for his ability to throw the ball. Hadl signed with the San Diego Chargers in 1962 despite being the first-round draft choice of the Detroit Lions of the NFL. He became a starter as a rookie when Jack Kemp was injured and then waived to Buffalo. Within several years, Hadl had established himself as one of the most effective quarterbacks in the league, leading the AFL in passing in 1965, finishing second in 1966, and throwing for more than 3,300 yards in both 1967 and 1968. In 1973, he was traded to Los Angeles, where he led the Rams to the best record in pro football and was named the NFL player of the year. He finished his career with stints in Green Bay and Houston. In his 16-year career, he was selected to six AFL All-Star Games or AFC-NFC Pro Bowls and was the number-five passer of all-time in yardage, with 33,503 yards, while throwing 244 touchdown passes.

Lamonica, not Namath, actually was the quarterback most people had expected to see playing against the Colts in Super Bowl III. He wasn't one of Notre Dame's most heralded quarterbacks, and he had backed up Jack Kemp in Buffalo for the first four years of his career, but Oakland head coach Johnny Rauch traded for Lamonica in 1967, and installed him as the starter. In his first year with the Raiders, the "Mad Bomber," as Lamonica was known, led the AFL in passing, was named the league's player of the year, and took Oakland to Super Bowl II. Two years later, he again was the MVP in the AFL, after throwing 34 touchdown passes and leading the Raiders to the best record in pro football. Although Lamonica finished his career on the bench behind Ken Stabler, he was the perfect executor of Al Davis's vertical passing game in his heyday. In each of his first three years with the Raiders, he threw for more than 3,000 yards, and he led the AFC in passing in his fourth. Lamonica frequently saved some of his biggest games for the playoffs: In a 1968 AFL Western Conference playoff game, he threw for 347 yards and five touchdown passes—three in the first quarter—as the Raiders beat the Chiefs 41-6. In the 1969 playoffs, he threw six touchdown passes (including three in the first quarter again) as the Raiders destroyed the Oilers 56-7.

Norm Snead

N orm Snead and Craig Morton spent much of their long careers—16 years for Snead and 18 for Morton—as bitter rivals. Morton once even replaced Snead on the same team.

Eagles, 1964-1970

Snead was the first-round draft choice of Washington in 1961 after a brilliant career at Wake Forest. An immediate starter in the NFL, Snead preferred the deep game to a controlled passing attack. He was part of one of the most famous trades of all time in 1964, when he was sent to Philadelphia for Sonny Jurgensen. Snead's career often followed a strange up-and-down pattern, in which mediocre years were followed

by outstanding ones. In 1966, he passed for only 1,275 yards and eight touchdowns, but the next season he set Philadelphia records with 3,399 yards and 29 touchdown passes. In 1968, injuries held him to 1,655 yards, but the next year, Snead passed for 2,768 yards. Snead spent 1971 as a reserve with Minnesota, but the next year he led the NFL in passing with the New York Giants. In 1974, he was traded to San Francisco to make room for Morton. For all of the ups and downs, Snead finished as one of the most prolific passers of all time, with 30,797 career yards.

Vikings, 1971

Giants, 1972-74, 1976

49ers, 1974-75

Craig Morton

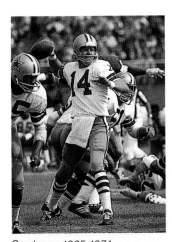

Cowboys, 1965-1974

Giants, 1974-76

Broncos, 1977-1982

Morton had to wait longer to take over as a starter. Dallas's first-round draft choice in 1965, the former University of California star sat on the bench for four years until Don Meredith retired. In his first two years as a regular, Morton was bothered by injuries, although in 1970 he led the Cowboys to Super Bowl V, where they lost to the Colts. Midway through the 1972 season, Dallas head coach Tom Landry decided to go with Roger Staubach as his quarterback. Morton started in 1973 when Staubach was injured in a preseason game, but his days in Dallas were numbered. In mid-1974, the Cowboys traded Morton to the Giants. In 1977, he was traded again, this time to Denver, where he got a new lease on life. In Morton's first three years in Denver, the Broncos, who never had made the playoffs in their first 17 years, went three consecutive times, including playing in Super Bowl XII against Dallas. Morton kept his magic until the end of his career. In 1981, his next-to-last season, he completed 17 of 18 passes for 308 yards and four first-half touchdowns in a game against San Diego. He retired with 27,908 career passing yards, still sixteenth all-time.

Morton with Tom Landry in 1969

Roman Gabriel   John Brodie

Brodie fires a touchdown pass against the Rams in 1968.

Roman Gabriel, a talented and handsome quarterback from North Carolina State, was the Rams' number-one draft choice in 1962. Gabriel became the regular starter in his second year, but midway through the next season, head coach Harland Svare replaced him with Bill Munson, a rookie from Utah State. When Munson was injured late in his second year, Gabriel took over again. The game of musical quarterbacks ended when George Allen became head coach and stuck with Gabriel, who responded with a series of outstanding seasons. In 1967, he passed for 25 touchdowns and led the Rams to the best record in the NFL (11-1-2), and, in 1969, he was named the NFL's player of the year. Gabriel was one of the first truly big quarterbacks (6-4, 220). He remains one of the strongest players ever to play the position. His forte was finding the open receiver 40 to 60 yards downfield and easily completing a pass despite two or three defensive players hanging on him, desperately trying to bring him down. In 1973, the Rams traded Gabriel to Philadelphia, where he immediately injected some offense into the Eagles with 3,219 passing yards and his fourth Pro Bowl appearance. In his 16-year career, Gabriel passed for 29,444 yards—the eleventh-most ever—and 201 touchdowns.

Gabriel finished as an Eagle.

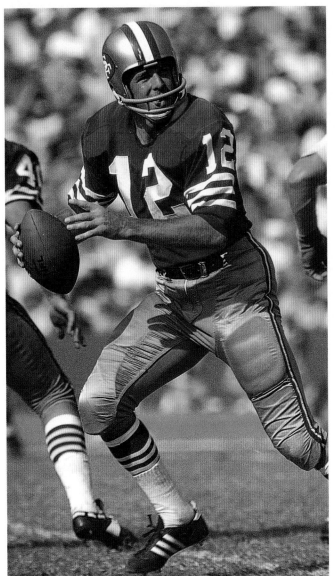

For 17 years, San Francisco's John Brodie, one of the greatest players *not* in the Hall of Fame, was one of the most consistent—and dangerous—passers in the NFL. An All-America at Stanford in 1956, when he led the nation in passing and total offense, Brodie was the 49ers' number-one draft choice. After serving an apprenticeship behind Y.A. Tittle, Brodie became the regular starter in 1960. He held the job almost until he retired after the 1973 season. Brodie led the NFL with a 9.1-yard average per attempt in 1961, with 3,112 yards and 30 touchdown passes in 1965, with 230 completions and 3,020 yards in 1968, in overall passing in 1970, and with 2,642 yards in 1971. He also took the 49ers to their first three divisional titles (1970-72) and was named the NFC player of the year in 1970. Brodie passed for a total of 31,548 yards (the ninth-most ever) and 214 touchdowns.

Jim Hart
Charley Johnson

In the early 1960s, the St. Louis Cardinals had one of the best young passers in football in Charley Johnson. But Johnson was cut down in an unusual manner—by the U.S. military—and the Cardinals replaced him with another of the best—and longest-lasting—passers, Jim Hart.

Johnson actually was drafted as a future by the old Chicago

A young Jim Hart, 1968.

Cardinals in 1960, in the midst of a brilliant career—academically and athletically—at New Mexico State. Johnson became a starter midway through his second year and proved a fast learner. The next season he passed for 3,280 yards and 28 touchdowns, both second-best in the NFL. In 1964, he led the NFL with 3,045 passing yards, but injuries forced him to miss part of the next two seasons. Before the 1967 season, Johnson was drafted into the Army, leaving the starting job to young Hart, who kept it despite Johnson's return in 1969. Johnson spent two years in Houston before ending his career in Denver,

where he finished among the AFC's top four passers three consecutive years (1972-74) and led the AFC with 20 touchdown passes in 1973. Johnson passed for 24,410 career yards and 170 touchdowns.

When Hart joined the Cardinals as a free-agent rookie out

Charley Johnson with the Oilers in 1970

of Southern Illinois, hardly anyone noticed. But when he retired 19 years later, everyone knew who he was. Hart was the club's starter from 1967, when he passed for 3,008 yards, until 1982, when he was succeeded by young Neil Lomax. In Hart's most successful years (1973-77), he was teamed with head coach Don Coryell. In that period, he led the Cardinals to three consecutive seasons of 10 victories, took them to two NFC East titles, and was selected to the Pro Bowl four times. Hart spent his final year as a backup to Joe Theismann in Washington. He remains the number-four passer of all-time in yardage, and finished his career with 5,076 attempts for 2,593 completions, 34,665 yards, and 209 touchdowns.

Johnson was Denver's leading passer for three years before giving way to Steve Ramsey.

Billy Kilmer

San Francisco made Billy Kilmer—who had led the nation in total offense at UCLA—its first-round draft choice in 1961 because he seemed a perfect candidate for head coach Red Hickey's innovative Shotgun offense. Although the offense didn't last, Kilmer did. The multi-faceted Kilmer (who also played basketball for John Wooden) began his career primarily as a runner, averaging more than five yards a carry in each of his first two seasons be-

Billy Kilmer was an outstanding runner in 1961-62.

Kilmer with the Saints, 1967

fore he broke a leg late in 1962. After missing an entire season, he returned, but he was generally ineffective and remained a backup to John Brodie. In 1967, Kilmer was grabbed in the expansion draft provided new franchises by New Orleans, for whom he became a starter, leading the Saints in passing three consecutive years. In 1971, Redskins head coach

George Allen traded for Kilmer, who, teaming with Sonny Jurgensen, led Washington to four consecutive playoff appearances, including the NFC berth in Super Bowl VII. Although people gave up on Kilmer each year because his passing didn't have the grace of Jurgensen's, his gutsy play, leadership, and ability to come back from adversity kept him with Washington through 1978. He finished his career with 20,495 yards and 152 touchdown passes.

Kilmer guided Washington to Super Bowl VII, but was limited to 104 yards and intercepted three times by Miami's "No Name Defense."

Greg Landry

ot many Americans had heard of Greg Landry when he joined the Detroit Lions from the University of Massachusetts, but he quickly showed that he had all of the skills to be an outstanding NFL quarterback. After a couple of years as a backup to Bill Munson, Landry split the job in 1970, when he completed 61 percent of his

Landry played two years with the Chicago Blitz/Arizona Wranglers of the USFL.

passes and averaged 10 yards per carry. In 1971, his first year as a starter, Landry finished second in the NFC in passing behind Roger Staubach and set an NFL record for quarterbacks with 530 yards rushing. The next year, he ran for 524 and led the NFC with nine rushing touchdowns. Landry's passion for running caused him to be injured frequently. His battle-scarred knees and subsequent immobility contributed to his being traded to Baltimore in 1979.

However, an injury to Bert Jones allowed Landry to play, and he responded with 2,932 passing yards. Landry finished his long NFL career in 1984 in Chicago, with a career total of 16,052 passing yards.

James Harris
Joe Ferguson

James Harris and Joe Ferguson are perfect examples of how NFL careers can change. Both started in Buffalo with great expectations, and both figured to be the Bills' quarterback of the future at one time. One was, one wasn't.

Based on what he did as a rookie reserve out of Grambling, Harris was projected as the Bills' starter in 1970. That year, however, Buffalo selected Dennis Shaw in the draft, and he not only earned the starting job, he went on to rookie-of-the-year honors. Harris hardly played again until he was picked up by the Rams as a backup in 1973. In his second year in Los Angeles, Harris suddenly became the starter when John Hadl was traded to Green Bay. He responded by leading the Rams to the NFC title game, finishing

Harris (12) and Simpson both were Buffalo rookies in 1969, though O.J., the first pick in the draft, got the headlines.

second in the NFC in passing, and being selected to the Pro Bowl, where he was named the game's most valuable player after throwing two fourth-quarter touchdown passes to produce a 17-10 victory. Some things rarely change in L.A., and Harris soon became embroiled in a quarterback controversy. In 1976, Harris lost the starting job late in the season despite having passed for 439 yards against Miami and having led

the NFC in passing. Shipped to San Diego the next year, Harris spent most of the last five years of his career as a backup to Dan Fouts, although he did have one last fling when Fouts held out several weeks in 1977.

Two years after Harris left Buffalo, Ferguson appeared. He had been a top Heisman Trophy contender at Arkansas, but a disappointing senior season took him out of the national spotlight. When Bills head coach Lou Saban decided to put his eggs in O.J. Simpson's basket, he saw Ferguson as a guy who wouldn't break them.

Joe Ferguson and daughter Kristen call it a game.

Ferguson became a starter as a rookie and remained in the job long after the Bills had learned to emphasize the pass. He remained a starter through his last year in Buffalo (1984), while becoming the Bills' career passing leader. He then played as a backup at Detroit and Tampa Bay. Ferguson finished the 1988 season (with Tampa Bay) not only as the twelfth-most productive passer of all time with 29,263 yards and 193 touchdowns, but as the top active passer in pro football.

Archie Manning

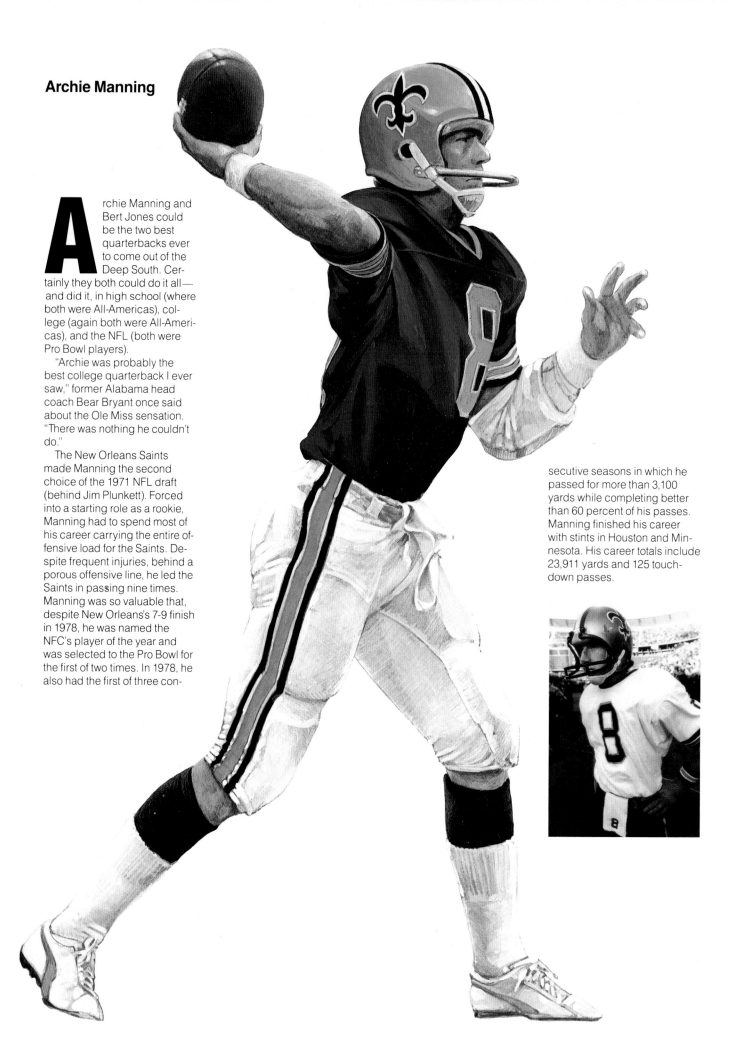

Archie Manning and Bert Jones could be the two best quarterbacks ever to come out of the Deep South. Certainly they both could do it all—and did it, in high school (where both were All-Americas), college (again both were All-Americas), and the NFL (both were Pro Bowl players).

"Archie was probably the best college quarterback I ever saw," former Alabama head coach Bear Bryant once said about the Ole Miss sensation. "There was nothing he couldn't do."

The New Orleans Saints made Manning the second choice of the 1971 NFL draft (behind Jim Plunkett). Forced into a starting role as a rookie, Manning had to spend most of his career carrying the entire offensive load for the Saints. Despite frequent injuries, behind a porous offensive line, he led the Saints in passing nine times. Manning was so valuable that, despite New Orleans's 7-9 finish in 1978, he was named the NFC's player of the year and was selected to the Pro Bowl for the first of two times. In 1978, he also had the first of three con-secutive seasons in which he passed for more than 3,100 yards while completing better than 60 percent of his passes. Manning finished his career with stints in Houston and Minnesota. His career totals include 23,911 yards and 125 touchdown passes.

Bert Jones

Like Manning, Jones, the son of former Cleveland Browns great Dub Jones, was the second player selected in the draft (1973) after being an All-America at LSU. After two years of sharing the Colts' quarterback job with Marty Domres, Jones took over in 1975 and led Baltimore, which had had only two victories in 1974, to three consecutive AFC East titles. Jones never finished lower than third in AFC passing in those three years, leading the conference with

3,104 yards in 1976 and 224 completions in 1977. Jones was injury-plagued in the latter stages of his career, although he did pass for 3,134 yards in 1980 and 3,094 in 1981. He finished his career after one year with the Rams, having passed for 18,190 yards and 124 touchdowns.

Few father-son combinations could keep up with the Joneses, especially on their home field.

Danny White

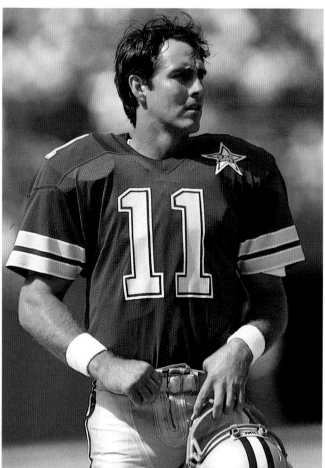

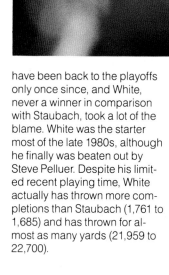

Few quarterbacks ever got dealt tougher hands than Danny White and Steve Bartkowski. White had to follow Roger Staubach in Dallas, and Bartkowski had to play for weak Atlanta teams. Each played valiantly in his own way, but neither ever overcame his draw.

White was drafted by Dallas in 1974 after setting NCAA records at Arizona State for most total offense yards per play for both a season and a career. After initially playing for Memphis of the World Football League, White joined the Cowboys in 1976 as a punter and backup quarterback. In 1980, with the retirement of Staubach, White became the starter. That year he passed for 3,287 yards and 28 touchdowns and took the Cowboys to the title game. The next year, White's last-minute pass almost reversed the 49ers' 28-27 lead in the final moments of the NFC Championship Game. In 1983, White set team records with 3,980 yards and 29 touchdown passes as Dallas went to the playoffs for the ninth year in a row. But the Cowboys have been back to the playoffs only once since, and White, never a winner in comparison with Staubach, took a lot of the blame. White was the starter most of the late 1980s, although he finally was beaten out by Steve Pelluer. Despite his limited recent playing time, White actually has thrown more completions than Staubach (1,761 to 1,685) and has thrown for almost as many yards (21,959 to 22,700).

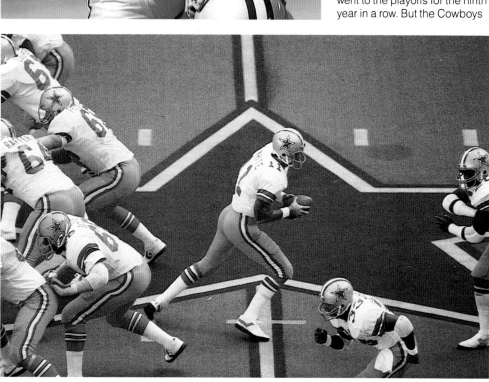

After leading the nation in passing and being a consensus All-America at California, Bartkowski was the first player selected in the 1975 draft. Despite having the size (6-4, 215), arm, and intelligence to be a superstar, Bartkowski had to put up with playing behind an offensive line that couldn't protect him from frequent hits that led to nagging and sometimes serious injuries. Nevertheless, "Peachtree Bart" led Atlanta in passing nine times in his first 10 years, including 1983, when he led the entire NFL. In 1978, Bartkowski set a team record with 2,489 yards, and the Falcons made the playoffs for the first time ever. Two years later, he passed for 3,544 yards and 31 touchdowns as Atlanta went 12-4 to win its first division title. In 1981, he broke his own mark, with 3,830 yards, while leading the NFL for the second year in a row with 30 touchdown passes. In 1985, Bartkowski was replaced by David Archer. The next year he finished his career with the Los Angeles Rams, having passed for 24,124 yards and 156 touchdowns.

Steve Bartkowski

Lynn Dickey

Dan Pastorini

I n 1971, there was no doubt that the Houston scouting staff could recognize a good quarterback. That year the Oilers selected Dan Pastorini of Santa Clara with the third pick in the draft, then came back with their second choice (in the third round) to select Lynn Dickey of Kansas State, the Big Eight Conference's all-time passing

Pastorini gave Dickey a ride after a season-ending injury in 1972.

leader. Unfortunately, only one quarterback can start for any team. Pastorini became a fixture in Houston, while Dickey went on to even bigger success in Green Bay.

Despite coming from a school not exactly known as a football power, Pastorini made an immediate impact in the NFL. As a rookie he not only beat out Dickey, he forced veteran Charley Johnson to the bench. With the starting job in tow, he then led the Oilers in passing nine consecutive seasons. Pastorini's greatest mo-

ments came in his last two years with the Oilers, after the arrival of Earl Campbell. In the 1978 AFC Wild Card Game, Pastorini completed 20 of 29 passes for 306 yards as the Oilers upset Miami 17-9. The next week he threw three touchdown passes in the second quarter as Houston jumped to a 21-0 lead and coasted to a 31-14 win over New England. After two consecutive appearances in the AFC Championship Game (1978-79), Pastorini was traded to Oakland in 1980. He earned the starting job, but a broken leg knocked him out for the season and he never was a regular starter again, finishing with the Rams and Eagles. In his career, he threw for 18,515 yards and 103 touchdown passes.

Dickey started out as a pro on the bench, and, after missing 1972 with a hip injury, it looked as if he might be a career reserve. But in 1976 Dickey went to Green Bay in a trade for John Hadl, and everything changed. After two years as a starter, Dickey suffered a broken leg in 1978, missing the entire season and limiting his action to that of a backup in 1979. He returned in 1980, setting team records for attempts (478), completions (278), and yards (3,529). In the next five years, Dickey continued to be one of the best passers in the NFL, breaking his own marks in 1983 with 484 attempts, 289 completions, and 4,458 yards (second-most ever in the NFC), as well as a team record 32 touchdown passes. In his career, Dickey passed for 23,322 yards and 141 touchdowns.

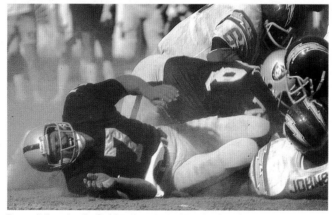

Pastorini's reign in Oakland ended with a broken leg.

Tommy Kramer

There never was any doubt that Tommy Kramer was going to be a pro football player. An all-state quarterback at Robert E. Lee High School in San Antonio, Kramer was the most sought-after player in Texas. He then went to Rice, where he led the nation in passing and total offense and was named the consensus All-America quarterback in 1976. The first-round draft choice of the Minnesota Vikings, Kramer became a starter in 1979 after the retirement of Fran Tarkenton. He wasted no time establishing his pre-eminence among NFL quarterbacks, passing for 3,397 yards his first year, 3,582 the next, and 3,912 in 1982. Although plagued by injuries frequently since, Kramer has had several outstanding seasons, including 1986, when he led the NFL in passing and had his fifth 3,000-yard passing season. In 1987 and 1988, Kramer gave way to Wade Wilson most of the time, but he remains a dangerous quarterback. Kramer has passed for 23,869 yards and 152 touchdowns in his career.

Brian Sipe

Brian Sipe is the classic example of a quarterback nobody wanted to give a chance, but who kept insisting until he got one. Then he proved himself to be among the best in the game. Sipe played for Don Coryell at San Diego State, where he led the nation in passing in 1971. But he still wasn't taken until the thirteenth round of the NFL draft by Cleveland. Then Sipe, who was considered too slight (6-1, 195) and without the arm strength to play in the NFL, backed up Mike Phipps for four years. But he took over in 1976 and slowly became one of the most respected quarterbacks in the NFL. Sipe's best year was 1980, when he led the Browns to the AFC Central title, led the NFL in passing, became the third quarterback in history to pass for 4,000 yards in a sea-

son (4,132), and was named AFC player of the year. He held the starting job in Cleveland through the 1983 season. Sipe retired from the NFL with 23,713 yards passing and 154 touchdown passes, then played in the USFL.

Joe Theismann   # Steve Grogan

Joe Theismann and Steve Grogan couldn't be less similar, yet they are two of the most successful quarterbacks of the past 15 years.

Theismann, an All-America and the runner-up for the Heisman Trophy at Notre Dame, was thought to be too small (6-0, 184) to play in the NFL. Despite being drafted by Miami, he began his pro career in Canada before joining the Washington Redskins in 1974. Used initially as much as a punt returner as a quarterback, Theismann ultimately wrested the starting job from Billy Kilmer in 1977. He had several outstanding seasons, but it wasn't until the appearance of head coach Joe Gibbs that he really reached his prime. In 1981, Gibbs's first year, Theismann passed for 3,568 yards. The next year he led the NFL in passing and helped the Redskins to a victory in Super Bowl XVII, where he threw two touchdown passes. He was named NFL player of the year. In 1983, he guided the highest-scoring offense in the history of the NFL by passing for 3,714 yards and 29 touchdowns; led the 14-2 Redskins to Super Bowl XVIII; and was named player of the game in the Pro Bowl. Theismann's career came to a sudden end during a Monday night game November 18, 1985, against the Giants, when he suffered a compound fracture of his right leg. The Redskins' career passing leader (ahead of Sammy Baugh and Sonny Jurgensen), Theismann passed for 25,206 yards and 160 touchdowns in his career.

Grogan was far from a national celebrity at Kansas State and was the fifth-round draft choice of New England in 1975. But he beat out Jim Plunkett for the starting job as a rookie. Known more as a runner than as a passer early in his career, Grogan scored 12 touchdowns in 1976 and ran for 539 yards in 1978 when the Patriots became the first NFL team ever to have four players rush for more than 500 yards in a season. However, he also was a consistent and steady passer. He threw for 3,286 yards and an AFC-high 28 touchdowns in 1979; aver-

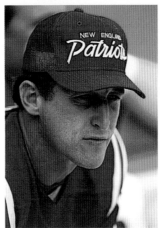

aged a conference-leading 8.1 yards per pass in 1980; and led the AFC with an 8.6-yard average in 1981. In 1984, Grogan was replaced by Tony Eason as the starter, but his experience allowed him not only to call the plays for his replacement but to play when needed at crucial times. Grogan's fourth-quarter performance against Miami in the 1986 season finale allowed the Patriots to win the AFC East championship. He is New England's all-time passing leader with 24,574 yards and 169 touchdown passes.

Phil Simms

Who are the only two active NFC quarterbacks to pass for 4,000 yards in a season? The answers are Phil Simms and Neil Lomax.

Simms achieved the feat in 1984, just when it looked as if he might no longer be around the NFL. The Giants' first-round draft choice in 1979 out of Morehead State, Simms started each of his first three seasons, al-

though two of them were cut short by shoulder injuries. In 1982, a knee injury in a preseason game cost him the entire season. The next year, he fractured a thumb and missed 14 games. But in 1984, he was back with a vengeance, setting club records for attempts (533), completions (286), and yards (4,044). The next year, he passed for 3,829 yards, including 513 (the third-most ever in the NFL) against Cincinnati. He was selected to his first Pro

Neil Lomax

Lomax joined the Cardinals after the most productive passing career in the history of college football. At Portland State, he passed for 13,220 yards and 106 touchdowns. He has continued the same pattern in the NFL. After beating out 16-year veteran Jim Hart as a 1981 rookie, Lomax improved each year, finally passing for 4,614 yards and 28 touchdowns on a 61.6 completion percentage in 1984. Lomax passed for more than 3,200 yards in three of the four seasons from 1985-88. In his first eight years, he became the Cardinals' number-two passing leader (behind Hart, who played 18 years) with 22,771 yards and 136 touchdowns.

Bowl, where he threw three second-half touchdown passes to earn player-of-the-game honors. But even that performance fell short of his efforts in Super Bowl XXI. Against the Denver Broncos, Simms completed 22 of 25 passes for 268 yards and three touchdowns as New York won 39-20. He was named the game's most valuable player. The Giants' career passing leader, Simms has thrown for 23,174 yards, including the three most-productive years in team history.

This patch—a memorial to Carl (Spider) Lockhart who died in 1985—was worn by the Giants in 1986, the season they won Super Bowl XXI.

Ken O'Brien

Ken O'Brien and Boomer Esiason both were surprises at draft time— O'Brien, from California-Davis, because he went in the first round in 1983 with players such as John Elway, Jim Kelly, and Dan Marino; and Esiason, from Maryland, because even though he was the first quarterback selected in 1984, he didn't go in the first round at all. Both men, however, have lived

up to their high promise. O'Brien didn't play a single down with the Jets in his rookie season, but he became the starter late in 1984 and has maintained that role since. He led the NFL in passing in 1985, his first full year as a starter. O'Brien totaled 3,888 yards and 25 touchdowns while throwing only 8 interceptions. The next year, he led the Jets to a 10-1 start. From 1984-88, O'Brien passed for 14,243 yards.

Boomer Esiason

Esiason finally received the respect he deserved in 1988, when he led the NFL in passing and guided the Bengals to Super Bowl XXIII. After a year learning from veteran Ken Anderson in 1984, Esiason took over as the starter in the third game in 1985. In each year since, he has passed for at least 3,300 yards. "He has one of the best throwing arms in the game," said Cincinnati head coach Sam Wyche. "He has a strong arm that is also very accurate. And he is very mobile. Most importantly, though,

Boomer is a smart quarterback. We throw a lot of things at him, and he never gets fazed in the slightest. If we asked him to call the plays for both teams one game he could do it." With 14,825 yards in only five years, it probably seems to many coaches that Esiason *has* been playing offense both ways.

Ron Jaworski
Randall Cunningham

I t isn't often that a team can lose one great quarterback and immediately come up with another. But that is what happened in Philadelphia with Ron Jaworski and Randall Cunningham.

Jaworski first joined the Eagles in 1977 after three years with the Los Angeles Rams, who had drafted him in the second round out of Youngstown State. In Los Angeles, Jaworski, nicknamed "Jaws" or the "Polish Rifle," was part of a quarterback controversy with James Harris and Pat Haden. The Rams sent Jaworski to the Eagles in ex-

change for tight end Charle Young. The combination of Jaworski and head coach Dick Vermeil made a quick impact in Philadelphia. After having had two 4-10 seasons in a row under Mike McCormack, the Eagles made the playoffs in Vermeil's third year, and went four years in a row. In 1980, when the Eagles won the NFC East with a 12-4 record and advanced to Super Bowl XV, Jaworski led the NFC in passing, was named to the Pro Bowl, and was selected the NFL's player of the year. Injuries slowed Jaworski in 1985 and 1986, and new head coach Buddy Ryan replaced him with Cunningham. He spent 1987-88 with Miami, then was picked up as an unprotected free agent by Kansas City in 1989. Jaworski is the number-two active passer (in yards) and ranks seventeenth all time with 27,805 yards.

Jaworski (right) and Cunningham bridged the generation gap.

D espite his almost unbelievable athletic abilities, Cunningham was somewhat of a surprise selection by the Eagles after he finished his college career at Nevada-Las Vegas. The brother of former USC and New England fullback Sam Cunningham began his career as a specialist quarterback on third-down plays because he was both a running and passing threat. Having gained valuable experience, he was able to move in when Jaworski injured a finger on his passing hand in 1986. Despite starting only five games that year, Cunningham rushed for 205 yards. His running has remained a constant threat, while his passing has improved dramatically—from

1,391 yards in 1986 to 2,786 yards in 1987 to 3,808 yards in 1988. He led the Eagles in rushing in both 1987 (with 505 yards) and 1988 (with 624). In the 1989 Pro Bowl, he led the NFC to an easy victory and was named player of the game.

Bobby Hebert   Warren Moon

Warren Moon and Bobby Hebert both had to come into the NFL from other leagues. Both joined weak teams. And both have been among the keys to making those teams solid playoff teams with legitimate Super Bowl aspirations.

Moon was a standout quarterback at the University of Washington, but he wasn't even drafted by an NFL team. So he went to Canada. In six years in Edmonton, Moon passed for 21,228 yards, helped the Eskimos to five consecutive Grey Cups, passed for 5,000 yards in a season twice, and was named the CFL's most valuable player in 1983. The next year, he joined the Oilers as a free agent and has been the starter ever since. Blessed with a powerful arm, great mobility, and an ability to inspire his teammates, Moon has helped make the Oilers one of the best teams in the AFC. He has led Houston to the playoffs in each of the last two years. Meanwhile, he has continued to improve himself, as shown by his selection to the Pro Bowl despite missing a month of the 1988 season with an injury. In his five years in the NFL, Moon has passed for 14,669 yards and has thrown 78 touchdown passes.

Hebert was a highly regarded prospect after playing at Northwestern State (Louisiana), but he signed with Michigan of the USFL. After three years, and appearances in two title games, Hebert signed as a free agent with the Saints in 1985. He started the season's final five games and the first three the next year before he broke his foot. Hebert became the full-time regular in 1987, and led the Saints to a 12-3 record, the second-best in the NFL. In 1988, he really showed his ability by passing for 3,156 yards while the Saints went 10-6.

Jim Kelly

Kelly was in a league of his own in the USFL.

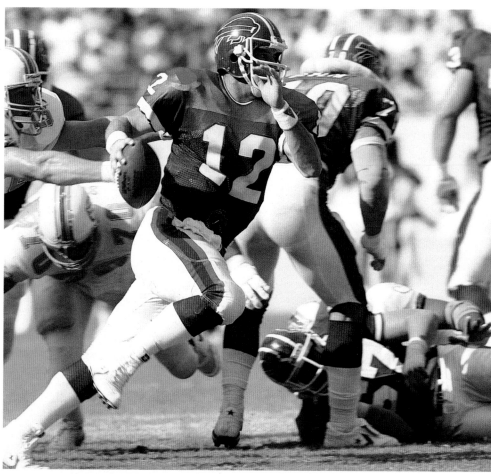

Jim Kelly and Bernie Kosar—two members of the NFL's three-quarterback University of Miami connection (along with Vinny Testaverde)—each entered the NFL with reputations almost too big to live up to. But each has done it.

Kelly was the third quarterback taken in the 1983 draft. Rather than sign with Buffalo, however, he joined the Houston Gamblers of the USFL. In two years, he set the league on fire, passing for 9,842 yards and 83 touchdowns. He joined the Bills in 1986 and promptly established himself as one of the best in the NFL by completing 59.4 percent of his passes for 3,593 yards. A sensational percentage passer, he has completed 59.7 and 59.5 percent the past two years. More than anything else, Kelly has proven to be the leader Buffalo's offense needed. In 1988, he led the Bills to their first division title since 1980 and a 12-4 mark, tied for the best record in the NFL.

Miami alumnus Kelly gets an icy reception from Kosar at a 1984 Hurricanes game.

Bernie Kosar

Kosar is not the best athlete among NFL quarterbacks, but he unquestionably is one of the brightest and most astute. Kosar graduated after only three years at Miami, during which time he took the Hurricanes to their first national championship. The Browns selected him in a supplemental draft in 1985, and he became a starter as a 22-year-old rookie. In each of his four years, Kosar has led the Browns to the playoffs, including 1986 and 1987, when they came close to trips to the Super Bowl before losing to Denver in consecutive AFC Championship Games. In the 1987 title game, he completed 26 of 41 passes for 356 yards. The 1987 season also was his best statistically. He led the AFC in passing with a 95.4 rating, 3,033 yards, and 22 touchdowns. The year before, he set a personal best with 3,854 yards. "Kosar is so good that people have to try to think of weaknesses to pin on him," says former Cleveland head coach Marty Schottenheimer. "They point to his lack of mobility. Well, Bernie doesn't need to be mobile, because he is so smart he can see exactly what is happening, and he is so quick that he can put the ball just where he wants it—like that."

Doug Williams

At the beginning of the 1987 season, Doug Williams was the subject of trade rumors. At the end of the season, he was honored as the record-setting most valuable player in Super Bowl XXII. Williams entered the NFL as the first-round draft choice of Tampa Bay in 1978 after leading the nation in total offense at Grambling. He became a starter as a rookie, then led the Buccaneers tp the NFC Championship Game the following year, losing 9-0 to the Los Angeles Rams. Williams started for Tampa Bay for five years, es-

Williams started two years for the Oklahoma/Arizona Outlaws.

tablishing himself as the franchise's all-time passing leader, before signing with the Oklahoma Outlaws of the USFL in 1983. After two years in the USFL, during which he passed for 6,757 yards, Williams signed with the Redskins in 1986. He spent most of two seasons as a backup, before earning the starting role in the 1987 playoffs. Williams responded by leading Washington to Super Bowl XXII, where he set four records, including 340 passing yards and four touchdown passes (see page 165). Although plagued by injuries in 1988, Williams still passed for 2,609 yards and 15 touchdowns, raising his NFL career totals to 16,413 yards and 99 touchdowns.

Sammy Baugh joined the Redskins in 1937 and Williams arrived in 1986. The patch cited the team's fiftieth year in D.C.

Williams and defensive end Lee Roy Selmon (left) were the arm and hammer of the young Buccaneers.

The Subject Is Quarterbacks

An Anthology

"Playing quarterback in the NFL is so tough it is almost impossible. The basic reason is that there is a degree of excellence required that is so high it is virtually unimaginable to outsiders."

Paul Brown
Pro Football Hall of Fame Head Coach
Cleveland Browns, Cincinnati Bengals

Who's the Greatest of Them All?

W ho was the best quarterback of all time? Who would make the all-time, all-pro team chosen by long-term scouts and personnel directors, the men who would know best?

In an attempt to find out, 14 personnel experts, men whose careers spanned the decades from the 1920s to the 1980s, were questioned. They only could choose players whom

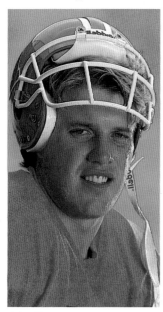

John Elway

they had studied closely, whether in person or on film. Each personnel expert was asked to rank his three top quarterbacks of all time in order to determine a consensus. The personnel experts also were promised confidentiality to insure open and honest responses.

Eight men were mentioned a lot by the experts, including five who received support as the best ever.

One name kept popping up —not as the best ever, but with the potential to be.

"John Elway was the best college quarterback I have ever seen," one scout said. "He

came into the NFL with people saying he had it all, and he still does. He has carried the Broncos to two Super Bowls by his own sheer athletic ability, but he still hasn't gotten the credit he deserves because they never have won. But there hasn't been another quarterback in the NFL —now or in the past thirty years —who could have gotten either of those teams into the Super Bowl, much less both of them. In Elway, we might be looking at the guy who will be the best ever before he's done. I just hope Denver can win some so he'll get the credit he deserves."

"Elway is virtually superhuman," agreed an NFC scout with more than 25 years experience. "If he were with a good team they'd be thinking about changing the rules so they could vote him into the Hall of Fame right now. Give him a team like the 49ers or the Bears and he might not lose a game for the next ten years. If he keeps playing like he does on his good days, there will be no other quarterback who will be able to be mentioned in the same breath."

Despite that praise, a number of scouts don't think that Elway even is the top quarterback in the game at the moment. That praise is reserved for a man who is a confirmed winner—in fact one of the great winners of all time— Joe Montana.

"The thing about Joe Montana is that he is so consistent," said a scout who saw all of the top eight quarterbacks play in person. "He could run and pass and be a leader and pull out the big play and inspire his teammates and do everything you want a quarterback to do virtually from the moment he arrived in the NFL. Earlier, actually. If you saw any of his perform-

Dan Fouts

Joe Montana

Sammy Baugh (33), Sonny Jurgensen

ances at Notre Dame—especially the Cotton Bowl game against Houston—you know what a real comeback is like.

"Montana had it all early in his career when he won the Super Bowl XVI most valuable player award. He had it all at the height of his career, when the 49ers won Super Bowl XIX. And he has it all now, as he showed when they won Super Bowl XXIII. Montana probably won't continue to play as long as some quarterbacks have, but he will play as long as he wants, and he will be at the top of the game as long as he chooses to play."

A current AFC personnel director said, "In a much more competitive league than it was when Otto Graham and Bobby Layne were taking their teams to titles, or even when Terry Bradshaw and the Steelers won

four Super Bowls, Joe Montana has won three Super Bowls. And unlike the Steelers, who won their first two Super Bowls with a magnificent defense, the 49ers have won primarily because of Montana. He has been the key to their team all along. As a guy who can get the job done that a quarterback is supposed to do—win—Montana is one of the two or three best ever."

A man who played, coached, and scouted in the NFL made a similar comment about a different player.

"There have been few quarterbacks who I would rate as total producers," he said. "By that, I mean someone who produced yards, points, leadership, big plays, and wins. Some guys get the yards but no wins. Some get the wins, but they don't really do it themselves—they let their teammates do the work. I don't

know if I could rate him as the best ever, but Dan Fouts wouldn't rate any lower than second on my list. He did everything asked of him and produced the most impressive

Norm Van Brocklin

passing attack in the history of the NFL—no matter what kind of yards Dan Marino has thrown for lately. If the Chargers had had any kind of defense, they would have won as many Super Bowls as the Steelers, and Fouts would be doing the color for all the nationally televised games right now. You'd still see his picture plastered every-where."

"Only Sonny Jurgensen was a better passer than Fouts," said a retired scout who worked with a number of teams through the decades. "I would put Fouts in my top five of all time, but even he can't stand with Sonny. As a passer, Sonny was next to God, and I'm not sure even God could throw the deep out as well as Sonny."

Not only did Jurgensen get considerable mention as the best quarterback of all time, he was a hands-down winner as the best "pure" passer ever. There were others, but it seemed the consensus was Jurgensen.

"Johnny Unitas remarked that Jurgensen was the best passer he had ever seen," said one NFC personnel expert. "Who am I to argue with that? Sonny was simply the best at getting the football to a receiver. The quick release, the arm strength, the catchable ball, the perfect timing, the perfect placement—he had everything. I expect to go the rest of my life and never see a passer as good as Jurgensen."

"Some people like to say that Sammy Baugh was the best passer," said a retired scout who remembers Baugh and his contemporaries clearly. "Howard Cosell popularized the notion that Namath was the best passer, but what did Howard Cosell know? Now people like to point at Marino and say he might be the best there's been.

"Well, you know what? They're all wrong. Norm Van Brocklin was better than any of those guys, and I didn't know if anyone could be the passer the Dutchman was. Then came Jurgensen, and I realized, 'Well, Van Brocklin is okay.' If anyone tells you that there was someone who was a better passer than Jurgensen, do me a favor—laugh at him."

Like Jurgensen, one of his contemporaries also got some strong support as the best over-

Johnny Unitas

Some think Unitas was the best quarterback ever...

all quarterback in history.

"Johnny U. stands alone as a quarterback," one scout said. "He was cool, he was daring, he was flawless. He had perfect passing form. He was the ultimate thinker and leader. He could fire a team up or keep them cold and calculating. He could do anything and everything. I don't think there will be another one like him."

"Unitas gave you such a broad range of abilities," agreed a long-time personnel director. "He could go an entire game without throwing a pass, just calling the correct running play, time after time. Or he could throw the ball twenty times in a quarter if he had to, or if he didn't have to but just felt

like it. More than any other quarterback, the defense never knew what Johnny Unitas was going to do. He was the ultimate master of running an offense."

Some think Unitas was the best quarterback, but many think Baugh was the best overall. Some of those think he was the best quarterback as well.

"When you look at the best football player in the history of the game, or at least since the thirties, since I never saw Jim Thorpe play," said one old-timer, "there are only a few players you can consider. Bob Waterfield of the Rams is one, Don Hutson of the Packers is another, and Mel Hein could be a third. But the best has got to be Sammy Baugh. He was the best punter ever, he was among the finest passers, he was a marvelous defensive back—one of the best in the game at the time. He could do anything on a football field a coach could have asked. Baugh revolutionized the game, and how many players can really claim to have done that?"

"Who cares how good a player he was overall?" another scout said. "That isn't the key to what you're asking. The simple

*Bob
Waterfield*

fact is that he was the best quarterback who ever put on a uniform. He totally modernized the passing game, and he set records that stood for years and years. If Sammy Baugh were playing with the rules today, he would be completing eighty-five percent of his passes. He'd have people hanging on his skinny, little frame, but then he'd whip that ball out of there sidearm and it would go about sixty yards and land perfectly in his receiver's arms, about three inches over the defender's hand. There just hasn't been anyone like him."

An executive who was in personnel and scouting for years said, "Baugh might not have been perfect, but he was a damned-sight closer to it than anyone else I've ever seen. He could beat you in so many ways. He just scared the hell out of you, yet you had to like and admire him because he was just so good. I had teammates who used to have pools before every game. If you could knock the opposing quarterback out of the game—Paul Christman or Bob Waterfield or Sid Luckman

or Charlie Conerly—then you got to keep the pool. But they never would have dreamed of doing such a thing when we played Washington. Baugh was too big a figure for that. He was both mythical and mystical, I guess. Everybody respected him...a little in awe of him. We knew then just what we know now—he was the best ever."

With all of that praise for Baugh, Unitas, and Jurgensen, it's hard to believe that two players could have received more support as the best quarterback. But two contemporaries actually tie for the honor, with four votes each. Considering the respect they had for each other, Otto Graham and Bobby Layne wouldn't have minded being tied.

If indeed winning is the most important thing a quarterback can do, then Otto Graham was truly the best ever. He spent four years with the Cleveland Browns in the short-lived All-America Football Conference and then six more years in the NFL. In those 10 seasons, he took the Browns to 10 cham-

OTTO GRAHAM
QUARTERBACK, CLEVELAND BROWNS

Otto Graham

pionship games, winning seven of them (and losing twice to Layne's Lions). In four years in the AAFC, he led the league in passing three times and guided the Browns to a 52-4-3 record and four titles. When Cleveland joined the NFL, Graham took the Browns to a six-year record of 62-16-1 and league titles in 1950, 1954, and 1955, while leading the league in passing in 1953 and 1955. But Graham was much more than just a marvelous passer.

"Graham was the heart and soul of that Cleveland machine," said a scout who played for a rival NFL team at the time. "Some people say he was just a robot, carrying out Paul Brown's orders, but that is nonsense. You could tell that when the year after Graham left, the Browns fell to fourth place with a 5-7 record. The difference between that and ten championship games was Otto Graham."

"There have been a lot of great passers and a lot of great field leaders," said another scout. "You want to throw the ball, you look at Sonny Jurgensen, with the best arm ever. You want a leader who players will die for, you get Bobby Layne. You want the most poise ever in the game, there is Johnny Unitas. But if you want the man who was all of that—the guy who could pass long, short, or medium; who could scramble and who could run; who had as good a grasp of the game as his coach, Paul Brown; who could lead by example, by intimidation, and by being emotional; and who, if it came down to it, like in the 1954 title game [when Graham threw three touchdown passes and ran for

three more as the Browns beat Layne and the Lions 56-10], could just go win it himself, then the man you want, and the only quarterback you could consider, would be Otto Graham."

Amazingly, the praise was just as lavish for Layne.

"Layne wasn't the prettiest quarterback you ever saw," said a scout whose career took him from the NFL to the AFL and back to the NFL. "But he was the best. His passes somehow found the receiver, even if they had to go for a leisurely flight around a marshland with the other ducks first. And he didn't look like Jim Brown running, but he ran for more than 2,400 yards. He also could kick, and, the year after Doak Walker retired, he led the league in scoring. If you wanted someone stylish, you could take Unitas, but if you wanted the absolute best for getting the job done, Bobby Layne was your guy."

Layne stayed around the NFL longer than Graham—15 years with the Chicago Bears, New York Bulldogs, Detroit Lions, and Pittsburgh Steelers. His greatest years were with the Lions, whom he led to four divisional and three NFL titles in eight years. Then the fun-loving Texan gave Pittsburgh the best teams it had had to that point.

"The most important thing about Layne was his leadership," said one scout. "Oh, he was a great clutch player and probably ran the two-minute offense better than any quarterback in the history of the game. But it was his magnetic personality that set Layne apart. He was the king in Detroit, and everyone just followed him. He took them right to the top."

A scout who played with or against both of them and who refused to name a best quarterback said, "Layne or Graham, it doesn't really matter. One would win you a championship, the other would win you a championship. The one was arguably the all-time master of the game. The one might have been the best, the other might have been the best.

"Sound kind of similar? There's a reason for that. They were so far ahead of the others. They could each claim to be the perfect quarterback. I don't know if one was better than the other. I just know that they were the greatest."

Bobby Layne

GREATEST

When Good Isn't Good Enough

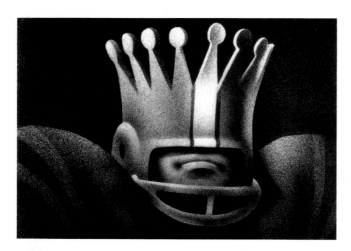

I t is a curse that goes with playing the most glamorous position in professional sports. No matter how good a quarterback you are, no matter what you do for your team, some fans don't think you are good enough.

John Elway hasn't won a Super Bowl yet, nor has Dan Marino. Joe Montana has won three, but detractors claim he doesn't have the powerful arm he had a few years ago.

"Fans can be very fickle,"

said former Giants quarterback Charlie Conerly, who experienced both sides of popularity in his years in New York. "One year a guy will interrupt your dinner with your wife at a restaurant to ask for your autograph. Then he'll offer to pay for your meal. The next year, when you're at the same place— same wife, same table—the

Babe Parilli (below) struggled in Green Bay, Cleveland, Oakland, Boston, and New York, but Jay Schroeder (right) might tell him about Washington.

same guy will call you a jerk and tell you you're too old to play."

The basic reason for this seems to be that there always is a better quarterback somewhere else. For every Rudy Bukich in Chicago (who actually led the NFL in passing in 1965), there is Bart Starr in Green Bay or Frank Ryan in Cleveland leading his team to a conference title.

So unless a quarterback leads the league in passing *and* leads his team to a championship, he's just another guy. Of course, that's only happened

three times—most recently in 1976, when Kenny Stabler led the NFL in passing and the Raiders won Super Bowl XII. So most quarterbacks are. . .well, just not as good as the fans figure they should be.

"The Redskins haven't had a good quarterback since Sonny Jurgensen," a Washington fan complained in print once, overlooking Billy Kilmer (who led the Redskins to Super Bowl VII), Joe Theismann (who took them to Super Bowls XVII and XVIII and passed for 25,206 career yards), Jay Schroeder (who

NFL quarter-backs: All they're asking for is a little r-e-s-p-e-c-t

Randy Johnson never was dealt a lucky hand in the NFL. He experienced only two winning seasons (both 8-6) during 10 years with the Falcons, Giants, Redskins, and Packers.

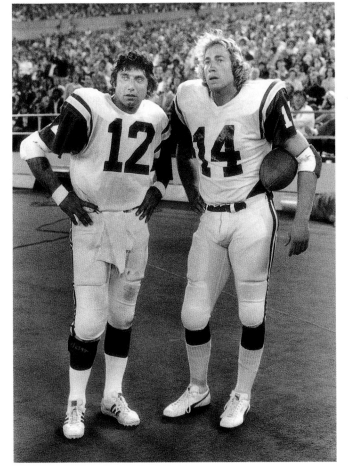

As Richard Todd (right) discovered, replacing Joe Namath in New York was about as easy as following John Wooden at UCLA or Vince Lombardi at Green Bay.

Does the name Rudy Bukich (with Pittsburgh here) ring a bell? He tied an NFL record in 1964 with 13 consecutive pass completions, and led the league in passing in 1965 when he played for Chicago.

THE HEISMAN HEX

Each year the Heisman Trophy is presented to the outstanding college football player in the United States. Whether it actually goes to the best player is a matter for debate, but what is certain is that it creates an enormous level of expectation for success in the National Football League for the winner.

Historically, the Heisman Trophy-winning running backs who have gone into pro football have been very successful. Starting in 1976, for example, eight consecutive running backs won the Heisman and each went on to rush for more than 1,000 yards in a season in the NFL and to earn selection to the Pro Bowl at least once.

On the other hand, while

Paul Hornung

some Heisman-winning quarterbacks have been quite successful, more have been disappointments. A number of quarterbacks or Single-Wing tailbacks, such as Nile Kinnick of Iowa, who was to be killed in World War II, and Dick Kazmaier of Princeton, chose not

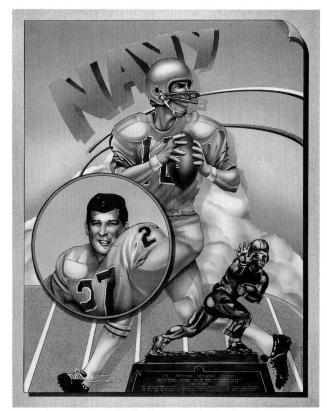

Roger Staubach and Joe Bellino (inset) both played at Navy.

to try pro football.

Other quarterbacks and tailbacks who were outstanding runners, such as Frankie Sinkwich of Georgia, Les Horvath and Vic Janowicz of Ohio State, and Paul Hornung of Notre Dame, were converted into halfbacks in pro football.

Some Heisman quarterbacks never were successful in pro football. Terry Baker of Oregon State and Gary Beban of UCLA both were moved to halfback before realizing they weren't going to play anywhere in the NFL. John Huarte of Notre Dame, Steve Spurrier of Florida, and Pat Sullivan of Auburn hung in there at quarterback—Spurrier for 10

years—but never really made it as regulars.

Only two Heisman-winning quarterbacks really have made it big in the NFL. Roger Staubach, who won as a junior at Navy, joined Dallas after four years in the U.S. Navy. He played 11 years, led the Cowboys to four Super Bowls, and was elected to the Pro Football Hall of Fame in his first year of

eligibility. Jim Plunkett of Stanford had an up-and-down career after being named rookie of the year in 1971. But he returned to lead the Raiders to victories in Super Bowls XV (in which he was named the most valuable player) and XVIII.

Two more recent Heisman winners still are looking to reach the limelight in the NFL. Doug Flutie, who won in 1984, started some games in 1988 for the New England Patriots, and appeared to have the magic—if not the physical dimensions—needed to win in the NFL the way he did at Boston College. And Vinny Testaverde of Miami still has big-time potential despite a slow and painful start in the pro game.

Below is a list of all the Heisman Trophy-winning quarterbacks or Single-Wing tailbacks who have played in the NFL.

Pat Sullivan

1938	Davey O'Brien, TCU	Philadelphia 1939-1940
1942	Frankie Sinkwich, Georgia	Detroit 1943-44; N.Y. Yankees (AAFC) 1946-47; Baltimore (AAFC) 1947
1943	Angelo Bertelli, Notre Dame	L.A. Dons (AAFC) 1946; Chicago Rockets (AAFC) 1947-48
1944	Les Horvath, Ohio State	L.A. Rams 1947-48; Cleveland (AAFC) 1949
1947	Johnny Lujack, Notre Dame	Chicago Bears 1948-1951
1950	Vic Janowicz, Ohio State	Washington 1954-55
1956	Paul Hornung, Notre Dame	Green Bay 1957-1962, 1964-66
1962	Terry Baker, Oregon State	L.A. Rams 1963-65
1963	Roger Staubach, Navy	Dallas 1969-1979
1964	John Huarte, Notre Dame	Boston 1966-67; Philadelphia 1968; Kansas City 1970-71; Chicago Bears 1972
1966	Steve Spurrier, Florida	San Francisco 1967-1975; Tampa Bay 1976
1967	Gary Beban, UCLA	Washington 1968-69
1970	Jim Plunkett, Stanford	New England 1971-75; San Francisco 1976-77; Oakland 1978-1981; L.A. Raiders 1982-86
1971	Pat Sullivan, Auburn	Atlanta 1972-75
1984	Doug Flutie, Boston College	Chicago Bears 1986; New England 1987-88
1986	Vinny Testaverde, Miami	Tampa Bay 1987-88

Steve Spurrier

King Hill was the Chicago Cardinals' bonus pick in 1958, but he never quite lived up to his first name while playing 12 seasons for three teams.

The pass always is cleaner on the other sideline

Playing in Los Angeles often was frustrating for Vince Ferragamo, but he must have found some enjoyment in it—he came back after Canada.

passed for 4,109 yards in 1986), and Doug Williams (the most valuable player in Super Bowl XXII).

Respect is what it's all about. There aren't many NFL quarterbacks who receive the respect they deserve.

For example, Y.A. Tittle was one of the greatest passers. But in San Francisco the banners read, "With Tittle, no title." When the 49ers lost at home, 60,000 fans left Kezar Stadium hating Tittle.

In New York, a quarterback never has a chance.

The New York press and fans virtually tried to run Conerly out of town in the 1950s. Once, when he and his wife went to a basketball game at Madison Square Garden, the public-address announcer commented that they were there. Booing rocked the Garden for more than five minutes. Signs hanging from the upper deck of the Polo Grounds read, "Back to the Farm, Charlie" and "Hang Up the Cleats, Conerly."

Giants fans had a run of quar-

Bob Berry played well in Atlanta, but the Falcons had a cumulative five-year record of 26-41-3 while he was there.

terbacks they found easy to hate: Tittle, Earl Morrall, Fran Tarkenton, Norm Snead, Craig Morton, and Phil Simms. Jets fans did the same on the other side of town. The objects of their disaffection: Al Dorow, Dick Wood, Richard Todd, Ken O'Brien, and every other quarterback not named Namath.

In Chicago, Ed Brown led the league in passing in 1956 while taking the Bears to the NFL title game, but the fans called for Zeke Bratkowski. A few years later, Billy Wade actually scored both touchdowns as the Bears won the 1963 NFL Championship Game. In 1964, he and Rudy Bukich were almost booed out of town when the Bears faltered, in part because the team's offensive attack was decimated by the deaths of running back Willie Galimore and end John Farrington in an automobile accident in training camp.

Vince Ferragamo was big (6-3, 217) and talented, but he never was the toast of the town in Los Angeles. Drafted by the Rams in 1977, he became the starter late in the 1979 season when Pat Haden suffered a hand injury. Ferragamo not only survived in the role, he thrived, leading the Rams through the playoffs and into Super Bowl XIV, where he passed for 212 yards in a 31-19 loss to Pitts-

Tony Eason was drafted ahead of Ken O'Brien and Dan Marino in 1983, and no one in New England has let him forget it.

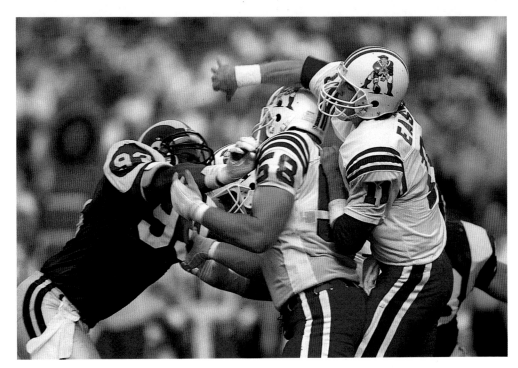

LITTLE GUYS

They are multi-talented, highly paid professionals who can do things few others can. But they are oddities. They are short quarterbacks.

"The worst discrimination in the world isn't color, it's size," said the late Buddy Young, a former great halfback who stood only 5 feet 5 inches tall. "When I came into the league, I was five-five and weighed one sixty-five. The [New York] Yanks acted like I was some kind of sideshow, like I was supposed to go out with the band at halftime."

Little quarterbacks have been in the NFL for years. The first great one was Davey O'Brien, the Heisman Trophy winner from Texas Christian, who stood only 5-7 and weighed just 150 pounds when he joined Philadelphia in 1938. Eagles owner Bert Bell insured his little rookie against injury with Lloyds of London. But O'Brien never missed a game, and he set NFL records for passing yards in a season (1,324) and completions in a game (21).

The next year, O'Brien set records for attempts and completions for a game (60 and 33) and season (277 and 124). He then retired to join the FBI.

Eddie LeBaron, 5-7, played 11 years in the NFL and one in Canada. He succeeded legendary Sammy Baugh in Washington, and was the expansion Dallas Cowboys' first quarterback in 1960. LeBaron led the NFL in passing in 1958 and was named to the Pro Bowl four times.

"You run your deep pattern and look back and nobody's there," former Dallas end Billy Howton once said, describing what it was like trying to catch a long pass thrown by LeBaron. "You can't see him. And, suddenly, it looks like the ball

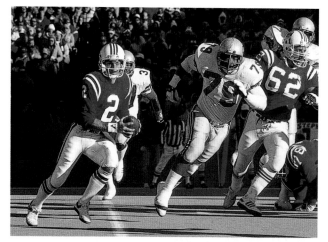

New England fans expect big things from Doug Flutie.

Pat Haden finds trouble in the land of the giants.

is coming out of a silo."

The Cowboys tried another smallish quarterback a couple of years later. Jerry Rhome, who was listed at something between 5-9 and 6 feet, had been a record-setting passer at Tulsa. But with the Cowboys he never was a starter.

Doubts about players' listed program heights are not unusual. All-time passing yardage leader Fran Tarkenton was listed at 6 feet. Many question whether Tarkenton was ever anything near that.

One man who has built a reputation partly because of his size is New England quarterback Doug Flutie, the former Heisman Trophy winner from Boston College. People still say that Flutie will have problems passing in the NFL because of his height (5-10). But somehow Flutie threw four touchdown passes against the Bears in 1988.

"I always will have to live with the fact that I'm short for a football player," Flutie said. "But that certainly isn't going to stop me. I was short in college and I overcame it. I'll do the same in the NFL. It's like anything else. If someone gives you an extra challenge, you just have to work a little harder to succeed."

The wee shall overcome: Future G-man Davey O'Brien (8) set an NFL record with 33 completions in his final NFL game in 1940.

Eddie LeBaron makes fellow Washington quarterbacks Sammy Baugh (33) and Harry Gilmer (52) look larger than life.

Is everything bigger in Texas? Not backup quarterbacks, as pint-sized Jerry Rhome (13) proved in the mid-1960s.

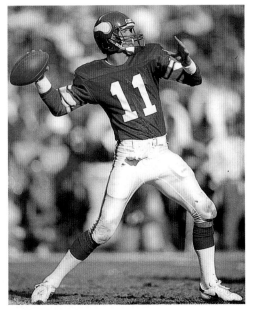

n 1983, Bill Kenney passed for 4,348 yards, but he still isn't mentioned among the NFL's best quarterbacks.

burgh. But, despite encouraging performances in 1980 (3,199 yards) and 1983 (3,276), Ferragamo never became consistent enough to please the Rams' fans, who had become accustomed to winning teams. His one-year escapade with the CFL's Montreal Alouettes in 1982 didn't help his popularity any, either.

In Atlanta, rookie Randy Johnson was pressed into service with the expansion Falcons in 1966. For several years he struggled with little help. Then he was replaced by Bob Berry. But Berry lasted only as long as it took the Falcons to get Bob Lee. The revolving door continued until Steve Bartkowski was drafted number one in 1975.

A number of quarterbacks toiled in virtual anonymity—at least until they threw their next interception. Babe Parilli played 16 years of pro football (including one in the Canadian Football League) and Cotton Davidson a dozen (again, with one in Canada).

Bill Kenney is the number-two passer in Kansas City Chiefs history, and he was benched as soon as Steve DeBerg arrived in 1988. DeBerg is a guy who can tell you something about respect.

"Steve is one of the best young quarterbacks in the league," former San Francisco head coach Bill Walsh said in 1979. "He is a born leader who can take control of a team and really make it go places."

A year later, Walsh didn't sound quite the same. "DeBerg plays just well enough to get you beat," he said. "His limitations are...unacceptable in the NFL today."

In Seattle, head coach Chuck Knox has had similar feelings about free agent quarterback Dave Krieg.

"Krieg is not as consistent as we would like," Knox said after a loss a couple of years ago. "To be a top NFL quarterback, you really have to be able to throw the ball with consistency. I don't know if Krieg will ever really develop that."

However, entering the 1989 season, Krieg was rated as the fifth most-efficient passer in NFL history.

Dave Krieg can't shake the inconsistent label, but only Dan Marino and Johnny Unitas threw 100 scoring passes in fewer games.

NO RESPECT

Roots: College Quarterback Factories

No school has a monopoly on producing NFL quarterbacks. Dave Krieg came from Milton College, which doesn't exist anymore. Jeff Kemp played at Dartmouth, not a university that is generally considered a football factory. And Pete Beathard was a star at USC, a school known more for its tailbacks and offensive linemen than for the men who call the signals.

Still, four schools could have claimed the title of "Quarterback U" at various times during the past several decades. Stanford and Alabama have the longest history of producing outstanding quarterbacks, but Brigham Young and Miami have made impressive inroads in the last decade.

The University of Alabama has produced players who have accounted for the most passing yardage in NFL history. The first great Crimson Tide quarterback to make it in the pros was Harry Gilmer, who was the "bonus" choice (first player selected) by the Redskins in the 1948 draft. Gilmer played eight years with Washington and the Detroit Lions, although he never was a regular starter.

In 1956, the Green Bay Packers used their seventeenth-round draft choice to take an Alabama quarterback who had been successful as a sophomore and junior before he was benched as a senior. After a disappointing professional start, Bart Starr became a regular when Vince Lombardi took over in 1959. Starr led the Packers to five NFL titles and eventually was named to the Pro Football Hall of Fame.

When Paul (Bear) Bryant became the head coach at Alabama in 1958, he recruited a continuous line of future pro quarterbacks.

"Pat Trammell probably was the best of all Alabama quarterbacks," Bryant said years later, speaking of the man who led

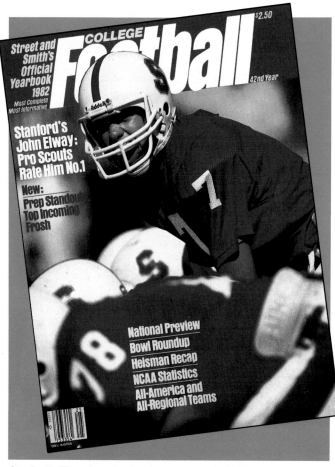

Stanford's Elway faced extensive coverage in 1982.

the Crimson Tide to the 1961 national championship. "He would have played in the NFL if he hadn't decided to be a doctor. He could really put points on the board and win ball games. He was a tremendous leader with all the confidence in the world. The players followed him around like they were following their mamas."

Trammell died of cancer in 1969, the same year his successor at Alabama—Joe Namath—led the New York Jets to an upset victory over the Baltimore Colts in Super Bowl III. Despite having been benched for part of his junior year and playing with injuries as a senior, Namath was the first draft choice of both the AFL Jets and the NFL St. Louis Cardinals in 1965. In 1967, he became the first player—professional, college, or high school—to pass for more than

4,000 yards in a single season.

Namath was succeeded at Alabama by Steve Sloan, who led the Crimson Tide to the national title in 1965. Sloan played briefly with Atlanta, but left to go into coaching. He now is the athletic director at Alabama.

One of Bryant's biggest success stories was the man who followed Sloan.

"Kenny Stabler had ability coming out his ears," Bryant said. "He had a great touch passing, he could run the ball outside, and he was quick as a cat. His junior year was the best year any of our quarterbacks ever had."

Stabler went on to have a fabulous pro career with the Oakland Raiders that was climaxed with a victory in Super Bowl XI. Stabler's success under Bryant convinced the coach he should install a pro-style attack for his

next quarterback, Scott Hunter.

"We really handicapped Scott because we didn't do a good job of recruiting while he was here," Bryant said. "He personally had it all—the arm, the mind, and the guts of a burglar. As a passer, he was the best we had in my years at Alabama."

The year after Hunter turned pro, Bryant adopted the Wishbone. Typically, two of his quarterbacks, Richard Todd and Jeff Rutledge, made the transition and became successful NFL quarterbacks.

"I had to learn about the passing game when I entered the NFL," Todd said. "But the transition wasn't difficult because Coach Bryant had given me a winning attitude, discipline, and the ability to perform under pressure—the things that really count in football."

Stanford quarterbacks also learned all of those things through the years, but they also received intensive schooling in the passing game.

The first great Stanford quarterback was Frankie Albert, the little magician who remains one of the most effective fakers, passers, and runners of the T-formation in pro or college history. Albert was a two-time All-America for Clark Shaughnessy at Stanford in 1940-41. After spending several years in the service during World War II, Albert signed with the San Francisco 49ers of the All-America Football Conference, with whom he played from 1946 to 1952. (The 49ers joined the NFL, beginning with the 1950 season.)

But after Albert left, Stanford didn't really become a Mecca for great passers for another decade. In 1951, Chuck Taylor was hired as head coach.

"Passing could keep us in almost every game," Taylor said, "and could allow us to upset a team that was physically stronger than we were. So we decided to go with a style unique at the time. We would establish the passing game first, not the running game. It was the start of that strategy in football."

Frankie and Johnny—and a Few Others—Made the Grade for Stanford

Schonert (14), Benjamin (7), and Dils helped arm the 1977 Cardinal.

Bobby Garrett, Class of '53

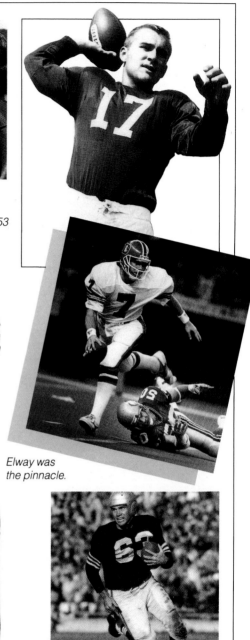

Elway was the pinnacle.

Brodie stayed near the Bay.

Plunkett won the 1970 Heisman.

Albert got the train rolling.

Taylor's new program began with Gary Kerkorian, whose passes to All-America end Bill McColl put Stanford in the 1952 Rose Bowl. Kerkorian, who later played four years in the NFL, was succeeded by Bobby Garrett, the first of half a dozen Stanford quarterbacks to lead the nation in passing. Garrett, later Cleveland's top draft choice, played briefly for the Packers. A stuttering condition adversely affected his pro career.

Taylor's top quarterback was his last. John Brodie led the na-

tion in passing and total offense in 1956 and was named All-America over contemporaries such as Paul Hornung, Milt Plum, Sonny Jurgensen, and Len Dawson. Brodie then joined the 49ers, with whom he played for 17 years, leading the team in passing 11 times and finishing his career as one of the top five passers in National Football League history.

When Taylor moved up to assistant athletic director, his successor was Cactus Jack Curtice, who also developed a national passing leader—Dick

Norman. He played one year for the Bears.

John Ralston took over as head coach at Stanford in 1963 and tried to change the Indians' offensive philosophy. "I thought I could get enough players to line up and take on those [USC] Trojans and [UCLA] Bruins," Ralston said. "But I quickly found out that I was wrong. So I went back to what Chuck Taylor [who was then the athletic director] was promoting. That was throwing the football all of the time, which became a lot easier when we got a sophomore

named Jim Plunkett."

As a senior, Plunkett took Stanford to its first Rose Bowl in 20 years. He finished as the NCAA's career total offense leader, won the Heisman Trophy, and was the first selection of the 1971 NFL draft, by the New England Patriots. After being named rookie of the year, Plunkett had an up-and-down career with the Patriots and 49ers before winding up in Oakland. There, and then in Los Angeles, he led the Raiders to victories in two Super Bowls—XV (where he was named most val-

FROM STEEL MILLS TO FOOTBALL FIELDS

I mmigrants came to the United States from around the world, and many found themselves living and working in terrible conditions. Few places were more depressing than Pittsburgh and the surrounding towns of western Pennsylvania, where smoke from the steel mills filled the skies and soot covered the streets.

Today many of the mills are closed, and there are fewer than half as many jobs in the steel-making business around Pittsburgh as there were in 1980. For some, life isn't any better than it was for their grandfathers decades before.

But there still is one way to get out, one way to make it big. It's the same route that existed four decades ago—football.

"It is virtually impossible to tell you how important football

is in that part of the country," said George Blanda, a member of the Pro Football Hall of Fame and a product of western Pennsylvania.

"Kids in the area play football all the time because they see it as their only way of getting off that treadmill, of going to college, of making something of themselves. It is their one hope for the good life."

Blanda should know. It is something he did, leaving Pennsylvania to

play for Bear Bryant and the University of Kentucky in the early 1950s, and then following that with a record 26 years in professional football.

Blanda is only one of an astonishing number of NFL quarterbacks to come from western Pennsylvania. There were the Hungarians, like Joe Namath; the Lithuanians, like Johnny Unitas; the Italians, like Joe Montana and Dan Marino; the Irish, like Jim Kelly; and more.

"Western Pennsylvania is

truly a phenomenal part of the country for football," said Joe Horrigan of the Pro Football Hall of Fame. "Pro football was born in the Pittsburgh area almost a hundred years ago, and it has continued to be a center for it ever since. Today, it turns out an amazing number of players, not just quarterbacks. Look at the Hall of Fame class of 1988. Three of the four were from that area. Mike Ditka was from Carnegie, Fred Biletnikoff from Erie, and Jack Ham from Johnstown."

But it is the run of quarterbacks that is the most spectacular. They include Arnold Galiffa, Johnny Lujack, Terry Hanratty, and Chuck Fusina, and each was a consensus All-America in college.

"Hope and sports go together in this area of the country for the youngsters," says Larry Bruno, who was Namath's coach at Beaver Falls High School. "Football is a way for the kids to be someone. But it is more than that. Through the years, it was a way for the immigrant families to get some recognition. If the son was a star football player, it gave a little bit of glory to the whole family or even the whole community."

So football gives every kid a dream that he can match the success story of another young man from a working-class family in Pittsburgh. That kid got a football scholarship to Louisville, and even went to training camp with the Steelers before he was cut. After he came home, and started playing semipro ball for the Bloomfield Rams for $6 a game, he got a phone call to try out with the Baltimore Colts. Then Johnny Unitas made it in a big way, eventually ending up in the Hall of Fame in Canton, Ohio, a two-hour drive from Pittsburgh.

"Unitas is a hero for all the kids in western Pennsylvania," said Montana, who is an equally popular folk legend there.

"Everyone knows what Unitas accomplished and that to a great extent it was because of his perseverance and willingness to keep working. He is a great role model for all young kids in the area."

Jim Kelly, East Brady
Dan Marino (below), Pittsburgh

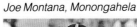

Joe Montana, Monongahela

Terry Hanratty, Butler

George Blanda, Youngwood

Johnny Unitas, Pittsburgh

Joe Namath, Beaver Falls

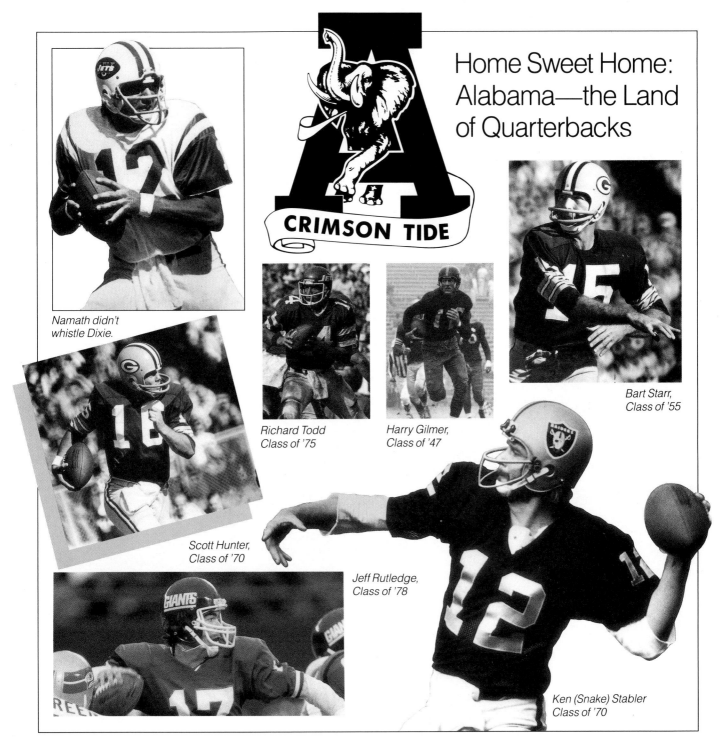

Home Sweet Home: Alabama—the Land of Quarterbacks

CRIMSON TIDE

Namath didn't whistle Dixie.

Richard Todd
Class of '75

Harry Gilmer,
Class of '47

Bart Starr,
Class of '55

Scott Hunter,
Class of '70

Jeff Rutledge,
Class of '78

Ken (Snake) Stabler
Class of '70

uable player) and again in XVIII.

Plunkett's successor at Stanford was a man who had to sit on the bench three years while waiting for his chance to play. But when Don Bunce got his chance, he made the most of it. He took Stanford back to the Rose Bowl in 1971, where he was named most valuable player after leading a 13-12 upset over undefeated Michigan. Bunce first played in the Canadian Football League, then went to medical school. Today, he is the Stanford team doctor.

Ralston left to join the Denver

Broncos in 1973, but that didn't stop the influx of quarterbacks. New head coach Jack Christiansen coached Mike Boryla, who later played for Philadelphia, and Mike Cordova.

Christiansen was followed in 1977 by pass master Bill Walsh, who had ideas similar to Taylor's. "Only a limited number of college teams are able to play conservatively and overwhelm their opponents physically," he said. "So we decided to utilize a high-percentage passing offense." With Walsh's ball-control passing game, Stanford fea-

tured the nation's leading passer in each of his two years— Guy Benjamin (1977) and Steve Dils (1978). Each would play for three NFL teams.

In 1979, Rod Dowhower's only year as head coach, Turk Schonert became the third Stanford quarterback in a row to lead the nation in passing. He then joined the Cincinnati Bengals, for whom he has been a backup to Ken Anderson and Boomer Esiason.

Dowhower also gets credit for

recruiting Stanford's—and arguably college football's—best quarterback ever, John Elway. After a star-spangled career, Elway finished second in the Heisman balloting. He was the first player selected in the 1983 NFL draft, one of the richest ever in quarterback talent. Since then, he has led Denver to the playoffs four times, including appearances in Super Bowls XXI and XXII.

In recent years Stanford, like Alabama, has taken a backseat to two other schools that have emphasized the pro-style pass-

ing game—Brigham Young and Miami.

The first star quarterback at each school actually played more than two decades ago. In 1962-63, George Mira of Miami was one of the nation's leading passers. He was drafted by the 49ers as the man expected to replace Brodie. But he never panned out as the 49ers hoped, and he played for three teams in his seven-year NFL career.

Several years later, Virgil Carter of BYU led the nation in passing, while also setting an NCAA record with 599 yards to-

tal offense in one game. Relatively small at 6-1 and 185 pounds, Carter was an occasional starter for the Chicago Bears and Cincinnati Bengals, for whom he played three years each.

BYU's passing fortunes really began to change in 1972 when LaVell Edwards became head coach. Edwards's first project was Gary Sheide, who finished second in the nation in passing in 1974. He was followed by Gifford Nielsen, an All-America in 1976, who broke his leg and missed much of his senior sea-

son in 1977. Nielsen had a productive six-year pro career with the Houston Oilers.

When Nielsen, who had been a Heisman Trophy contender, was injured, he was replaced by sophomore Marc Wilson. Wilson went on to lead the nation in total offense in 1979, when he was named the All-America quarterback. He then played eight years with the Oakland and Los Angeles Raiders, for whom he started much of his career.

Wilson's replacement was the most productive major universi-

ty quarterback ever. Jim McMahon led the nation twice in passing and twice in total offense. He still is the top-ranked passer in college history. Selected by the Chicago Bears in the first round of the 1984 draft, McMahon usually started when healthy. In 1985, he led the Bears to a 15-1 regular season, followed by a smashing triumph in Super Bowl XX.

McMahon was succeeded by Steve Young, who became another record-setting All-America before going on first to the USFL, then the Tampa Bay Buc-

Brigham Young Turned Football Into an Air Show

Marc Wilson, Class of '79

The Oilers rated Nielsen high.

McMahon had the BYU arm, but not the BYU image.

Steve Young is a great passer and a direct descendant of Brigham Young; Virgil Carter (right) was just a great passer.

Extreme Caution Advised: Another Hurricane Passing

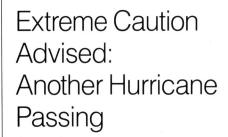

Walsh (above) joined the NFL early, forfeiting a year of eligibility; Kelly (below) joined the NFL's Buffalo Bills after two seasons in the USFL.

Testaverde just moved cross-state.

Mira played in Miami before the factory officially opened.

Cleveland won the "Kosar Supplemental Draft" lottery in 1985.

caneers and the 49ers. A backup to Joe Montana, Young is considered one of the brightest future stars in the NFL.

Young's replacement—Robbie Bosco—led the Cougars to a national title in 1984 before being drafted by the Packers. Injuries prevented him from having a successful career, so he went into coaching.

BYU's run of quarterbacks this decade is impressive, but it's no more admirable than Miami's. At one time in 1982, the Hurricanes had Jim Kelly, Bernie Kosar, and Vinny Testaverde all on the same team.

"I think the reason we all were at Miami was because of Howard Schnellenberger's pro-style system," Kosar said. "For a dropback quarterback, it was ideal. And all three of us wanted to play in the NFL."

All three of them made it there in the first round. Although Kelly didn't receive much acclaim from the media in 1982 because of competition from players such as John Elway, Dan Marino, and Todd Blackledge, pro scouts certainly noticed him. He played with the Houston Gamblers of the USFL before joining the Buffalo Bills in 1986. He has helped make the Bills one of the best teams in pro football.

The year Kelly turned pro, Kosar led the Hurricanes to the national championship. Then, after graduating early, Kosar was selected by the Cleveland Browns in a supplemental draft. He has led the Browns to the playoffs four consecutive years.

Testaverde almost transferred from Miami when he was beaten out by Kosar, but he stayed on and benefited from it. He became the starter when Kosar turned pro, then capped his career in 1986 by winning the Heisman Trophy and being named All-America. The Tampa Bay Buccaneers made him the first choice in the draft.

The latest quarterback from Miami is Steve Walsh, who led the Hurricanes to the national championship in 1987 and was named All-America as a junior in 1988. He forfeited his senior season to join the NFL.

M any standout NFL quarterbacks got their starts in other leagues. Several others left the NFL to play in rival leagues. Since the 1940s, four defunct leagues produced quarterbacks who went on to success in the NFL. The league that had the greatest influence was the All-America Football Conference, which existed from 1946-49.

Following World War II, seven significant quarterbacks or Single-Wing tailbacks chose to play at least part of their careers in the AAFC, rather than the NFL. None was better than Otto Graham of the Cleveland Browns. Graham, who went on to play six years with the Browns in the NFL, led his team to all four AAFC titles. After finishing second in the league in passing behind Glenn Dobbs his first year, Graham led AAFC passers for three consecutive years. In four years in the AAFC, he threw for 10,085 yards and 86 touchdowns, was named all-AAFC each season, and was the league's most valuable player in two of the three years one was named.

"Unlike some of the other leagues that came along later, the AAFC truly was on a competitive level with the NFL," Graham said. "The good teams in both leagues were really good and the poor teams were really poor. I don't think the Browns left any doubt when we entered the NFL that we were the best team in football, no matter what anybody had been saying for four years."

The AAFC's only most valuable player other than Graham was Dobbs, who never played in the NFL after starting his four-year career with the Brooklyn Dodgers and finishing it with the Los Angeles Dons. After being named most valuable player in 1946, Dobbs was traded to the Dons in 1947 because of the play of Bob (Hunchy) Hoern-

Graham and Albert: From a League of Their Own

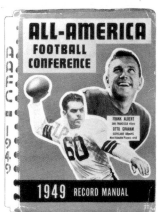

Frankie Albert (above left) and Otto Graham both were so good in 1948 that they had to share the AAFC most valuable player trophy. But the AAFC championship trophy—all four of them, in fact—belonged to Graham and the Browns.

schemeyer, a tailback who ran better than he passed.

Hoernschemeyer played four years in the AAFC, then joined the Detroit Lions in 1950. Because the Lions had Bobby Layne at quarterback, Hoernschemeyer was moved to halfback. He led the team in rushing four consecutive seasons, helping Detroit win two NFL titles.

Orban (Spec) Sanders may have been an even better tailback than Dobbs or Hoernschemeyer. Although he had been a third-string halfback at Texas, the New York Yankees saw potential in Sanders and installed him as their starter. In

1946, he led the AAFC in rushing. The next year, he became the only pro player ever to both rush and pass for more than 1,000 yards in the same season, throwing for 1,442 yards, while leading the league with 1,432 yards rushing. Sanders didn't play pro football in 1949, but he was talked into returning by the New York Yanks of the NFL. In 1950, his only year in the NFL, Sanders tied an NFL record by making 13 interceptions in a season.

AAFC teams that ran the T-formation also had success getting outstanding players to run their offenses. Three other NFL

quarterbacks started their careers in the AAFC. Frankie Albert, who was named the league's co-most valuable player with Graham in 1947, started all four years for the San Francisco 49ers, with whom he stayed when the team joined the NFL. George Ratterman played three years with the AAFC's Buffalo Bills before spending seven years with the Yankees and Browns in the NFL. And Hall of Fame member Y.A. Tittle, who was drafted on the first round by the Detroit Lions of the NFL, chose to play two years with the AAFC Baltimore Colts before entering the

Orban (Spec) Sanders was a multi-threat tailback and a genuine gate attraction for the AAFC's New York Yankees. In three seasons, he rushed for 2,900 yards and 33 touchdowns, and passed for 2,829 yards and 23 scores.

George Ratterman, a collegiate hero at Notre Dame, was nicknamed "The Kid" because of his adolescent appearance and slender build (6-1, 175). One of the AAFC's best passers, for the Buffalo Bills, he later backed up Otto Graham at Cleveland.

His Brooklyn Dodgers finished 3-10-1 in 1946, but tailback Glenn Dobbs earned the AAFC's first most valuable player award after leading the conference in passing and punting. The next year, Brooklyn traded Dobbs to the Los Angeles Dons, who were looking for a name to compete with the Rams' Bob Waterfield. Dobbs did that, helping the Dons attract 304,177 fans in seven games in 1947.

NFL with the same team in 1950.

"The AAFC was successful on the field because there were so few teams and so few markets but so many outstanding players at that time," Tittle said. "In 1946, when the AAFC started with eight teams, there were only ten in the NFL. So there was great talent to go around. Some of the later leagues had problems because by then there were twenty-six or twenty-eight NFL teams, including one in every important market."

Other than the American Football League (1960-69), the next pro football league to take on the NFL was the World Football League in 1974. In its first year, WFL rosters included former NFL quarterbacks Virgil Carter (with the Chicago Fire), John Huarte (Memphis Southmen), and George Mira (Birmingham Americans). One of the league's co-most valuable players was rookie quarterback Tony Adams of the Southern California Sun, who later would spend four years with the Kansas City Chiefs.

The WFL folded midway through the 1975 season, but it introduced two quarterbacks to professional football who later had long and successful NFL careers—Danny White of Memphis and Pat Haden of the Sun. Each eventually directed his NFL team—the Cowboys and Rams, respectively—to NFC Championship Games. Haden got his chance to play with the Sun because of an injury to Daryle Lamonica, who had left the Oakland Raiders for a lucrative contract in 1975.

"I don't know if I ever would have played pro football if it hadn't been for the Sun," Haden said. "Most NFL scouts thought I was too small to play and they were turned off because I had to leave during my rookie year to go to Oxford [where Haden was a Rhodes scholar]. I'm not sure I could have gotten back into the NFL the next year without having done well in the WFL."

A decade after the WFL, the United States Football League came into existence. Although well-financed, its plan to play during the spring months helped doom the new league. However, it did feature several quarterbacks who have become prominent NFL players.

The USFL's star quarterback was Jim Kelly, who signed with

The Rams selected diminutive, but brainy Pat Haden on the seventh round of the 1975 draft, but the USC star chose to sign with another local club, the WFL's Southern California Sun, which played at Anaheim Stadium.

Cajun sensation Bobby Hebert, now the Saints' quarterback, led the Michigan Panthers to the USFL championship in 1983 and was named most valuable player.

The USFL's Los Angeles Express never fully exploited Steve Young's talents. In 1984, he became the first pro player to rush for 100 yards and pass for 300 in the same game.

the Houston Gamblers rather than the Buffalo Bills of the NFL. Kelly set pro football passing records in Houston before he finally joined the Bills in 1986.

Steve Young, an All-America quarterback from BYU in 1983, signed with the Los Angeles Express of the USFL. But injuries and questionable personnel moves eventually forced him to play halfback. When the USFL folded, Young moved to the Tampa Bay Buccaneers. He later was traded to the San Francisco 49ers. He started several games in 1988 as the 49ers put together another successful season, but he didn't play in the 49ers' victory in Super Bowl XXIII.

Another USFL star to move on to the NFL is Bobby Hebert of the New Orleans Saints. Hebert led Michigan to the first USFL championship. He played three years before moving to the Saints. He helped New Orleans to the first winning record (12-3) in its history in 1987.

The most valuable player in Super Bowl XXII also was a former USFL player. Doug Williams had played the early years of his career with Tampa Bay before going to the USFL's Oklahoma Outlaws. When the league failed, he joined the Washington Redskins. In the Super Bowl, he passed for 340 yards and four second-quarter touchdowns in a 42-10 victory over Denver.

Williams wasn't the first Washington quarterback to take his team to a victory in a Super Bowl after having played in another league. Joe Theismann started his pro career in Canada. When he was drafted by Miami in 1971 out of Notre Dame, Theismann figured to disappear behind Bob Griese. So he headed north, became a successful pro, and then entered the NFL with the Redskins, where he eventually became a Super Bowl champion after earning his spurs returning punts for head coach George Allen. That scenario was not unique.

"No one in the NFL was particularly interested in me when I graduated from the University of Washington," said Warren Moon, the Pro Bowl quarterback for the Houston Oilers. "Not only wasn't I drafted, people didn't exactly line up for me as a free

Joe Theismann passed for 2,440 yards and led the Toronto Argonauts to the CFL Grey Cup his rookie season, 1971.

Edmonton was a strange setting for a Los Angeles kid, but Warren Moon threw for 21,228 yards in six years with the Eskimos.

Few players have moved south to Minnesota, as Joe Kapp did.

agent. So when Edmonton was interested, I packed my bags to give it a try. My intention in going to Canada was to show that I could play. When I felt I had showed that, I wanted to prove the same thing against the best —the NFL."

After becoming the first pro player to pass for 5,000 yards in a season (which he did twice with Edmonton), Moon signed as a free agent with the Oilers, immediately became a starter, and helped turn Houston into a Super Bowl contender.

The first Super Bowl team quarterbacked by a former Canadian player was the Minnesota Vikings in Super Bowl IV. Joe Kapp had joined the Vikings in 1967, the same year head coach Bud Grant also came to Minnesota from Canada.

"There are some basic differences in the game that make the strategies and style of play different," said Grant, who led the Vikings to four Super Bowls. "The major ones are that the end zones are twenty-five yards deep, the field is wider and longer, you get a single point for a rouge [anytime the ball is punted or kicked into or beyond the end zone and not returned out of it], there are only three downs to make a first down, each team has twelve men on the field, and there is unlimited offensive motion by backs and receivers."

"I didn't adjust well to all the differences in Canada," says Vince Ferragamo, who left the Rams to play for Montreal in 1981, then returned to Los Angeles after one season. "My season up there was a mess all the way around. The extra man, the motion, the wider field. . .it's really just a different game."

Conversely, some successful quarterbacks in Canada didn't adjust well to the NFL. Dieter Brock, one of the CFL's all-time greats, played two years with the Rams, but never could generate the passing game expected of him. Tom Clements, another CFL star, tried out with the Kansas City Chiefs but never got to play.

"It was frustrating not making it in the NFL after doing so well in college [at Notre Dame] and in the CFL," Clements says. "I was truly disappointed because I wanted to play in the NFL, where all the best players eventually go."

OTHER LEAGUES

Throwing Caution to the Wind in the AFL

The battle lines were clear in the argument over whether the American Football League was equal to the NFL in the early 1960s.

"The AFL definitely is an inferior product," said Allie Sherman, the head coach of the NFL's New York Giants at the time. "They just throw the ball up and down the field and don't bother to play any defense. What is the thrill to the fan of having a good offense, when in reality it is just that there is no defense?"

"The AFL could have been playing competitive football with the NFL from 1962 or 1963 on," said Sid Gillman, who was the head coach of the Los Angeles/San Diego Chargers and who had coached the NFL's Los Angeles Rams from 1955-59. "The first year or two there was a dramatic difference in the overall quality of the leagues, although the top teams in the AFL—the Oilers and the Chargers—would have been able to play with any NFL team. The NFL had more solid foundations, better defenses, and perhaps better offensive lines. But we had more exciting skill players than the NFL."

Both arguments are somewhat true. The AFL *didn't* have the strong defenses that the NFL had, and that perhaps helped make the offenses even more dominant. But AFL of-

The job was a tossup in training camp (above), but Tom Flores (15) eventually beat out Babe Parilli (10) and Paul Larson (12) to become Oakland's starting quarterback in 1960.

Butch Songin (left) returned from the Canadian League to quarterback the Patriots in 1960-61. He was traded to the New York Titans in 1962.

The AFL football (opposite page) was about the same as the NFL's —it was just used differently.

Send Us Your Tired, Your Poor...Your Second-String NFL Quarterbacks

The Giants were one of Shaw's three NFL teams.

Kemp played five games for Pittsburgh in 1957.

Washed up? Blanda played 16 more years.

Parilli was Green Bay's first-round draft pick in 1952.

Dawson spent two forgettable seasons with Cleveland.

fenses would have scored a lot of points anyway, because the AFL had many outstanding passers and receivers. Many of them continued to be successful when the AFL merged with the NFL in 1970.

"There still is a certain skepticism over even the better quarterbacks from the early days of the AFL," said Joe Horrigan of the Pro Football Hall of Fame. "That is because a number of them—players like Babe Parilli, Len Dawson, Jack Kemp, and Cotton Davidson—weren't successful in their early years in the NFL. Then they went to the AFL and became stars. So people figure the competition wasn't as good. But that argument is unfair, because certain quarterbacks who stayed in the NFL took quite a while to become stars, too—players like Earl Morrall."

The quarterbacks from the AFL's first couple of years didn't exactly read like a who's who at the time. Sure, there were George Blanda in Houston,

JACKY LEE: LEND-LEASE QUARTERBACK

Few trades in the history of professional sports have been more unusual than one consummated between the Denver Broncos and the Houston Oilers of the American Football League in 1964.

In the first three years of their existence, the Broncos had lived and died on the arm of quarterback Frank Tripucka. But Tripucka suddenly retired after the second game of the 1963 season. Then, after two victories, quarterback John McCormick was knocked out of action with a severe knee injury, leaving the Broncos with rookie Mickey Slaughter, with whom they went winless the final 10 games of the season.

Desperate for an established quarterback, Broncos head coach Jack Faulkner made a deal with the Oilers in August, 1964. Denver sent all-league defensive tackle Bud McFadin, a first-round draft choice, and cash to the Oilers in exchange for the services of quarterback Jacky Lee for two years, at which point he would return to Houston.

Unfortunately for Denver, and Faulkner (who was fired after an 0-4 start), Lee never worked out as hoped. He finished tenth in passing in an eight-team league, while Slaughter actually played well enough to finish ninth. Lee threw 11 touchdown passes

Denver should have hung onto Bud McFadin (64).

and 20 interceptions, and the Broncos finished 2-11-1.

In 1965, Lee played behind Slaughter and McCormick most of the year, finishing with only 692 passing yards. The Broncos no longer were interested in keeping him, and in 1966 he went back to Houston, where he was fourth string, behind Blanda, Don Trull, and Buddy Humphrey.

Some of Cotton Davidson's (19) best games were played in the shadow of the Oakland courthouse at Frank Youell Field.

Davidson with the Dallas Texans, and Kemp with the Los Angeles/San Diego Chargers, but they each had been out of pro football for a year, and only Blanda really had been an NFL starter prior to that. Tom Flores was a rookie in Oakland, as was Johnny Green in Buffalo. And two men in their 30s—Frank Tripucka of Denver (32) and Butch Songin of the New York Titans (36)—were fresh from long careers in Canada.

In 1960, it was the receivers who were special—Bill Groman and Charley Hennigan in Houston, Don Maynard and Art Powell with the New York Titans, Chris Burford with the Dallas Texans, and Lionel Taylor in Denver.

It would be another couple of years before the big names who dominated the rosters for the rest of the decade showed up. In 1963, Vito (Babe) Parilli became Boston's regular quarterback, Len Dawson joined the

Texans, and John Hadl was a rookie in San Diego. So was the man who would become his battery mate and the best receiver in the history of the AFL —Lance Alworth.

In 1963, Daryle Lamonica was a rookie with Buffalo, and the ageless Tobin Rote signed with the Chargers after three years in Canada. San Diego needed a quarterback besides Hadl because of a *faux pas* in 1962. When starter Jack Kemp broke his hand, the Chargers' Gillman tried to slip him through waivers to the reserve list. But Buffalo claimed Kemp for the $100 waiver price.

So the game of pass-and-catch was set in the younger league. And how they played it! In 1961, Blanda set a pro record with 36 touchdown passes. The next year he gave up 42 interceptions. One year, Houston's Jacky Lee threw 12 touchdown

passes—as a reserve who never started. Tom Flores averaged 18.6 yards a completion in 1963.

In 1961, Hennigan caught 82 passes for 1,746 yards and averaged 21.3 yards per catch. His teammate, Groman, averaged 23.5 yards and caught 17 touchdown passes. The same year, Taylor became the first pro to make 100 receptions in a season, a record that lasted only three years—until Hennigan caught 101. And, in 1965, Lance Alworth made enough leaping, diving, carnival catches to finish second in the AFL.

Alworth averaged an amazing 23.2 yards per catch while totaling 1,602 yards.

"At no time have as many good passers and receivers been put together in as confined a group as in the mid and late years of the AFL," said Hall of Fame coach Weeb Ewbank, who coached the New York Jets from 1963 to 1973. "Before Super Bowl III, people were horrified when Joe Namath said that there were four AFL quarterbacks better than the Colts' Earl Morrall [who had been named the NFL's most valuable player].

But look at who was in the league that year. It was an all-star cast of passers: Namath, Lamonica, Hadl, Dawson, and [Bob] Griese. It was an amazing cast."

The next season, 1969, Griese, a peerless percentage passer, ranked tenth in the league in passing. Mike Livingston, who split time with Dawson, actually ranked fourth (compared to Dawson's sixth). Steve Tensi of Denver and Pete Beathard of Houston also ranked ahead of Griese. But statistically, the best of them all

was rookie Greg Cook, who averaged a still-existing rookie record of 9.4 yards per attempt for a weak Cincinnati team.

"The AFL will always be remembered as a passing league because of the great passers and catchers it had," said Tom Bass, an assistant coach with the Bengals at the time. "Not that it didn't have the running backs, because it had guys like Keith Lincoln, Mike Garrett, Jim Nance, Dickie Post, Floyd Little, and Matt Snell. But it was the guys throwing the ball who gave it its personality."

It Was Better to Receive in the Younger League

Charley Hennigan had 1,746 yards receiving in '61.

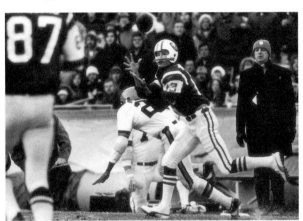

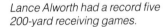
Lance Alworth had a record five 200-yard receiving games.

Lionel Taylor was the first to catch 100 passes in a season.

Chris Burford was an important possession receiver for the Chiefs.

Don Maynard was Namath's favorite receiver.

Art Powell was one of the early Titans.

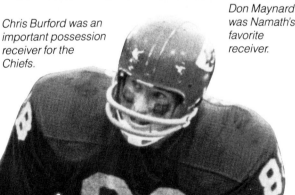

Franchise Quarterbacks

Every once in a while, a "franchise" player comes along, someone who supposedly is singlehandedly going to have a winning impact on an entire team. Sometimes, that player is a running back. Usually he is a quarterback.

Franchise quarterbacks have existed from the very beginning of the NFL draft. In 1937, the Boston Redskins (who would move to Washington before the season) drafted Texas Christian All-America Sammy Baugh. That year, Baugh led the NFL in passing and took Washington to the NFL title.

Two years later, Philadelphia chose TCU Heisman Trophy winner Davey O'Brien in the draft. O'Brien turned out to be a record-setting passer, but he couldn't do much for the Eagles' record. Philadelphia won only one game in both 1939 and 1940. O'Brien then retired from pro football to work for the FBI in Washington, D.C. The Eagles' two-year "franchise" did not quite have the effect Baugh would have in his 16-year career with the Redskins.

With the primitive scouting techniques used through the first several decades of the draft, it is not surprising that as many franchise picks were busts as successes. In 1948, the Bears selected Bobby Layne and the Lions chose Y.A. Tittle, both of whom would have Hall of Fame careers, although neither with those respective teams. The next year, the Packers used the third pick in the draft to take Nevada-Reno quarterback Stan Heath, who played only one year.

Through the final five years of the bonus pick (1954-58), franchise quarterbacks were anything but. In 1954, Cleveland took Bobby Garrett of Stanford. The next year, George Shaw of Oregon went to Baltimore. And, in 1956, Gary Glick of Colorado A&M was selected by Pitts-

Baugh, from TCU, was the first to be called a "meal ticket."

Dallas waited four years as Staubach served his tour of duty.

burgh. Paul Hornung of Notre Dame (1957) made it in Green Bay—but as a running back, not a quarterback. King Hill of Rice ingloriously finished off the bonus picks by going to the Chicago Cardinals in 1958.

Although Terry Baker of Oregon State, the first selection of the 1963 draft, was one of the great disappointments ever, the 1960s definitely were a more productive time for franchise quarterbacks. In 1962, Roman Gabriel and John Hadl both were early picks; both men more than lived up to expectations by passing for more than 29,000 yards and being named the NFL's player of the year during their careers.

In 1965, Joe Namath was the first pick of both the St. Louis Cardinals of the NFL and the New York Jets of the AFL. He signed with the Jets for the largest contract ever at that time, giving the AFL a major victory over the NFL.

"In certain ways, Namath was the first modern franchise quarterback," said Jack Butler, a long-time NFL personnel man. "He was scouted with modern techniques like we use today, as opposed to the *Street and Smith* scouting of earlier days. Both teams wanted him badly, and he showed why."

In the early 1970s, "the franchise" started rolling off the quarterback production line. The first pick of the 1970 draft was a big, tall, lanky, emotional kid from Louisiana Tech. Some people said Terry Bradshaw didn't have the experience or the smarts to make it in pro football. But the Steelers didn't buy it, and they got a Hall of Fame player who led them to four Super Bowls.

The next year was one of the two greatest ever for franchise quarterbacks. The top three players in the 1971 draft were quarterbacks—Jim Plunkett of Stanford, Archie Manning of Mississippi, and Dan Pastorini of Santa Clara. Each lived up to his billing and had a long NFL career. Plunkett was the rookie

of the year, but he had his ups and downs after that before leading the Raiders to two Super Bowl victories. Manning never was a winner in New Orleans, but he established himself as one of the most talented, if snake-bit, players in the history of the game. Pastorini was a long-term starter with the Oilers, helping them to the AFC Championship Game two years in succession in the late 1970s.

Franchise quarterbacks came in all rounds in 1971. Lynn Dickey, who would have a long and productive career, went to Houston in the third round, and Joe Theismann, eventually an NFL most valuable player, was picked by Miami in the fourth.

A franchise quarterback has continued to enter the NFL every couple of years since (al-

Louisiana Tech's Bradshaw helped Pittsburgh win four Super Bowls.

Montana took his miracle finishes from Notre Dame to San Francisco.

Johnny Who? He Was the Pride and Joy of the Bloomfield Rams

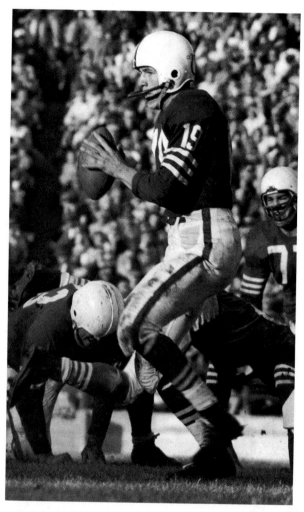

Johnny Unitas's drive down the road to glory began with a flat tire. The Steelers drafted Unitas out of the University of Louisville in 1955, but they waived the lanky passer in training camp, so he spent the '55 season playing for the Bloomfield Rams, a semipro team in the Pittsburgh area. The next summer, Baltimore Colts general manager Donald Kellett made the shrewdest 80-cent phone call of his life, persuading Unitas to come for a tryout. He did. The rest is, as they say, history.

though in 1983 there were six of them). In 1973, Baltimore made Bert Jones of LSU the number-two pick of the draft. Two years later, Atlanta made California All-America Steve Bartkowski the top selection overall.

In 1977, St. Louis thought it had a steal when it tabbed local hero Steve Pisarkiewicz from Missouri in the first round, leaving Rice All-America Tommy Kramer for the Vikings. Kramer still is in Minnesota, but Pisar-

kiewicz played only two years in St. Louis. He is remembered chiefly for being the cause of the argument between Cardinals owner Billy Bidwill and head coach Bud Wilkinson that ended in Wilkinson's being fired.

Pickings generally were slim for quarterbacks from the mid-1970s until 1983, although San Francisco got future superstar Joe Montana on the third round in 1979. That draft also produced Jack Thompson of

A VINTAGE YEAR: THE CLASS OF '83

The 1983 draft was a dream come true for NFL scouts and personnel directors. No position in the draft was deeper than quarterback—six were selected in the first round. All six have started at one time or another, and four have gone on to be NFL stars.

There never was any doubt about who the first player taken would be.

"I run out of superlatives when talking about John Elway of Stanford," Mike Hickey, the New York Jets' director of player personnel, said at the time. "He's the best I've seen since I've been scouting.

"When evaluating Elway, negatives are brought up that aren't negatives for most people. He has such high potential that we end up nit-picking to try to find something wrong. Elway simply is atypical—he has no weak points."

After being selected by Baltimore, Elway was traded to Denver, where he has excelled

Stanford's Elway was number one in '83—he still might be.

Hurricane Kelly took Houston and Buffalo by storm.

as predicted, leading the Broncos to two AFC titles.

The biggest disappointment of the draft was the second quarterback taken. Todd Blackledge, who had been a fourth-year junior on Penn State's national championship team and was eligible to be drafted if he graduated on time, seemed to have all the qualifications.

Kansas City took him with the seventh pick of the draft. But Blackledge never really succeeded as a starter, and he was traded in 1988 to Pittsburgh.

Two quarterbacks went in succession in the middle of the first round in 1983. With the fourteenth choice, Buffalo drafted Jim Kelly of Miami. Then New England immediately took Tony Eason of Illinois.

Kelly signed with the Houston Gamblers of the USFL, where he played until joining Buffalo in 1986. Since then, he has helped turn the Bills into divisional champions.

"Eason is a very intriguing football player," Hickey said at the time. "He has top speed, a strong arm, good size, and he's been trained in a pro-style offense. I think his best times are

The 1983 NFL Quarterback Lottery: Pick Six

Blackledge has faltered since taking Penn State to a national title.

Twenty-six teams passed up a chance to draft Marino.

The Patriots wasted no time in grabbing Eason of Illinois.

around the corner because he's still learning."

Eason didn't take long to learn. He was starting by the end of his second season, and in 1985 he led the Patriots to Super Bowl XX. But problems set in. Injuries, and a lack of confidence that seemed to stem from them, reduced his efficiency in recent seasons.

Two more quarterbacks were drafted late in the first round. The New York Jets surprised some by selecting Ken O'Brien of Cal-Davis with the twenty-fourth pick. But, despite some doubts about O'Brien because of the level of competition he had experienced, he has produced at a very high level, leading the NFL in passing in 1985.

Thanks to O'Brien, most New Yorkers can locate UC-Davis.

The final quarterback selection of the first round—Dan Marino of Pittsburgh—was made by Miami with the twenty-seventh pick. One reason Marino still was around that late was that he had gone down in the ratings of many scouts.

"I think Marino is being downgraded too severely simply because of his outstanding junior year," Hickey said. "Everyone just expected so much of him and the team that when it didn't materialize, they blamed Marino. He still is the quality quarterback he was as a junior."

Marino not only started as a rookie, he led the AFC in passing and was selected to start in the Pro Bowl. The next year, he led the entire league in passing while setting NFL records for yards and touchdown passes. Assuming fate is kind, Marino could end up as the most productive passer in NFL history.

The Patriots had high hopes when they made Stanford's Jim Plunkett the top name on the 1971 draft board (above). He eventually won two Super Bowls, but with the Raiders.

The Rams gave up two players and three draft picks to get Jim Everett from Houston midway through the 1986 season.

Washington State (Cincinnati). He was a disappointment with the Bengals and, later, Tampa Bay. In 1981, California's Rich Campbell turned out to be a wasted pick for Green Bay. In 1982, one of two franchise quarterbacks, Ohio State's Art Schlichter, flopped, while BYU's Jim McMahon became successful, though he was frequently injured.

The past several years, every great quarterback has been compared to the class of 1983 (see page 142). There was Steve Young in the 1984 supplemental draft (to Tampa Bay), Bernie Kosar of Miami in a 1985 supplemental draft (to Cleveland), Jim Everett of Purdue in 1986 (to Houston and, ultimately, the Los Angeles Rams), and Heisman Trophy winner Vinny Testaverde of Miami in 1987 (to Tampa Bay). Each has had success so far, and each has superstar potential.

The latest franchise was just taken in 1989. Troy Aikman of UCLA went to the Dallas Cowboys with the first draft pick.

"Aikman has it all," said Dick Steinberg, the director of player personnel for the New England Patriots. "He is big. He has a quick, strong arm. And he has those intangibles—vision, timing, and anticipation. He also moves exceedingly well.... He is the type of player that doesn't come along very often. I think it would be fair to classify him as a franchise."

Trading for a Quarterback

Quarterback trades break down into three basic types: a quarterback for a quarterback; a quarterback for various position players, draft choices, or a combination; and the draft position that *will be* a quarterback or an unsigned draft choice for other players or draft choices.

"A quarterback for a quarterback trade is unusual," says Kansas City general manager Carl Peterson, one of the NFL's most knowledgeable personnel experts. "That kind of move means that the two teams have to differ entirely in their opinions about the two players. The one has to think that the other's quarterback is superior to its own, and vice-versa."

The most famous swap of quarterbacks came before the 1964 season, when new Philadelphia coach Joe Kuharich traded Sonny Jurgensen to the Washington Redskins for Norm Snead. Snead was a productive player who would enjoy a 16-year NFL career in which he passed for more than 30,000 yards. Jurgensen, however, would become one of the best passers of all time and eventually was selected to the Pro Football Hall of Fame. The trade was one of several that incensed Philadelphia fans, who immediately started calling for Kuharich's head.

Another trade with similar results came in 1967. The Oakland Raiders sent starting quarterback Tom Flores and split end Art Powell to Buffalo for backup quarterback Daryle Lamonica and split end Glenn Bass. Although Bass didn't make the Raiders, Lamonica led the AFL in passing in 1967 and the AFC in 1970, was named AFL most valuable player in 1967 and 1969, and led the Raiders to their first appearance in a Super Bowl, in game II. Meanwhile, Flores never became a starter for the Bills.

Perhaps the most controver-

Eagles Get Caught With Small Trade Deficit

Norm Snead (top left) was an efficient seven-year starter for Philadelphia, but coach Joe Kuharich (left) never was forgiven for the one who got away—future Hall of Famer Sonny Jurgensen (top right).

sial trade of all time involving a quarterback for a player at a different position occurred in 1961 when the San Francisco 49ers sent veteran quarterback Y.A. Tittle to the New York Giants in exchange for young guard Lou Cordileone. Cordileone played one year in San Francisco, while Tittle led the Giants to three consecutive NFL Championship Games. In 1962, Tittle set an NFL record with 33 touchdown passes; he broke the record the next year with 36. He later was named to the Pro Football Hall of Fame.

The Giants made another blockbuster trade for a quarterback three years after Tittle retired. In 1967, they sent two first-round and two second-round draft choices to the Minnesota Vikings for Fran Tarkenton. Five years later, the Vikings sent Snead, receiver Bob Grim, rookie running back Vince Clements, and two high draft picks to the Giants for the return of Tarkenton. The Giants struggled with and without Tarkenton, but the master scrambler led the Vikings to appearances in Super Bowls VIII, IX, and XI.

No team has traded more quarterbacks than the Los Angeles Rams. Former owner Daniel F. Reeves loved the draft and the young players it would bring. For years it seemed he would draft the best players in the country, tire of them, and trade them off so he could draft more. Many of those traded proved to be championship quarterbacks. In 1958, the Rams shipped Norm Van Brocklin to Philadelphia for guard Buck Lansford, defensive back Jimmy Harris, and a first-round draft pick in 1959 that the Rams

BOBBIE 'BLONDE BOMBER' LAYNE

Pittsburgh lost its rights to Bobby Layne in 1948, but got him in a 1958 trade.

used to select running back Dick Bass. In 1960, Van Brocklin led the Eagles to the NFL championship, defeating Vince Lombardi's Packers for the title.

In 1961, the Rams traded Billy Wade to the Bears for defensive back Erich Barnes and quarterback Zeke Bratkowski. Two years later, Wade led the Bears to the NFL title.

In 1962, Los Angeles sent Frank Ryan to Cleveland. Two years later, he quarterbacked the Browns to the NFL championship.

In 1963, the Rams dealt a quarterback for the third year in a row. Bratkowski became an outstanding backup to Bart Starr in Green Bay, playing on three consecutive league championship teams with the Packers.

San Franciscans left their hearts with Y.A. Tittle (right), who was traded cross-country for Lou Cordileone (left) in 1961.

Daryle Lamonica (left) departed Buffalo and came to be known as the "Mad Bomber" with the Raiders; Tom Flores left Oakland and came to be known as an unspectacular backup.

Years later, the Rams still liked to trade championship quarterbacks. In 1977, backup Ron Jaworski was sent to Philadelphia for tight end Charles Young. Three seasons later, Jaworski had the Eagles in Super Bowl XV.

Recently drafted or about-to-be-drafted quarterbacks are regularly involved in trades today, but the first such major trade occurred in 1948. That year, the Chicago Bears traded halfback Ray Evans to Pittsburgh for the first-round choice the Bears used to select Bobby Layne. Evans played one year in the NFL; Layne made it to the Hall of Fame after a brilliant career with Detroit.

Van Brocklin (left) had the biggest laugh in the huge trade of '58, leading Philadelphia to the 1960 NFL title. The results were mixed for Los Angeles. Lansford and Harris (middle) played a total of only four years for the Rams, but Bass (right) retired as the leading rusher in franchise history.

The Colts felt jinxed when Elway (left) slipped from their grasp, but Hinton developed into an all-pro.

Another Hall of Fame player involved in such a trade was wide receiver Paul Warfield. In 1970, Cleveland, desperate for a quarterback who could provide insurance for starter Bill Nelsen, traded Warfield to Miami for the draft choice that allowed the Browns to select Purdue All-America quarterback Mike Phipps. Seven years later, Warfield rejoined the Browns. By then, the disappointing Phipps had moved on from Cleveland and into obscurity.

In recent years, several quarterbacks have been traded before they ever joined the team that drafted them. In 1983, John Elway, the first player selected in the draft, refused to sign with Baltimore. The Colts traded him to Denver for another first-round pick, tackle Chris Hinton, backup quarterback Mark Herrmann, and a number-one draft choice. Three years later, the Oilers traded Jim Everett, who had balked at signing with them, to the Rams for two players and three draft choices. And in 1988, the Cardinals traded 1987 number-one pick Kelly Stouffer to Seattle after he held out for an entire year.

Quarterback trades are relatively uncommon, at any time of the year, but a truly rare occurrence is a quarterback trade during the regular season.

"Quarterbacks need to know a team's entire system, and that is basically impossible to pick up without some kind of learning period," said former great Archie Manning. "Therefore the quarterback is the one player you don't see traded very often during the regular season. He is not going to help a team nearly so much as if he had been obtained during the preseason."

But Manning was traded twice, both times in the middle of a season. The first time was in 1982, when Manning, who had been the heart and soul of the New Orleans Saints for a decade, was traded to Houston for tackle Leon Gray. The next year, Manning was on the move

The numbers weren't right in Phoenix, so Stouffer held out for a trade to Seattle.

again, going to Minnesota with tight end Dave Casper for draft choices.

"I couldn't make a real contribution to either team right away," Manning said. "It was very disappointing for me and probably for the Oilers and the Vikings. I think coaches need to think about that kind of move and how much a new quarterback can really do for them."

Despite the obvious logic of this, occasionally a new quarterback really can make a difference—even in midseason. After two games of the 1958 season, the Lions traded Bobby Layne to the Steelers for Earl Morrall and two draft choices. The results were amazing: The defending NFL-champion Lions dropped to 4-7-1, while Layne propelled the Steelers to their first winning season in a decade.

Getting old, established quarterbacks isn't always a cure-all, however. The Rams picked up Joe Namath, Bert Jones, and Steve Bartkowski late in their careers, and none was an important factor for them. Nor was Johnny Unitas in his final year in the NFL, which was spent in San Diego.

"We didn't have the best of luck with the established quarterbacks we got in trades," said Jack Faulkner, the director of football operations for the Rams. "But in a sense that isn't surprising. You need to remember that when you're trading a quarterback, there aren't going to be a heck of a lot of steals. It isn't a position people tend to overlook."

Broadway Joe's act got less than rave reviews on L.A.'s Wilshire Boulevard.

Johnny U. looked as out of place in a Chargers uniform as a 20-piece orchestra in a discotheque. The legendary 18-year veteran played sparingly in his final season.

ANATOMY OF A TRADE

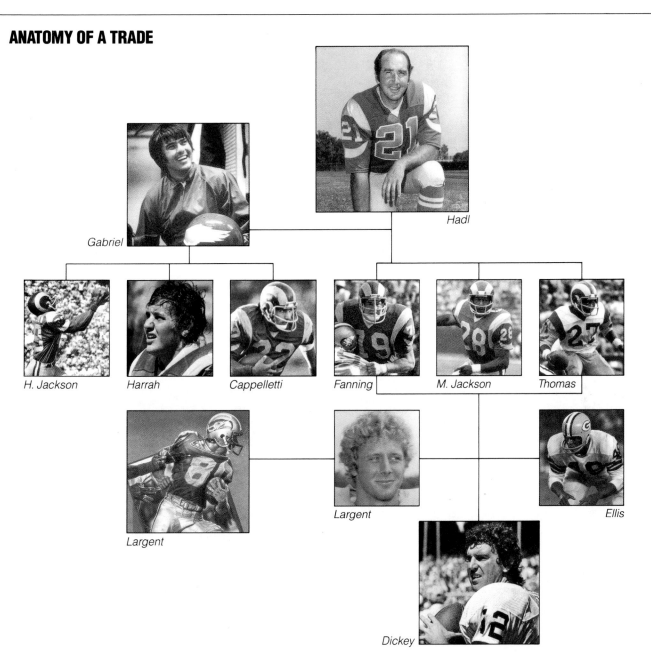

Gabriel

Hadl

H. Jackson

Harrah

Cappelletti

Fanning

M. Jackson

Thomas

Largent

Largent

Ellis

Dickey

I n 1973, Rams general manager Don Klosterman felt Los Angeles needed an experienced backup for quarterback Roman Gabriel. So Klosterman traded Pro Bowl defensive lineman Coy Bacon and running back Bob Thomas to the San Diego Chargers for quarterback John Hadl, who had become expendable when the Chargers drafted Dan Fouts from the University of Oregon and obtained veteran great Johnny Unitas from the Baltimore Colts.

But Gabriel was uncomfortable with the acquisition of Hadl and requested to be traded. Klosterman sent him

to the Philadelphia Eagles, in exchange for wide receiver Harold Jackson plus first-round picks in 1974 and 1975.

Gabriel had five successful years in Philadelphia, but the Rams made out even better. Hadl was named the NFC player of the year in 1973, Jackson gave the Rams five superb years, and the draft choices proved to be Heisman Trophy winner John Cappelletti of Penn State and guard Dennis Harrah, who would lead the Rams' offensive line for the next 13 years.

But the trade wasn't over for the Rams. The next year Hadl had a slow start, and the Rams traded him to Green

Bay for the Packers' first three draft choices in 1975 and first two in 1976. The 1975 picks included defensive tackle Mike Fanning and cornerback Monte Jackson, who would play in two Pro Bowls. The first selection with Green Bay's choice in 1976 was cornerback Pat Thomas, like Jackson a two-time Pro Bowl player.

Green Bay didn't totally lose on the Hadl deal, however. In 1976, the Packers traded Hadl, cornerback Ken Ellis, and a fourth-round draft choice to the Houston Oilers for quarterback Lynn Dickey. Hadl finished his career two years later, Ellis played for the Oilers for less than a season,

and the draft choice never played for the Oilers. Dickey, meanwhile, became the Packers' offensive leader for the next decade, setting numerous team passing records.

Even then, the Hadl saga had one last chapter. The player who was taken by the Oilers with the fourth-round Hadl pick was traded to Seattle before the 1976 season for an eighth-round choice in 1977, which became wide receiver Steve Davis of Georgia, who never played in the NFL. In Seattle, the fourth-round pick was a slow-footed wide receiver from Tulsa. Steve Largent went on to become the leading pass receiver in NFL history.

On Game Day

Similar patterns of thought clutch the minds of all professional football players as the game draws near: excitement, anticipation, purpose, anxiety. The starting quarterback is acquainted with all of these elements, and another that is less universal. He also carries the weight of leadership. He knows that he will receive disproportionate praise for victory...and unfair derision for defeat. He wouldn't have it any other way.

ON GAME DAY

152

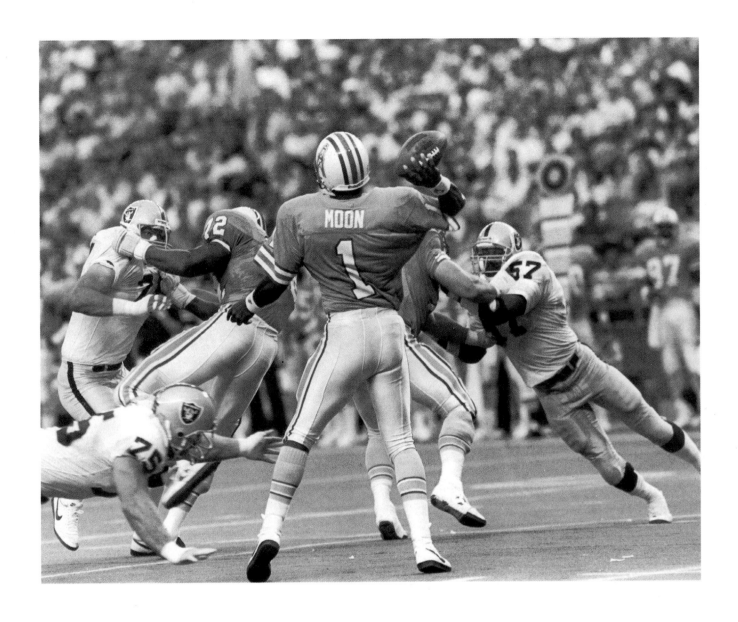

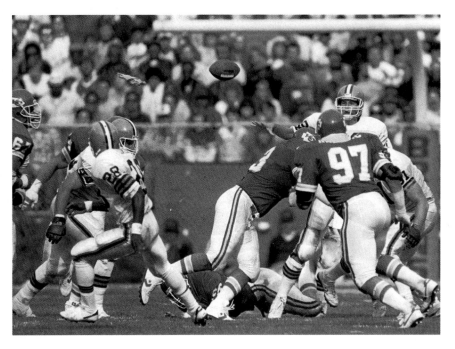

157

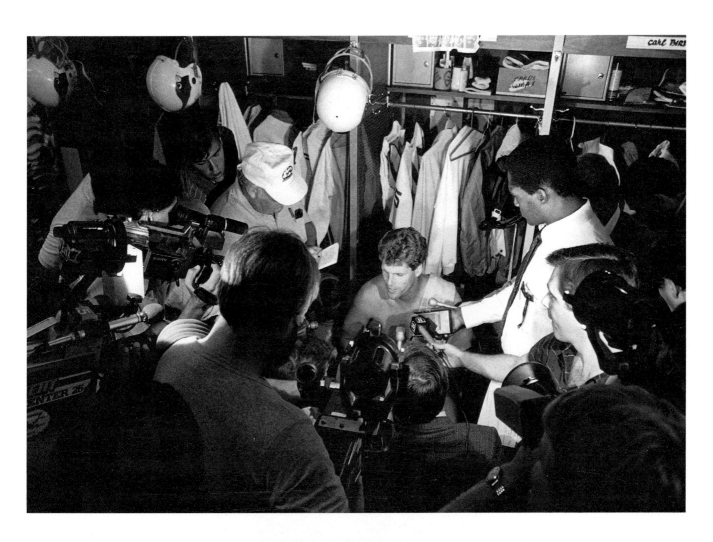

Black Quarterbacks: They Have Overcome

"My first year in the NFL," Washington quarterback Doug Williams said about his time in Tampa Bay, "a reporter asked me how long I had been a black quarterback. I told him that I'd always been a black quarterback."

That was 1978. Things have changed in pro football over the past decade. No longer is a black quarterback unusual, a topic for conversation. Black quarterbacks in the NFL have made the ultimate step forward—they have become recognized not as black quarterbacks, but simply as quarterbacks.

The transition hasn't been hurt by the fact that some of the best quarterbacks in the NFL are black: Two of the four Pro Bowl quarterbacks in 1989, including the game's most valuable player, Randall Cunningham, were black, as is Williams, the MVP of Super Bowl XXII.

But it wasn't always so. For years, the black quarterback was unknown in pro football. The color barrier that existed in the sport had been broken down by Marion Motley and Bill Willis of the Cleveland Browns and Kenny Washington and Woody Strode of the Los Angeles Rams in 1946. But the quarterback position was different.

It took a number of strong men to struggle against the belief by NFL coaches that blacks were not qualified to play the position. They were men who not only had to fight all the normal football fights, but who had to overcome the racial overtones, the criticism, and the myths.

The first black quarterback broke in slowly—not into the game, but into the position. George Taliaferro actually began as a Single-Wing tailback with the Los Angeles Dons of the All-America Football Conference in 1949, sharing the posi-

Fritz Pollard: The Trendsetter Who Didn't Know He Was

Fritz Pollard simply was playing the game he loved. It wasn't until years after his retirement that the American sporting world realized what a pioneer he was. Pollard not only was one of the league's best passers in the days before anyone played quarterback as we know it, he also was the first black head coach (actually co-coach, along with Elgie Tobin) in pro football. Pollard's Akron Pros finished atop the American Pro Football Association with an 8-0-3 record in 1920.

tion with Glenn Dobbs.

When the AAFC went out of business at the end of that season, Taliaferro joined the New York Yanks of the NFL, for whom he played halfback in 1950 and 1951. However, in that season, he also was tried at quarterback, finishing with 33 passing attempts for 251 yards. His excellent overall play earned him selection to the Pro Bowl. Like most of the Yanks, Taliaferro spent 1952 with the Dallas Texans, the last team in the NFL to become extinct, then moved on to the newly formed Baltimore Colts in 1953. Each year Taliaferro split his time between halfback and quarterback, and each year he was selected to the Pro Bowl, becoming the first, and still one of only two, players to go to the Pro Bowl with three different teams.

In Taliaferro's final Pro Bowl season, the first black man to play only quarterback in the NFL came on the scene. Willie Thrower played only the 1953 season with the Chicago Bears, backing up George Blanda and Tommy O'Connell.

It wasn't until 1968, however, that the first black quarterback to start regularly for a team arrived in pro football, and even then it was not by design. When starter Steve Tensi of the Denver Broncos was injured, his replacement was Marlin Briscoe, a rookie from Nebraska-Omaha, who had been drafted to play wide receiver. Briscoe passed for 1,589 yards and 14 touchdowns and helped the Broncos to five victories. The next year, however, Briscoe was back at

Randall Cunningham is one of the latest and greatest in a line of black quarterbacks who have overcome the once-insurmountable color barrier. Cunningham, fast and strong, was named most valuable player in the 1989 Pro Bowl. He passed for 3,808 yards and 24 touchdowns during the 1988 season.

wide receiver. Although easily interpreted as a racially motivated position switch, it actually wasn't a bad career move for Briscoe—he ultimately led the AFC in receiving in 1970.

More than any other, James Harris was the significant pioneer. Harris's ascendancy had its genesis at Grambling, where he quarterbacked two Southwestern Athletic Conference championship teams before being drafted by Buffalo in 1969. However, Harris started only three games between 1969 and his release in 1971.

Signed by the Rams as a free agent in 1973, Harris was penciled in as John Hadl's backup. But when Hadl was traded to Green Bay midway through the 1974 season, Harris became the starter. The Rams won the NFC West in 1974 and 1975. In the latter season, Harris was voted to the AFC-NFC Pro Bowl, where he threw two fourth-quarter touchdown passes and was named the game's most valuable player.

Each year Taliaferro split his time…and each year he made the Pro Bowl.

The appropriately named Willie Thrower, a promising passer from Michigan State, never found his stride in the NFL. He played only one year, backing up George Blanda for the 3-8-1 Bears in 1953.

George Taliaferro from Indiana University was the first black man to be drafted by an NFL club. The Bears selected him in the thirteenth round in 1949, but he elected to sign with the Los Angeles Dons of the AAFC. Taliaferro's versatility took him to three Pro Bowls.

Most of Marlin Briscoe's nine NFL seasons were spent as a wide receiver (he earned two Super Bowl rings as a Miami Dolphins receiver in games VII and VIII), but he was Denver's quarterback of record for most of his 1968 rookie year, when he passed for 1,589 yards.

Super Boost

Dave Mays played three NFL seasons with Cleveland (1976-77) and Buffalo (1978). He started five games for the Browns in 1977.

Joe Gilliam led the 1974 Steelers to a 4-1-1 record before he was replaced by Terry Bradshaw. Pittsburgh went on to win the Super Bowl.

Williams: "I don't think it was too hard on me to be a quarterback in the NFL, and I think a lot of the credit for that has to go to James."

James Harris became the first black quarterback to lead an NFL team to a championship when he directed the Rams to the NFC West title in 1974. He was the NFC's leading passer in 1976, but was traded to the San Diego Chargers in 1977.

James Harris - 1975 Pro Bowl MVP

Unfortunately, Harris became involved in a three-way quarterback controversy in Los Angeles. In 1976, even a 436-yard passing performance against Miami and leading the NFC in passing didn't help. Pat Haden, a former star at USC, eventually was named the starter. Harris was subsequently traded to San Diego, where he played five years—primarily as a backup—before retiring.

"James Harris was my hero growing up," Williams said. "I grew up in Zachary, Louisiana, which is only about twelve miles from Grambling. Everything I did, I did to emulate James Harris. I don't think it was too hard on me to be a quarterback in the NFL, and I think a lot of the credit for that has to go to James, who broke the ground for all of the black quarterbacks."

"There have been some pretty outstanding black quarterbacks in the NFL the last decade," said an NFC personnel director. "Joe Gilliam in Pittsburgh, Doug Williams, Warren Moon, and now Randall Cunningham, who might not only be the best black quarterback ever, he might be the best quarterback in the game right now, period. But if James Harris had ever had a coach who was sold on him the way Buddy Ryan is on Cunningham, then everybody would recognize him as the best. Harris was a phenomenally talented athlete, a simply marvelous passer, and an inspirational leader."

One of Harris's greatest contributions was to serve as a role model and inspiration for many who followed him, including John Walton of Philadelphia, Dave Mays of Cleveland, Vince Evans of Chicago, and Williams.

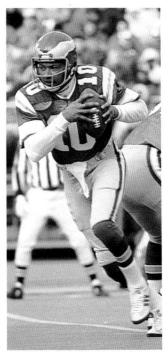

Two strong-armed black quarterbacks joined the NFL in 1976: Johnnie Walton (right), whom coach Dick Vermeil remembered from the Rams' 1970-71 taxi squad, was signed by the Eagles, and Parnell Dickinson (left) was drafted by Tampa Bay.

Houston's Warren Moon unquestionably rates among the NFL's top quarterbacks. Moon has size, mobility, and intelligence, but most of all he has a winner's touch—he has led teams to victory in the Rose Bowl, the CFL's Grey Cup, and the NFL playoffs.

DOUG WILLIAMS'S ENCHANTED EVENING

There were those who said he shouldn't even be starting in the Super Bowl. There were those who said he was starting only because Washington head coach Joe Gibbs had a personality conflict with quarterback Jay Schroeder. Fortunately, there were those who said he was the best quarterback on the team and had earned the job.

Whatever the reason, when the Redskins and Broncos lined up against each other in Super Bowl XXII on January 31, 1988, in San Diego, Doug Williams became the first black quarterback ever to start a Super Bowl.

It seemed appropriate. A decade earlier, Williams, one of the first regular black quarterbacks in the NFL, had led Tampa Bay to within one game of Super Bowl XIV. But Williams left the Buccaneers in 1983 to play in the United States Football League. When the USFL folded, he joined the Redskins in a backup role. Before the 1987 season, Williams was shopped around by Washington, but no deal was made. So Williams started the season as he had the year before, on the bench behind the promising young Schroeder. But when Schroeder

Second Quarter
Washington—Sanders 80 pass from Williams (Haji-Sheikh kick), :53. Drive: 80 yards, 1 play. Denver 10, Washington 7.
Washington—G. Clark 27 pass from Williams (Haji-Sheikh kick), 4:45. Drive: 64 yards, 5 plays. Key play: T. Smith 19 run. Washington 14, Denver 10.
Washington—T. Smith 58 run (Haji-Sheikh kick), 8:33. Drive: 74 yards, 2 plays. Key play: Williams 16 pass to G. Clark. Washington 21, Denver 10.
Washington—Sanders 50 pass from Williams (Haji-Sheikh kick), 11:18. Drive: 60 yards, 3 plays. Key play: Williams 10 pass to Sanders. Washington 28, Denver 10.
Washington—Didier 8 pass from Williams (Haji-Sheikh kick), 13:58. Drive: 79 yards, 7 plays. Key plays: T. Smith 43 run; Williams 21 pass to Sanders. Washington 35, Denver 10.

faltered, Williams became the starter, and Gibbs gave him the nod in the playoffs.

The postseason didn't start well for Williams. It included a lackluster 9-for-27 passing performance in the NFC Championship Game. But it all came together in the second quarter of the Super Bowl.

Still, there was a moment when it looked as if Williams wouldn't even make it to the second period of the game. Late in the first quarter, he fell while dropping back to pass and hyperflexed his left knee. Schroeder took his place.

But with the Redskins trailing 10-0, Williams re-entered the game with 14:17 left in the second period. That began the most amazing quarter in Super Bowl history. On five consecutive possessions, Williams led touchdown drives of 80, 64, 74, 60, and 79 yards. In the 18 plays and combined 5:47 those drives took, Williams completed 9 of 11 passes for 228 yards and touchdowns of 80, 27, 50, and 8 yards. By halftime, the Redskins had an insurmountable 35-10 lead.

Williams added one more touchdown drive in the third quarter to seal the 42-10 victory. Despite not passing often in the second half, he finished with a Super Bowl-record 340 yards and was named the game's most valuable player.

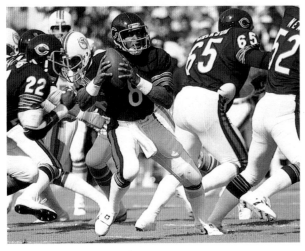

Vince Evans, an elusive running quarterback from USC, played in 62 games, starting 32, for the Bears from 1977 to 1983. His best season was 1981, when he passed for 2,039 yards and 11 touchdowns. Evans last played for the Raiders in the 1987 NFLPA strike games.

Williams led Tampa Bay to the 1979 NFC Championship Game, but it wasn't until the past three or four years that the stigma attached to being a black quarterback finally seemed to disappear. The acceptance coincided with the NFL arrivals of Moon and Cunningham.

"Warren Moon proved beyond a shadow of a doubt when he was in Canada that he had everything it took to be a top NFL quarterback," said Ladd Herzeg, the former general manager of the Houston Oilers. "We desperately wanted him when he let it be known he was going to come down to the NFL, and in the last four years he has shown why. He really has become the emotional and spiritual leader of the Oilers, as well as one of the top game performers in the NFL."

In 1988, Moon led the Oilers to the playoffs and was selected to the AFC-NFC Pro Bowl. The same happened to the Eagles' Cunningham, who had a record passing day against the Bears in the playoffs and then was named the Pro Bowl's most valuable player.

"I've been saying for three years that Randall is the best quarterback in football and has the potential to be the best ever," Eagles head coach Buddy Ryan said. "I think this year went a long way toward proving that. He is the best running quarterback in the game; he has the strongest, most powerful arm in the game; and he is simply the most dangerous player with the ball in all of football."

Quarterback Controversies

In Los Angeles, quarterback controversies are almost a way of life. If there isn't one now, there probably will be soon.

Not that quarterback controversies are the sole property of Los Angeles. After all, who can forget football's version of *Dallas*? —Meredith vs. Morton, Morton vs. Staubach, Staubach vs. Longley, White vs. Hogeboom. Not to mention the same scenario on other teams, among them Washington (Jurgensen vs. Kilmer, Kilmer vs. Theismann, Schroeder vs. Williams), Chicago (Luckman vs. Lujack vs. Layne, Concannon vs. Douglass), and Minnesota (Kramer vs. Wilson). But Los Angeles has turned the quarterback controversy concept into an art form. It doesn't seem to matter who is under center in Los Angeles, a significant portion of the fans and media always seems to favor someone on the sidelines.

One of the first quarterback controversies to gain national attention began in 1949, when ambitious rookie Norm Van Brocklin joined a team already quarterbacked by all-pro Bob Waterfield.

Waterfield had been the leader of the Rams since 1945, when he was the last quarterback in history to win the NFL title and the most valuable player award as a rookie. Waterfield led the NFL in passing in 1946, and in field goals in 1947. A local hero from UCLA, he seemed to have it all—looks, manners, a marriage with sex symbol Jane Russell, and—most important —an almost unbelievable natural talent. He may have been the best defensive back the Rams ever have had. But the private Waterfield was a reluctant celebrity in a town where making an impression was everything. He was serious, low-keyed, and reserved.

"Bob had a calming effect on the entire team," said Hall of Fame receiver Tom Fears. "He was as cool as a deep freeze. He was the same one point ahead or fourteen behind. He inspired utter confidence."

Van Brocklin was the emotional opposite. The Dutchman

Bob Waterfield (7) and Norm Van Brocklin appear to be brothers-in-arms, but the debate surrounding the two future Hall of Fame selections sometimes caused bad blood.

Bill Wade set Rams passing records in 1958, but was gone three years later. He led Chicago to the 1963 NFL title, though in 1964 he split time with Rudy Bukich, who originally was drafted by—surprise—Los Angeles.

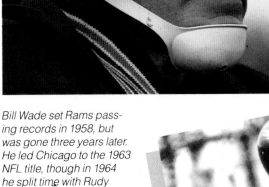

Frank Ryan, who had battled Wade for the Rams' job, was traded to Cleveland in 1962. With Jim Brown (32) pacing the ground attack, the Browns swept to the 1964 NFL title.

Van Brocklin, disgruntled as a part-time Rams starter, spent his last three seasons with Philadelphia. In 1960, he took the Eagles to the NFL championship. Los Angeles, coached by Bob Waterfield, finished 4-7-1 that season.

Made in L.A.: Rams Supply Championship Quarterbacks to the Rest of the NFL

was volatile, impatient, and acerbic. But he had a golden arm and was a leader the equal of Waterfield in an altogether different way.

Van Brocklin was torn between his ambition and his admiration of and friendship with Waterfield. When he first arrived in Los Angeles in 1949, he told head coach Clark Shaughnessy to give him a chance because he was the best passer the Rams had. Shaughnessy allowed Waterfield to guide the Rams to the NFL Championship Game.

The next year, however, Joe Stydahar became head coach of the Rams, and he tried alternating his quarterbacks—Waterfield playing the first and third quarters, Van Brocklin the second and fourth. The city, the team, and the coaches were split just as evenly.

Waterfield continued to be the consummate all-around player and leader, but Van Brocklin's passing truly was remarkable. In one quarter against Detroit, he put 41 points on the scoreboard. By the end of the 1950 season, Van Brock-

lin had earned the NFL passing title and the Rams had advanced to the NFL Championship Game, which Cleveland won 30-28.

The scenario continued in 1951 until the final game of the season, when Van Brocklin refused to call a play Stydahar sent in from the sideline. The coach put Waterfield in for the rest of the game. Waterfield threw five touchdown passes to edge Van Brocklin for the passing title. A heated discussion after the game resulted in Waterfield playing the first 50 minutes

of the championship game against Cleveland. But with the score tied 17-17 in the fourth quarter, the Dutchman came off the bench to throw a 73-yard touchdown pass to Fears to give the Rams the title.

The debate raged on the following season. Van Brocklin again led the league in passing, but Waterfield showed he could do it all. Against the Packers in Green Bay, he led the Rams from a 28-6 deficit with 12 minutes left to a 30-28 victory.

The issue seemed to be resolved when Waterfield, weary

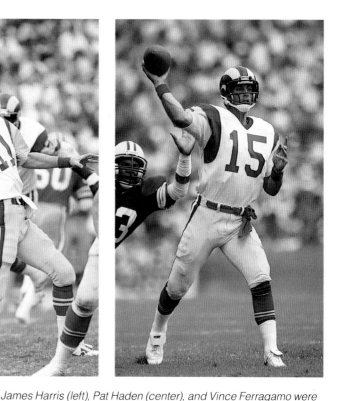

Passer Needed—Inquire With Rams (Only Serious Applicants Need Apply)

James Harris (left), Pat Haden (center), and Vince Ferragamo were just three of the numerous entrants in the Great Rams Quarterback Derby of the 1970s. Harris probably had the most natural ability; Haden, a USC graduate, was a local favorite; but it was Ferragamo who quarterbacked the team in its only Super Bowl appearance.

of the constant media battle, retired at the end of the 1952 season. Van Brocklin had two outstanding years, leading the NFL in passing again in 1954. Then a new Rams controversy began. In 1955, Sid Gillman became head coach of the Rams, and he started playing young Billy Wade, the Rams' bonus choice in 1952, on a rotating basis with Van Brocklin. In Gillman's first year, the Rams won the Western Conference title. Wade received significantly more playing time in 1956, and the Rams dropped to last.

"Van Brocklin's [lack of] speed was a terrible disadvantage in those years, when a quarterback had to run on the rollout," Gillman said. "Wade was a much younger and more mobile quarterback."

Ultimately, Van Brocklin demanded—and got—a trade, which sent him to Philadelphia in 1958. But nothing changed in Los Angeles except the faces. The year Van Brocklin left, the Rams drafted Frank Ryan. Within a couple of seasons, he and Wade were fighting it out in the media as well as on the field. When Wade left to lead the

Bears to an NFL title in 1963 (as Van Brocklin had done with the Eagles in 1960), it was Ryan vs. Zeke Bratkowski. That was followed by Bratkowski vs. rookie Roman Gabriel. Meanwhile, Ryan went to the Browns, whom he led to the NFL championship in 1964.

In the first round of the 1962 draft, the Rams selected Gabriel. The next year they chose Heisman Trophy winner Terry Baker. In 1964, they added Bill Munson. It wasn't until George Allen became the head coach in 1966 that Gabriel—who would be named the league's most valuable player in 1969— was given the job.

Meanwhile, in San Francisco, the 49ers had quarterback controversies of their own. The word wars started almost immediately upon their entering the NFL, when young Y.A. Tittle was the darling of the Frankie Albert haters. Later, Stanford's John Brodie was cheered over Tittle. When Tittle was traded to the New York Giants, Brodie became the target. But neither collegiate passing whiz George Mira nor Heisman Trophy winner Steve Spurrier could beat

out Brodie, until Spurrier put him on the bench for his last two seasons.

Few quarterback controversies were more hotly contested than the one in Dallas, where Craig Morton and Roger Staubach divided loyalties among fans, the media, and teammates. Morton had been a patient and well-liked backup to Don Meredith for four years before he became the starter after Meredith's surprise retirement in 1968. That same year, Staubach joined the Cowboys as a 27-year-old rookie.

In 1970, injuries to Morton allowed Staubach to play on-and-off, and he began developing a following despite the fact that Morton led the Cowboys to Super Bowl V, where they lost to Baltimore 16-13.

By 1971, nobody was more confused than Dallas head coach Tom Landry, who went so far as to alternate his quarterbacks by plays in one game early in the season. Midway through the year, Landry decided to go with Staubach. The Cowboys won their last seven

regular-season games and rolled through the playoffs, defeating Miami 24-3 in Super Bowl VI, where Staubach was named most valuable player.

Staubach suffered a shoulder separation the next season and Morton again led Dallas to the playoffs. But in an NFC playoff game against San Francisco, Staubach came off the bench in the second half and passed for two touchdowns in the final 1:48 to spark a dramatic 30-28 victory. Morton eventually was traded to the New York Giants.

At the same time Staubach and Morton were being played off against each other, three quarterbacks had a round-robin affair in Pittsburgh. In 1969, Terry Hanratty of Notre Dame was drafted as the Steelers' quarterback of the future. The next year, however, Pittsburgh had the first pick of the entire draft and selected Terry Bradshaw of Louisiana Tech. Despite up-and-down performances early in his career, Bradshaw earned the starting job and in 1972 helped take the Steelers to their first divisional title ever. Few people figured it was relevant when the Steelers chose Joe

Gilliam, a quarterback from Tennessee State, in the 1972 draft.

But Pittsburgh began a quarterback merry-go-round in 1973 when Bradshaw suffered a shoulder separation and Hanratty broken ribs. Gilliam took over, and, despite throwing a string of interceptions, played well enough to gain support over local-hero Hanratty and the talented Bradshaw.

In 1974, the three quarterbacks alternated in the preseason. Head coach Chuck Noll named Gilliam the starter before the regular season, and the Steelers began with a 4-1-1 record. However, his wide-open style conflicted with Noll's ideas of percentage football. After Gilliam completed only 5 of 18 passes against Cleveland, Noll reinstated Bradshaw. The big blond never saw the bench again, leading the Steelers to a divisional title and a 16-6 victory in Super Bowl IX. Bradshaw also took the Steelers to three more Super Bowl triumphs in the next five years. He was named most valuable player in games XIII and XIV.

In 1973, the Rams, who already had Gabriel and backup

Haden explains to Rams new-comer Joe Namath what it's like to be one of three starters. Namath played only a few games for the Rams.

James Harris, traded with San Diego for quarterback John Hadl and drafted Ron Jaworski. Feeling uncomfortable with the acquisitions, Gabriel demanded to be traded, and Hadl took over as the Rams' offensive leader. Hadl led the Rams to the best record in the NFL (12-2) and was named the NFC player of the year.

But Hadl started slowly in 1974 (the Rams were 3-2), and was traded to Green Bay for a load of draft choices. Harris became the starter and his popularity lasted until the Rams lost in the playoffs again. Late in the next season, Jaworski took over when Harris was injured and led the Rams to the NFC Championship Game.

In 1976, the Rams controversy started again in full force. Harris won the job in the preseason, then was injured before the first game. Jaworski led an opening-day victory, but suffered a shoulder separation, trying to score from the one-yard line. In the second game of the year, rookie Pat Haden—a product of USC and a local favorite—led the Rams to a 10-10 tie with Minnesota while outplaying Fran Tarkenton. When Harris returned, the position looked like a revolving door, with all three playing. Harris produced the Rams' best passing day in 25 years, with 436 yards against Miami. But after he was sacked mercilessly by Cincinnati, head coach Chuck Knox decided to go with Haden the last five games.

The next season, the Rams ended that quarterback controversy. . .and started another. They traded the stoic Harris to San Diego, and the vociferous Jaworski to Philadelphia. They then drafted Vince Ferragamo and signed an aging Joe Namath, who led the Rams to two early victories. He threw four interceptions in the fourth week before being forced out with injuries. Haden became the starter, and Namath didn't play again.

The debate returned two years later, after Haden broke a finger on his passing hand in a win over Seattle. Ferragamo took over and, with some brilliant passing in the playoffs, led the Rams to Super Bowl XIV. The controversy now involved Haden and Ferragamo, and it wasn't resolved until Haden, who won the job in the 1980 preseason, was injured in the opening game and knocked out for the year. Ferragamo set team passing records for yards and touchdowns in 1980, then, following a bizarre salary negotiation with new owner Georgia Frontiere, suddenly signed with Montreal of the CFL, relinquishing the job to Haden.

In the next half dozen years, the Rams' continuing controversy included Haden, Jeff Rutledge, Dan Pastorini, Bert Jones, Ferragamo (who returned after one year in Canada), Jeff Kemp, Dieter Brock, and Steve Bartkowski. Los Angeles finally settled on the man who figures to be its first stable, long-term starter since Gabriel—Jim Everett.

The picture hasn't become totally clear in Los Angeles, however. The Rams merely have passed the mantle to the Raiders, a team with a long history of quarterback stability until recently. As soon as the Raiders left Oakland in favor of Los Angeles, things went crazy for their quarterbacks.

In their first five years in Los Angeles, the Raiders had a continuous media fight over Jim Plunkett and Marc Wilson. In 1988, Plunkett retired and the Raiders released Wilson. The not-surprising follow-up was a new controversy between young Steve Beuerlein and Jay Schroeder, who was acquired from Washington.

And the controversy continues. . . .

Tommy Kramer (9) succeeded Fran Tarkenton in 1979 and went on to compile the three most-productive seasons in Vikings history (1980, '81, and '85). But Kramer often rode an emotional roller coaster, and the team eventually rotated him with Wade Wilson, (11) fanning controversy in the Twin Cities.

Shooting Stars

A t the end of the 1939 season, Parker Hall looked like a shooting star of intergalactic proportions. The Cleveland Rams rookie tailback had set the league on fire with his performance in his first year out of Mississippi. He led the NFL in passing, setting single-season records for pass attempts (208) and completions (106). He finished fifth in the NFL in rushing (458 yards) and had a 41-yard punting average on a league-high 58 punts. Hall led the Rams to a 5-5-1 record after a 1-4 start, and was named the NFL's most valuable player.

But Hall's production decreased in each of the next three years. In 1942, he lost yards rushing, while throwing 19 interceptions and only seven touchdown passes. He then went into the service and played only one more year, in the All-America Football Conference.

Hall's story is not unusual. NFL history is dotted with players who enjoyed a successful year or two and then disappeared.

Still other players have had relatively undistinguished careers punctuated by a brief but brilliant game or season.

In the midst of an otherwise uneventful career, Mike Boryla of Philadelphia was selected to the AFC-NFC Pro Bowl in 1976 because all of the quarterbacks ahead of him were injured or unable to play. Boryla entered the game late. Only 5:39 remained, with the NFC trailing 20-9. Boryla first threw a 14-yard touchdown pass to Terry Metcalf, then followed with the game-winning pass, an eight-yard strike to Mel Gray. Boryla then disappeared.

The obvious question is how this can happen. If players are talented enough to be successful once, why doesn't that success continue? What is it that is so magical for them in that one season, one game, or even one play?

The answers are plentiful, but injuries are an obvious one. Johnny Lujack had a brilliant future with the Chicago Bears when he joined the team as the heir apparent to Sid Luckman in 1948. In only his second year, Lujack finished second in the NFL in passing while leading the league in yards (2,658) and touchdown passes (23). The next year he suffered a shoulder injury from which he never recovered. He finished the 1950 season with 21 interceptions and only four touchdown passes. He retired after the next year.

The personnel surrounding a quarterback and the way they are organized also can contribute to a sudden demise. Frankie Sinkwich was the NFL's most valuable player in 1944, his second year in the league. With a solid, if unspectacular, cast around him in Detroit, Sinkwich finished third in the NFL in rushing, first in punting, and sixth in passing, while running the Single Wing. But when he joined the Baltimore Colts of the AAFC midway through the 1947 season, Sinkwich was switched to the T-formation. He wasn't suited to it, nor were the players around him suited to his talents.

He spent most of the year riding the bench and playing unspectacularly (averaging 3.4 yards per carry) when he did get in.

Lujack's "Brilliant Future" Was Over in Just Four Years

Johnny Lujack's storybook 1949 season included a 52-21 victory over the Cardinals in which the former Notre Dame quarterback (32, shaking hands with Chicago Bears owner/coach George Halas) passed for six touchdowns and an NFL-record 468 yards.

Mike Boryla's heroic performance in the 1977 Pro Bowl was his last game in an Eagles helmet. Six months later he was traded to Tampa Bay, where he started only one game in two years before disappearing.

THE GREATEST QB WHO NEVER WAS

In one memorable season, Greg Cook of the Cincinnati Bengals showed he could have been not only a star, but an all-time great.

"If Cook hadn't gotten injured, he would have been the best quarterback of the 1970s," said Tom Bass, a former assistant coach with Cincinnati, Tampa Bay, and San Diego. "It is easy to say that this guy or that guy has it all, but Greg had more than that. He had everything—physically, mentally, emotionally—to be one of the greats of all time."

Cook was the Bengals' first pick (and the fifth overall) of the 1969 draft, after leading the nation in total offense at the University of Cincinnati with 3,210 yards (the second-most at the time). He had finished second nationally in passing.

Cook was an ideal physical quarterback (6-3, 213), and simply loaded with potential. He could read every move a defense made, could instill confidence in his teammates with a stare, could choose which finger to hit on a receiver holding out his hands at 20 yards (and then hit it).

In his first pro performance, in the Chicago College All-Star Game, he entered in the third quarter with the Jets leading 16-0. In slightly more than 20 minutes, Cook threw three touchdown passes as the All-Stars gave the Jets the scare of their lives before losing 26-24.

"Cook came into camp late and was therefore at a serious disadvantage," recalls Paul Brown, who was the Bengals' head coach at the time. "But it didn't matter. His performance was flawless in practices and in preseason games. He was just so superior to anyone else we had, and, we quickly learned, to anyone else any other NFL team had."

Cook quickly earned the starting job. In the Bengals' opening game against Miami, he threw two touchdown passes in a 27-21 victory. The next week, he passed for three scores and ran for a fourth

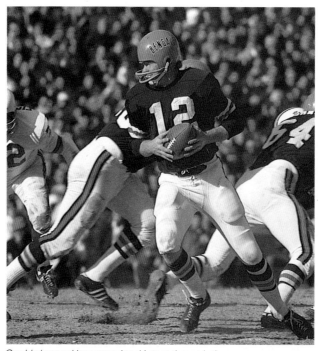

Cook's legend has remained intact through the years.

as Cincinnati upset San Diego 34-20. Then the Bengals shocked Super Bowl-bound Kansas City 24-19 to stretch their record to 3-0. However, Cook suffered a serious arm injury when he was hit by linebacker Willie Lanier, and he sat out the next four games, all losses. In Cook's first game back, he sparked a 31-17 upset of Oakland, the Raiders' only loss of the regular season. The next week, Cook threw four touchdown passes as the Bengals tied Houston 31-31. Additional injuries slowed Cook, however, and the Bengals didn't win the rest of the year.

"That was the year that Daryle Lamonica had his best year," says John Madden, who was the coach of the Raiders at

the time, "and the year that Len Dawson led the Chiefs to the Super Bowl. But Cook looked like the best quarterback in the league—better than Lamonica, better than Dawson, better than Namath, Hadl, or Griese. I thought that this kid was going to be better than anyone I had ever seen."

Indeed, Cook led the AFL in passing while setting a record for the highest pass rating by a rookie, and another still-existing mark for the highest average gain in a rookie season (9.41 yards per pass). He was named AFL rookie of the year by *UPI*.

Cook never recovered from his injuries, and retired before the 1972 season.

"Who can say who was the best quarterback ever?" Bass said. "I don't know if anyone will ever be able to answer that. But I do know that if Greg Cook had been healthy and had been able to play like he could have—even like he did his rookie year *after* he was first injured—then his name would be mentioned in the same breath as the other great ones. People today would think of Unitas and Layne and Tittle and Fouts and Cook at the same time."

A player's own attitude and desire also can have a lot to do with success—or a lack of it. Clint Longley of the Dallas Cowboys was a superbly talented backup to Roger Staubach. In his rookie season, 1974, Longley, subbing for the injured Staubach, threw two touchdown passes, including a 50-yard effort to Drew Pearson with 28 seconds left, to produce a dramatic, nationally televised 24-23 upset of Washington *(below, right)*. However, Longley felt that he should be the Cowboys' starter, and his emotions helped start a locker-room fight with Staubach in the 1976 preseason. Longley soon found himself in San Diego. A year after

that, he was out of football.

Coaching changes, loss of starting status, and age are other factors that lead to the here-today-gone-tomorrow syndrome.

In 1970, Buffalo's Dennis Shaw was AFC rookie of the year after throwing for 2,507 yards and ranking fifth in the conference in passing. But when Lou Saban became the Bills' head coach in 1972, he emphasized O.J. Simpson and the ground game. Shaw, an outstanding pure passer, wasn't the field leader and ball handler that Saban wanted. In 1973, he was replaced as the starter by rookie Joe Ferguson, who ran the team well, but mainly hand-

ed off while learning the Bills' new-style offense. Despite spending time with three other NFL teams, Shaw never again was a regular starter.

In 1965, Tom Matte, the Baltimore halfback who had been a running quarterback at Ohio State, became an emergency substitute for the Colts after quarterback Johnny Unitas suffered a leg injury and backup Gary Cuozzo separated his shoulder. Matte responded with a dramatic performance that led the Colts past the Rams 20-17. He led the game's ball carriers with 99 yards, set up the deciding field

goal, and handled the ball flawlessly. That victory got the Colts into a Western Conference playoff against Green Bay. Reading the plays off a wristband, Matte almost led the Colts to the NFL Championship Game. But a field goal by Don Chandler beat them 13-10 in overtime. The next week, against the Dallas Cowboys in the Playoff Bowl, Baltimore head coach Don Shula finally allowed Matte to open up the passing game. Matte passed for 165 yards and two touchdowns and the Colts won 35-3.

The next year, Matte was moved back to halfback, where he ultimately was named to two Pro Bowls.

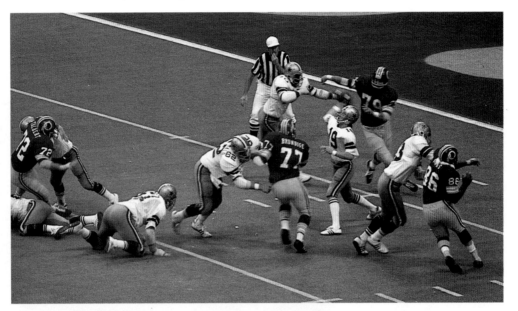

Dieter Brock was signed by the Rams in 1985 after 11 years in the CFL. He took Los Angeles to the NFC title game, but 34-year-old rookies don't hold much promise in the NFL—he was gone the next season.

Clint Longley's fiery temperament was an obstacle to his on-field accomplishments. The quirky quarterback from Abilene Christian occupied himself in the offseason by hunting rattlesnakes in the Texas desert.

Dennis Shaw got off on the right foot with an encouraging rookie season, but his career seemed to retreat thereafter. Shaw's production steadily declined in the '70s during stints with the Bills, Cardinals, Giants, and Chiefs.

Benchwarmers

There is a basic rule in the NFL about quarterbacks: One is not enough for a team that wants to make the playoffs. That is not to say that a team won't play only one quarterback all of the time if it can, but with the injuries inherent in professional football, a solid reserve quarterback is necessary insurance.

In fact, this seems to be more a truism with each passing year. Trying to get through 16 NFL regular-season games—not to mention four preseason games plus, hopefully, the playoffs—without a good backup is like going mountain climbing without a rope.

"It's very difficult to play a quarterback in this day and age who isn't extremely mobile," says former San Francisco head coach Bill Walsh. "Consequently, if a player is hampered at all, it's probably wiser to replace him. I think the second man at that position is going to be playing more each year because you have to have mobility and quickness, and it's very difficult to avoid the heavy contact with the heavy blitzing that's going on."

Although defensive linemen and blitzing linebackers haven't always been as big and strong and fast—translation: dangerous—as they are today, coaches, being creatures interested in security, always have wanted good backup quarterbacks. Sometimes, they have been lucky enough to get great ones.

One of the first great backups actually wasn't initially a quarterback, but a Single-Wing tailback. Frankie Filchock began his career with the Pittsburgh Pirates (they weren't named the Steelers until 1941), but was traded to Washington midway through the 1938 season. The

Redskins already had Sammy Baugh. The next year, Redskins head coach Ray Flaherty decided to protect Baugh by playing him only 30 minutes a game. Filchock proved his worth by outpassing Baugh two-to-one.

Although Baugh ultimately became an even more proficient passer out of the T-formation than the Single Wing, he struggled with the new position a bit in its first year in Washington, 1944. Meanwhile, Filchock, straight out of a stint in the U.S. Navy, adapted immediately and, while splitting time with Baugh, actually led the NFL in passing.

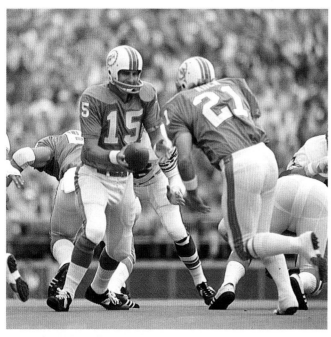

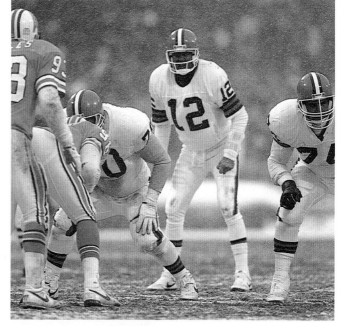

Earl Morrall spent a good part of his 21-year NFL career on the bench, but he was instrumental in bringing championships to Baltimore (left) and Miami (above). Morrall backed up at least three Hall of Fame quarterbacks.

Don Strock (left) found himself in a familiar situation—a relief role—when he signed with Cleveland (above) in 1988. Strock started 20 regular-season games in 14 years with the Dolphins.

One of Bob Lee's few starts for Minnesota was a 1977 NFC Divisional Playoff Game known for some reason as the "Mud Bowl." Playing in place of injured Fran Tarkenton, Lee (right) led the Vikings to a messy 14-7 victory over the Rams.

TO DeBERG'S CHAGRIN YOUTH IS SERVED...

Steve DeBerg knows how the plot of the soap opera goes. The bad guy gets the girl and starts to walk off with her. But, at the last minute, the good guy comes back into the picture, knocks off the villain, wins the girl's heart, and ends the show living happily ever after as the hero.

That's great...unless you happen to figure, like DeBerg, that you're the good guy, but you keep getting bad guys' roles. Actually, DeBerg has starred in this soap four times. Different characters, but the same ending. Central casting gets him the wrong part.

Depending on the story line, DeBerg usually inches his way to the starting position on some team, only to be joined, then supplanted, by that year's whiz kid.

DeBerg was the starter in San Francisco, before giving way to Joe Montana. He moved to Denver and was the starter there, until John Elway showed up. So he headed to Tampa Bay, where it was Steve Young, followed soon thereafter by Vinny Testaverde. He then went to Kansas City in 1988, where he and holdover Bill Kenney took turns holding the job.

DeBerg initially came into the NFL in 1977 as the tenth-round draft choice of Dallas, after having a record-setting senior year at San Jose State.

Cut by the Cowboys, he signed as a free agent with San Francisco. The next year, DeBerg not only saw his first pro action, he became a starter, passing for 1,570 yards in 11 games.

Before the 1979 season, Bill Walsh became the head coach of the 49ers. He installed a brilliantly conceived short-passing game and turned DeBerg loose. The result was a pair of NFL records: 578 attempts and 347 completions. DeBerg also passed for a team-record 3,652 yards.

"Steve is one of the best young quarterbacks in the league," Walsh said at the

Steve DeBerg, San Francisco

Steve DeBerg, Denver

Steve DeBerg, Tampa Bay

Steve DeBerg, Kansas City

time. "He is very accurate on short passes and has an outstanding grasp of the pro passing game."

Unfortunately for DeBerg, another player on the 49ers impressed Walsh even more. In the 1980 preseason, DeBerg received a blow to his throat, which caused him to suffer from severe laryngitis. The 49ers countered by

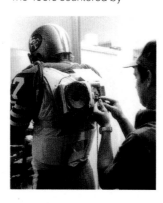

Not even turning up the volume on his temporary amplifier brought DeBerg the attention he deserved.

equipping him with an amplified backpack fitted under his shoulder pads, which allowed his teammates to hear him. The injury might or might not have contributed to a slow start, but, regardless, midway through the season, Walsh replaced DeBerg with Montana, who has led the team to three Super Bowl victories.

In the final week of the 1981 preseason, DeBerg was traded to Denver, where, after a year on the bench behind Craig Morton, he became the starter. But then Denver obtained John Elway, the first pick of the 1983 draft. That season, DeBerg and Elway shared the starting job, with the more experienced DeBerg actually outperforming Elway in general. For that, DeBerg was shipped off to Tampa Bay.

With the Buccaneers, DeBerg took over for early season starter Jack Thompson and passed for 3,554 yards and 19 touchdowns. But the next year the Buccaneers ob-

tained Steve Young, whom they broke in slowly but then made the starter late in the season. DeBerg played little behind Young in 1986, but then everything changed.

Before the 1987 season, Tampa Bay traded Young to San Francisco and drafted Heisman Trophy winner Vinny Testaverde. But DeBerg surprised everybody by earning the starting position in the preseason. Late in the season, despite having his best year, DeBerg was benched to make way for the young Testaverde.

The next move was to trade DeBerg to Kansas City, where he figured to back up Bill Kenney. But DeBerg surprised his doubters, won the starting job, and had an outstanding season. He looked as if he finally had found a place where he could be a long-term starter. But then the Chiefs realigned their front office and hired a new head coach, Marty Schottenheimer. Once again DeBerg faced an uncertain future.

Don't Feel Bad, Guys, Joe DiMaggio's Backup Didn't Play Much, Either

Filchock spent most of his career in Baugh's shadow, but in 1946 he was traded to the New York Giants. He responded by being named all-pro while leading the Giants to the NFL Championship Game in his only season with the team.

If Filchock was unlucky to spend so much time behind Baugh, George Shaw was doubly unfortunate. The former Oregon star began his career as a starter with the Baltimore Colts in 1955. But the next year, he suffered a broken kneecap in a game against the Bears and was replaced by free-agent rookie Johnny Unitas, who stayed in the Colts' lineup for the next 17 years. Shaw remained as Unitas's backup until he was traded to the Giants in 1959. In New York, Shaw played third fiddle in a unique two-quarterback system.

When Shaw was in New York, he saw one of the most unusual uses of quarterbacks in NFL history. The backup—Don Heinrich—actually was the starter. Frequently in the latter half of the 1950s, including 1956, when the Giants won the NFL title, Heinrich would start games for the Giants, before Charlie Conerly would come in at the beginning of the second quarter and play the rest of the game.

"The theory behind it," says Tom Landry, who was an assistant coach with the Giants at the time, "was you'd have Heinrich come in and probe the defense, see what they were doing, and you could discuss it with Conerly during the first quarter on the sidelines: 'This is what they're doing and this is what we planned, and here's what we ought to do.'"

But it wasn't just the system. According to Kyle Rote, an end on those New York teams, it was Heinrich who made the system work. "Heinrich wasn't the greatest passer in the world," Rote says. "But he had a great football mind, almost an instinct for the game, that let him find out everything a defense was doing. And he wouldn't hurt you being in there a quarter."

The expansion Minnesota Vikings traded for Shaw in 1961, perceiving him as their quarterback of the future. Shaw's future

Frank Filchock may have had a goofy smile, but he also possessed a fantastic arm. Unfortunately, Hall of Fame teammate Sammy Baugh kept Filchock from stardom.

The New York Giants' two-quarterback offense didn't have room for George Shaw, a pretty good quarterback who spent eight NFL seasons watching the likes of Johnny Unitas, Charlie Conerly, and Fran Tarkenton pass their ways into the NFL record books.

lasted only about 15 minutes. In the second period of the Vikings' first game, again against the Bears, Shaw was replaced by rookie Fran Tarkenton, who never saw the bench again.

Several quarterbacks who spent most of their days primarily as backups had amazingly long careers. Zeke Bratkowski was a rookie reserve behind George Blanda with the Chicago Bears in 1954. After also playing behind Ed Brown with the Bears, Frank Ryan with the Rams, and Bart Starr with the Packers, where he played on three NFL championship teams, Bratkowski retired in 1971.

A list of legendary quarterbacks must include King Hill, an 11-year veteran with three teams; Gary Cuozzo, who played with four clubs in 10 years; Mike Livingston, who spent six of his 13 years as Len Dawson's sub in Kansas City; Bob Lee, whose pinch-hit performances in pressure games during his 12-year career helped both the Vikings and Rams make it to the Super Bowl; Bobby Scott, who spent 10 years in the shadow of Archie Manning in New Orleans; and Marty Domres, who spent nine years with four clubs, including performing well enough to help convince the Baltimore Colts' management that an aging Johnny Unitas could be traded to San Diego.

The longest—and most impressive—career for a man who is thought of primarily as a backup, however, was that of Earl Morrall. Originally selected in the first round of the 1956 draft by San Francisco, Morrall backed up Y.A. Tittle for a year before becoming the starter in Pittsburgh. In 1958, Morrall went to Detroit in a trade for Bobby Layne. He backed up Tobin Rote, and eventually became a starter before going to the Giants in 1965, where he started until they obtained Fran Tarkenton in 1967.

Obtained by the Baltimore Colts before the 1968 season, Morrall became a starter when Johnny Unitas went down with an injury. Morrall then led the Colts to the best record in the NFL (13-1), led the league in passing, and was named the NFL's most valuable player. Although the season ended disappointingly with a 16-7 loss to the New York Jets in Super Bowl

They Also Serve Who Only Stand and Wait

One of Zeke Bratkowski's few moments of glory was this 1965 victory over Baltimore, when he set NFL playoff records by completing 22 of 39 passes for 248 yards.

III, Morrall gained his vindication two years later. In Super Bowl V, he came off the bench, where he had been relegated by the return of Unitas, to pass for 147 yards in the Colts' 16-13 victory over Dallas.

Released by Baltimore before the 1972 season, the 38-year-old Morrall was picked up by Miami, where his old coach, Don Shula, had moved in 1970. When Bob Griese suffered a broken leg and dislocated ankle early in the season, Morrall led the Dolphins through the only perfect season in NFL history, although Griese returned in time to start and lead the Dolphins to the Super Bowl VII victory. Morrall retired in 1976, ending a 21-year career.

Toward the end of Morrall's career, the Dolphins obtained a young quarterback who had led the nation in passing the previous year at Virginia Tech. Don Strock spent 14 years in Miami backing up Bob Griese, David Woodley, and Dan Marino before joining Cleveland in 1988.

Although he never was a regular starter, Strock captured the nation's imagination in a 1981 AFC Divisional Playoff Game. He replaced Woodley in the second quarter, with the Dolphins already trailing 24-0. In the next four periods—before the Chargers finally won 41-38 after 13:52 of overtime—Strock completed 29 of 43 passes for 403 yards and four touchdowns.

Several other recent backups have helped their teams win important games either in the playoffs or on the way to them. Gary Kubiak of Denver has bailed out the Broncos several times when John Elway has missed games with injuries; Jeff Kemp helped first the Rams and then the 49ers make the playoffs; Pat Ryan quarterbacked the Jets to a victory in a 1986 AFC Divisional Playoff Game; and Steve Young was a key figure in keeping the 49ers rolling in 1987-88 when Joe Montana was out with injuries.

Another reserve, Mike Tomczak of Chicago, ran up one of the best winning records of any quarterback in the NFL while replacing frequently injured Jim McMahon. In fact, based on his outstanding play at the end of the 1988 season, Tomczak could well be on his way out as a backup—and on his way in as a starter.

SOME MAKE WINNING LOOK EASY— FOR STOUDT, IT WAS ALMOST EFFORTLESS

In the second half of his NFL career, Cliff Stoudt was a walking, talking—though seldom throwing—trivia question. Stoudt, a fine college passer who broke most of Ron Jaworski's records at Youngstown State, received two Steelers Super Bowl rings before ever taking a snap in a regular-season game. Terry Bradshaw was the quarterback in charge in those days, and Stoudt usually was the third-stringer. Still, he was on the roster, and therefore lined up with Bradshaw, Lambert, Swann, et al. when they passed out championship jewelry in Pittsburgh. Stoudt got his first start in 1980, and he didn't do badly, passing for 310 yards in a 27-26 loss to Cleveland.

Super Bowl XIII

Super Bowl XIV

Mike Livingston, with a familiar look of patience, started for the Chiefs for most of four seasons, but before that he spent six as Len Dawson's reinforcement.

Gary Cuozzo graduated from dental school as number one in his class, but he usually was number two while playing for Baltimore, New Orleans, Minnesota, and St. Louis.

Steve Fuller's career got a promising start in Kansas City, but the Clemson graduate eventually settled into a backup role for the Chiefs, Rams, and Bears. He did lead Chicago to a playoff victory in 1984.

Disappointing Careers

In their college days, they were the greatest of the greats, and many are remembered as the finest players ever produced by their schools. But if they are remembered at all in the NFL, it is more frequently as the answers to trivia questions.

Pro football history is as full of disappointments as it is surprising success stories. For every unknown player from schools without national reputations, such as Walter Payton, there is an All-America who doesn't make it, such as Pat Sullivan. For every free agent who makes it big, such as Hall of Fame member Dick (Night Train) Lane, there is a high draft choice with everything going for him—until he dons his pro uniform, such as Terry Baker. And

Lee Grosscup, Giants

for every undersized, physically questionable player in NFL history, such as Fran Tarkenton, there is a perfect physical specimen, such as Leon Burns, who is in the stands rather than on the field.

Scouting and drafting are among the most important parts of a pro football club's operation. They also are among the most difficult. And nowhere is it harder than in judging quarterbacks.

Of course, there are many easily measured areas of ability. But there are just as many that aren't. One of the most impor-

Future Patriots GM Patrick Sullivan helps Huarte with his pads.

tant areas for quarterbacks is totally unmeasurable—their heart or their desire to play, to succeed, to win. That's why many quarterbacks who go in the low rounds of the draft end up playing, and many who go early disappear.

There are other reasons for a highly respected collegian not making it in the NFL.

First, a player can be what the pros call a P.R. All-America, a player who gains national attention because of his team's success, his school's history, or the efforts of his university's sports information director in convincing the media that the player is the best, whether he is or not.

Second, a quarterback's weaknesses can be hidden because of college formations that aren't used in the pros, or because of the style of play that a college team or conference uses. It is hard to picture a Wishbone quarterback as an NFL star, but Richard Todd was successful with the Jets after playing in Alabama's Wishbone.

Third, all factors—size, speed, arm strength, etc.—are less important in college football than in the NFL. NFL players are the cream of the crop, so the abilities that allow a player to dominate his college competition might not be enough to allow him to be successful when he is facing the best.

"The best example of success and the lack of it in recent years is to compare Jim McMahon with Art Schlichter," said Mike Hickey, the New York Jets' director of player personnel.

"When McMahon and Schlichter came out of college, there was a great debate over which of the two would and should be drafted first. Many people were deluded by physical comparisons. Schlichter was big, strong, and productive—seemingly the perfect NFL quarterback. McMahon was short, wore glasses, and needed a knee brace.

"However, some people who delved deeper felt that Schlichter had some personal problems that might affect his play. Obviously, they turned out to be right. Those who thought about

Ron VanderKelen, Vikings

McMahon should have seen through that front, too. Sure, he had those physical limitations, but he had had the same ones in college and had been the most productive passer in the history of college football. There was obviously something else there, something unmeasurable, something truly special."

Schlichter was only one in a long list of disappointing quarterbacks. One of the early ones was Angelo Bertelli, the 1943 Heisman Trophy winner from Notre Dame. In 1944, the Boston Yanks made him the first pick in the NFL draft, but he

Gary Huff, Bears

never signed with the team. After serving in World War II, Bertelli chose to go into the AAFC (Los Angeles Dons, 1946; Chicago Rockets, 1947-48). He spent most of his time on the bench in his unsuccessful three-year career in the new league, backing up two men who weren't exactly household names—Sam Vacanti and Al Dekdebrun.

Two years after they drafted Bertelli, the Yanks went for his successor at Notre Dame, Frank (Boley) Dancewicz. Although Dancewicz signed with Boston, he played little in his three years and wound up his career barely a 40 percent passer.

Despite their publicity, many Notre Dame quarterbacks were only moderately successful in their pro years.

"With all the publicity those

supposedly wonderful Notre Dame quarterbacks had, not one of their great ones was successful until first Joe Theismann and then Joe Montana," said a pro personnel director. "Daryle Lamonica had a splendid career, but he was a nobody when he still was at Notre Dame. As pros, the others—Johnny Lujack, Bob Williams, Ralph Guglielmi, George Izo, Terry Hanratty, and John Huarte—always will be remembered with clipboards in their hands, not footballs."

Huarte was one of the greatest disappointments of the 1960s. As a senior in 1964, he won the Heisman Trophy, beating out Roger Staubach, Craig

Morton, Joe Namath, Jerry Rhome, Gale Sayers, and Dick Butkus.

"When I won the Heisman, I thought I had a bright future in pro football," Huarte said. "But I got drafted by the New York Jets, who never were interested in giving me a chance. The same year, they drafted Joe Namath and they just handed him the job. I disappeared between the cracks."

Huarte must have felt there were a lot of cracks, because in the next decade he spent time with Boston, Philadelphia, Kansas City, and Chicago, where he finished his NFL career in 1972. He never got a starting job, but he did spend time as a backup to some of pro football's best passers, including Babe Parilli, Norm Snead, and Len Dawson. In 1974, he signed with the World Football League.

"Huarte was just one of those guys whom fate didn't want to let make it in the NFL," said George

Phipps was runner-up in the 1969 Heisman balloting, but he never really got off the ground for the Browns or Bears.

Boone, the director of player personnel for the Phoenix Cardinals. "After the Namath thing, he kept going to clubs that had experienced starters, so he could never get a foothold. Under the right circumstances, Huarte could have been a star."

That frequently has been the case through the years. One of the most effective college quarterbacks of the 1950s, Lee Grosscup of Utah, also just missed on his timing. He backed up Charlie Conerly in New York as a rookie and figured to be his successor. Then the Giants traded for Y.A. Tittle, and Grosscup disappeared into obscurity. Similar stories happened with two great college passers in San Francisco. George Mira and Steve Spurrier both had all the tools to be great pros. But neither could beat out John Brodie.

As often as not, however, it is the player himself who just can't perform as well as had been expected. Sometimes it becomes obvious why. Sometimes it remains a mystery.

It is easily apparent when the players just don't have the talent to transfer their col-

A Funny Thing Happened on the Way to the Hall of Fame

lege greatness to the NFL. Gary Glick was the bonus choice of the Pittsburgh Steelers in 1956 after a sensational career at Colorado State. But he ended up being moved to defensive back.

"Glick was one of those guys who was so successful in college because he could do literally everything well," said Fido Murphy, one of the most successful early NFL scouts. "But he couldn't do any of it well enough to be a pro quarterback. His passing was good enough for college, his running was good enough for college, and his leadership was good enough for college. But he was out of his depth in the NFL. Although none of them were as versatile as Glick, the same generality can be made about a number of other All-America quarterbacks, including Richie Lucas, Gary Beban, Mike

Jack Thompson, Buccaneers

Phipps, David Jaynes, and Chuck Fusina."

But what about the others, those who seemed to have pro skills and just never made it?

"Scouting mistakes," said an NFC personnel director. "The guys who are obvious stars and then don't make it. . .well, when you break them down in retrospect, you can see all of the problems and shortcomings they had. Usually they are things scouts should have been able to find out about, but overlooked. It is quite easy to become enamored of a prospect's obvious talents and then miss the subtle weak points.

"For example, Eldridge Dickey, whom the Raiders chose prior to Kenny Stabler in 1968, had fabulous raw talent, but no experience against top competition. He found it extremely difficult to pick up the Raiders' complicated offense. Jerry Tagge,

DISAPPOINTING CAREERS

Paul McDonald, Browns

who led Nebraska to two national titles, didn't have the arm strength to throw the ball long all day like an NFL quarterback needs to do. John Reaves and Jack Thompson, two superb college passers, were just the opposite. They both had magnificent arms, but they had problems with reading complicated pro defenses and with other more intense facets of the pro game. Gary Huff, a brilliant passer at Florida State, was hampered by a series of Chicago coaches who didn't understand the passing game and couldn't take advantage of his talents. And California's Rich Campbell was a precision passer, but first he didn't have good mobility and then he com-

Wilson never really looked comfortable in the Raiders' pocket.

pounded that by not having a strong-enough arm or a quick-enough release to get the ball away under a typical NFL pass rush."

Some current quarterbacks also are disappointments.

"Marc Wilson has all the physical tools to be a great quarterback," says an AFC personnel director. "You couldn't design a better guy from the standpoint of passing form and knowledge of the pro offense. But he doesn't have the heart to be a pro quarterback. He can't just take a team and make them win, because he isn't a winner himself."

It's easy for NFL scouts to knock these quarterbacks, but it also is true that they also have

contributed to various players' lack of success.

"Todd Blackledge was overrated when he came out of college partly because he had played on a national championship team and partly because he had been surrounded with such superior talent," says one NFC scout. "Despite his flaws, which include an unwieldy, mechanical passing motion and a lack of mobility, he had the one great season when he was a fourth-year junior, and everyone jumped on his bandwagon. So he figured he could go right into

Todd Blackledge, Steelers

the NFL without any more seasoning.

"Well, it soon became apparent that he wasn't as good as he thought he was or as some scouts thought he was. But the coaches in Kansas City figured he was a number one, so he had to play. So he ends up starting, getting benched, starting again, then getting benched again, and finally getting traded to Pittsburgh. It was too bad, because without a lot of that pressure, Blackledge might have gotten the coaching he needed to overcome some of the defects in his game.

"It's the same with many quarterbacks who haven't made it through the years. Sure, they have some problems, but most of them aren't that bad, or even that much worse than they looked in college. It's just that somewhere down the line they have had bad timing, or gotten a bad break, or made a mistake and lost confidence, or have listened to bad coaching or advice. With a little bit of luck here and there, some of the greatest disappointments over the years could have been some of the greatest players."

SAY, DIDN'T YOU USED TO BE TERRY BAKER?

No man exemplifies the lack of success even the greatest collegians can have in the pros better than Terry Baker, the most honored college football player of the 1960s, and a man who now is a successful attorney in Lake Oswego, Oregon.

Baker virtually owned college athletics in his senior year at Oregon State. In the 1962 football season, he led the nation in total offense, passing yards, touchdown passes, and passer rating. He finished his career as the second-most productive player in NCAA history, won the Heisman and Maxwell Trophies, was named AP, UPI, and *Sporting News* player of the year, was a unanimous All-America and an Academic All-America. Baker also was an Academic All-America point guard in basketball, helping his team to the Final Four of the NCAA tournament, and was a successful right-handed baseball pitcher (although he was a left-handed quarterback). He earned one of eight National Football Foundation and Hall of Fame postgraduate scholarships, earned Phi Beta Kappa academic honors, and was named *Sports Illustrated* man of the year, the first college football player ever so honored.

Ultimately, Baker was drafted by teams in pro baseball and basketball as well as by the Los Angeles Rams, who made him the first pick of the entire NFL draft.

"A lot of people look back today and question the Rams' selection of Baker with the first pick," said Dick Steinberg, the director of player development for New England. "But every scouting department in the league had him rated as the top pick that year. He would have gone first no matter who had the first choice.

"The guy could do it all: He averaged five yards a carry ...he was a high-percentage passer when not many were ...he had quick feet, a fast release, and perhaps the best

Elroy Hirsch crowns the Rams' number-one draft pick in 1963.

mind in all of college football. And he was a hell of a leader. Any doubts anyone had about him were blown away on that one play in the bowl game."

The play came in Baker's last college game, when he set an unbreakable record by racing 99 yards for the longest touchdown run in bowl history.

"That run was one of those times when in the flash of an eye adversity turns to opportunity," Baker said. "It was a bitterly cold day in Philadelphia, and we were playing Villanova in the Liberty Bowl. Villanova punted and the ball went into the end zone. But the officials put it on the one-foot line.

"On first down we ran a play that we shouldn't have—a roll-out in which I had to lose about five yards before getting into the play. A couple of their guys grabbed me in the end zone, and I barely slipped away. When I got to the line of scrimmage no one was near me, and I ran ninety-nine yards alone. We won 6-0."

"Terry not only won the Liberty Bowl for us," said Tommy Prothro, the Oregon State coach when Baker was there and later head coach for UCLA, the Rams, and Chargers, "but he flew to Kentucky the next day for a basketball tournament and he was named most valuable player.

"Terry was as fine a person as he was an athlete. His father deserted the family when

Terry was only five, and his mother raised three boys by working at Sears & Roebuck. When Terry signed with the Rams, it was the first time in his life that he had any money. The first thing he did was take his mother to the circus, because she had never been able to go before."

That was one of the last good things that happened to Baker in the pros, however.

"Maybe I was at the wrong place at the wrong time," Baker said. "The Rams were so unorganized that the coaches didn't know what was going on. I started my first game, and I was no more prepared than the man in the moon. I threw three interceptions, and I think [Rams head coach] Harland Svare lost confidence in me right there.

"I didn't have a strong arm, and it soon got sore because the amount of passing one had to do in the pro game was more than I could take."

Svare was convinced that there was more to Baker's arm troubles than arm troubles. After practice one day, he had Baker consult a psychiatrist.

"The guy took me in a room, turned off the lights, and asked me about my arm," Baker said. "I told him it hurt. He told me to think of someone, then asked me who it was. It was right after practice, so I was thinking about Harland.

"The psychiatrist stood up, turned on the lights, and said, 'I've solved your problem. Your arm hates Harland.' I was moved to halfback shortly after that."

Nagging injuries and a lack of speed kept Baker from being a standout halfback, and he was cut after the preseason in his fourth year by Svare's successor, George Allen. Contacted later in the season by the New York Giants, Baker passed up the chance to join them in order to remain full time in USC law school.

"Terry could have been successful in the NFL," Prothro said. "He was a lot like Brian Sipe, who wasn't given a chance until there was no one else. Terry would have made it. He could have been a superstar, if he had been given a real opportunity."

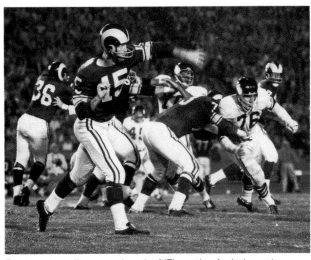

Baker eventually passed on the NFL, opting for jurisprudence.

DISAPPOINTING CAREERS

Quarterbacks as Coaches

A popular cliche about a successful quarterback is that he can be "a coach on the field." But for some reason, most successful NFL quarterbacks have made abominable head coaches. In fact, it is almost true that the more successful a man is as a quarterback, the less successful he is as a coach. After the 1920s, when coaches such as Jimmy Conzelman and John (Paddy) Driscoll also were players, six other Hall of Fame quarterbacks became head coaches. None achieved a winning record.

One of the first quarterbacks to become a head coach after his playing career was Earl (Dutch) Clark. Clark actually got a head start on the game by being the player-coach of Detroit his last two years, leading the Lions to successive 7-4 marks. However, as coach of the Cleveland Rams, he was much less successful. Clark never had a winning season, finishing with a 16-26-2 mark for four years.

"It is hard to figure why so frequently really good quarterbacks haven't made really good head coaches," said Chicago Bears head coach Mike Ditka, himself a Hall of Fame tight end. "They have all the leadership qualities it takes to be a coach, they certainly should have at least as good an understanding of the game as a player from any other position, and they make outstanding offensive assistants. So I don't know if there is anything you can lay your finger on to explain why they have had such difficulties as head coaches."

One quarterback who didn't have such difficulties was Tom Flores, who coached the Oakland and Los Angeles Raiders for nine years, during which time his team won Super Bowls XV and XVIII. Flores posted an impressive 91-56 record.

Only two other modern pro quarterbacks have served as

NFL head coaches as long as Flores. Bart Starr spent nine years with Green Bay, finishing with a 53-77-3 mark. The dean of all former quarterbacks in length of coaching service was Norm Van Brocklin, who had stints with two young teams—the expansion Minnesota Vikings from 1961-66 and as the second head coach of the Atlanta Falcons, from 1968-1974. Van Brocklin's record was 66-100-7.

One former NFL quarterback

currently in the league's head-coaching ranks has had some impressive accomplishments. Sam Wyche guided the Cincinnati Bengals all the way to Super Bowl XXIII, where they lost to San Francisco on a touchdown with 34 seconds remaining in the game.

The list on page 185 is of former NFL quarterbacks who have gone on to become NFL head coaches, including their NFL records when not serving as player-coaches.

Starr never fully escaped Vince Lombardi's shadow in Green Bay. He compiled two winning seasons in nine years before he was replaced by Forrest Gregg, another player from the Packers' glory days.

Though Bob Waterfield (with Bill Wade, above) was a brilliant, well-liked player, his 9-24-1 record as a Rams coach was one of the poorest in team history. He ultimately resigned under pressure eight games into the 1962 season.

Born to Lead—Until They Took Off Their Helmets and Shoulder Pads

Quarterbacks-Turned-Coaches

Frankie Albert	San Francisco 1956-58: 19-17-1
Sammy Baugh	N.Y. Titans 1960-61; Houston 1964: 18-24-0
Earl (Dutch) Clark	Detroit 1937-38; Cleveland 1939-42: 16-26-2
Jimmy Conzelman	Providence 1930; Chicago Cardinals 1940-42, 1946-48: 41-36-4
John (Paddy) Driscoll	Chicago Bears 1956-57: 14-10-1
Frankie Filchock	Denver 1960-61: 7-20-1
Tom Flores	Oakland 1979-81; L.A. Raiders 1982-87: 91-56-0
Harry Gilmer	Detroit 1965-66: 10-16-2
Otto Graham	Washington 1966-68: 17-22-3
Dan Henning	Atlanta 1983-86: 22-44-0
Cecil Isbell	Chicago Cardinals 1951: 1-1-0
Harvey Johnson	Buffalo 1968, 1971: 2-23-1
Ted Marchibroda	Baltimore 1975-79: 41-36-0
Alvin (Bo) McMillin	Detroit 1948-50; Philadelphia 1951: 14-24-0
Keith Molesworth	Baltimore 1953: 3-9-0
John Rauch	Oakland 1966-68; Buffalo 1969-70: 42-30-2
Gene Ronzani	Green Bay 1950-53: 14-31-1
Allie Sherman	N.Y. Giants 1961-68: 57-54-4
Bob Snyder	L.A. Rams 1947: 6-6-0
Bart Starr	Green Bay 1975-83: 53-77-3
Kay Stephenson	Buffalo 1983-85: 10-26-0
Norman (Red) Strader	N.Y. Yanks 1950-51; San Francisco 1955: 12-22-5
Norm Van Brocklin	Minnesota 1961-66; Atlanta 1968-74: 66-100-7
Bob Waterfield	L.A. Rams 1960-62: 9-24-1
Sam Wyche	Cincinnati 1984-88: 43-39-0

Sammy Baugh feuded with owner Harry Wismer for much of the New York Titans' first two AFL seasons. He then spent one 4-10 season in Houston, where he tutored George Blanda (above).

Otto Graham opened up the Washington offense, allowing Sonny Jurgensen (left) to set several league records, but his teams were one-dimensional, and their records showed it.

Norm Van Brocklin (seated next to Fran Tarkenton) became head coach of the newly formed Vikings just one year after quarterbacking Philadelphia to the NFL title.

Record Holders

Their names aren't exactly a who's who of pro football quarterbacks—Milt Plum, Richard Todd, Tommy O'Connell, and Jim Zorn. But when you look through the *NFL Record & Fact Book*, those are the names that stand out in the records section, rather than the marquee names the average football fan might expect to find. You won't find Terry Bradshaw, John Elway, Roger Staubach, or Jim Hart in the regular-season records section.

Plum might be the most surprising of all of the record holders. Generally thought of as a journeyman quarterback, he spent five years with Cleveland, six with Detroit, one with the Los Angeles Rams, and one with the New York Giants. But Plum not only led the NFL in passing in consecutive seasons (1960-61), he had the most efficient single-season passing performance in NFL history in 1960. Then a member of the Browns, he completed 151 of 250 passes for 2,297 yards and 21 touchdowns, while throwing only five interceptions. It all added up to a record 110.4 passer rating.

Many people have dismissed Plum's performance by saying that he had an easy time passing because Jim Brown and Bobby Mitchell were the Browns' running backs. But neither Plum's predecessor, Tommy O'Connell, nor his successor, Frank Ryan, nor any of the quarterbacks who played with Eric Dickerson or Walter Payton or Earl Campbell ever led the NFL in passing, much less established efficiency records.

Plum's success—and maybe even the fact that he got a chance—is somewhat surprising because his first year as a regular (1958, when he finished second in the league in passing) came one year after O'Connell set the NFL season record for the highest average gain per passing attempt

Cleveland's quarterback was Milt Plum in 1960, and no NFL passer ever has been more efficient.

(11.17). O'Connell, who obviously also was helped by the presence of Brown (then a rookie, like Plum), threw for 1,229 yards on only 110 attempts, after averaging only 5.7 yards per attempt in 1956.

Another player who was a sensation his first year as a starter was Jim Zorn, the initial quarterback for the Seattle Seahawks in 1976. Zorn set NFL rookie records for attempts (439), completions (208), and passing yards (2,571), marks that haven't been broken despite the increase to a 16-game season two years later.

But *The NFL Record & Fact Book* isn't a haven only for quarterbacks who probably *won't* make the Pro Football Hall of Fame. It also includes many of the biggest name quarterbacks in the history of the game.

Few men are mentioned more than Dan Marino of Miami. Marino, who has been selected to the Pro Bowl every year of his career except one (1988), holds season records for attempts

(623, set in 1986), completions (378, also in 1986), passing yards (5,084 in 1984), and touchdown passes (48, also in 1984). And if Marino continues to throw the ball as he has, he'll one day pass Fran Tarkenton, who holds the most NFL career marks.

Tarkenton, who played two stints for the Vikings, with five years with the Giants sandwiched in between, holds four major NFL career marks: attempts (6,467), completions (3,686), yards (47,003), and touchdown passes (342). Amazingly, if a quarterback could throw 20 touchdown passes a year for 17 seasons, he still wouldn't equal Tarkenton's record. But when a player can throw 48, 30, and 44 touchdown passes in consecutive years, as Marino did, he quickly can close in.

Tarkenton holds many of the basic career marks and Marino most season records, but the game records are spread across the board.

No one has thrown more passes in a game than George Blanda, who put the ball in the air 68 times against the Buffalo Bills in 1964. Blanda, then the quarterback for the Houston Oilers, also threw seven touchdown passes in a game against the New York Titans in 1961, tying a mark now shared by five players. In 1962, he set a record of more dubious distinction, throwing 42 interceptions in a 14-game season.

The record for most completions in one game is held by the New York Jets' Richard Todd, who completed 42 passes against the San Francisco 49ers in 1980.

The record for most yards in a game was set by Norm Van Brocklin of the Los Angeles Rams in 1951—554 yards against the New York Yanks.

"One of their defensive backs—a cocky little rookie—batted away one of the first passes I threw that day," Van Brocklin recalled later. "After the play, he said, 'That's the way it's going to be, Van Brocklin. Don't even try to throw in this area again.' So I passed at him all day long. Finally, after I had thrown for more than three hundred yards against just him, their coaches took him out. I asked him after the game if he felt he could stop every quarterback with just three hundred yards."

When it came to 300-yard games, no one was more consistent than Dan Fouts, who held many of the season passing marks before Marino's first great year in 1984. Fouts still holds NFL records for 300-yard games (51) and 3,000-yard seasons (6).

But even more consistent than Fouts, and the holder of a mark probably safer than Van Brocklin's yardage record, was Johnny Unitas, who passed for a touchdown in a staggering 47 consecutive games from 1956 through 1960. Despite all his touchdown passes, Marino reached only 30 games in a row, the second most ever, but still a long way behind Unitas.

If You're Looking for Burk, Kapp, or Zorn— Consult the Records

When O'Connell wasn't pitching out to Jim Brown in 1957, he was throwing for 11 yards a pop.

Major NFL Passing Records

Most Seasons Leading League:
6 Sammy Baugh, Washington, 1937, 1940, 1943, 1945, 1947, 1949

Most Consecutive Seasons Leading League:
2 Cecil Isbell, Green Bay, 1941-42
Milt Plum, Cleveland, 1960-61
Ken Anderson, Cincinnati, 1974-75, 1981-82
Roger Staubach, Dallas, 1978-79

Highest Pass Rating, Career:
92.0 Joe Montana, San Francisco, 1979-1988

Highest Pass Rating, Season:
110.4 Milt Plum, Cleveland, 1960

Highest Pass Rating, Rookie Season:
96.0 Dan Marino, Miami, 1983

Most Passes Attempted, Career:
6,467 Fran Tarkenton, Minnesota, 1961-66, 1972-78; N.Y. Giants 1967-1971

Most Passes Attempted, Season:
623 Dan Marino, Miami, 1986

Most Passes Attempted, Rookie Season:
439 Jim Zorn, Seattle, 1976

Most Passes Attempted, Game:
68 George Blanda, Houston vs. Buffalo, November 1, 1964

Most Passes Completed, Career:
3,686 Fran Tarkenton, Minnesota, 1961-66, 1972-78; N.Y. Giants 1967-1971

Most Passes Completed, Season:
378 Dan Marino, Miami, 1986

Most Passes Completed, Rookie Season:
208 Jim Zorn, Seattle, 1976

Most Passes Completed, Game:
42 Richard Todd, N.Y. Jets vs. San Francisco, September 21, 1980

Most Consecutive Passes Completed:
22 Joe Montana, San Francisco vs. Cleveland (5), November 29, 1987; vs. Green Bay (17), December 6, 1987

Highest Completion Percentage, Career:
63.22 Joe Montana, San Francisco, 1979-1988 (3,673-2,322)

Highest Completion Percentage, Season:
70.55 Ken Anderson, Cincinnati, 1982 (309-218)

Highest Completion Percentage, Rookie Season:
58.45 Dan Marino, Miami, 1983 (296-173)

Highest Completion Percentage, Game:
90.91 Ken Anderson, Cincinnati vs. Pittsburgh, November 10, 1974 (22-20)

Most Yards Gained, Career:
47,003 Fran Tarkenton, Minnesota, 1961-66, 1972-78; N.Y. Giants 1967-1971

Most Yards Gained, Season:
5,084 Dan Marino, Miami, 1984

Most Yards Gained, Rookie Season:
2,571 Jim Zorn, Seattle, 1976

Most Seasons 3,000 or More Yards Passing:
6 Dan Fouts, San Diego, 1979-1981, 1984-86

Most Yards Gained, Game:
554 Norm Van Brocklin, L.A. Rams vs. N.Y. Yanks, September 28, 1951

Most Games 300 or More Yards Passing, Career:
51 Dan Fouts, San Diego, 1973-1987

Most Games 300 or More Yards Passing, Season:
9 Dan Marino, Miami, 1984

Longest Pass Completion:
99 Frank Filchock (to Andy Farkas), Washington vs. Pittsburgh, October 15, 1939
George Izo (to Bobby Mitchell), Washington vs. Cleveland, September 15, 1963
Karl Sweetan (to Pat Studstill), Detroit vs. Baltimore, October 16, 1966
Sonny Jurgensen (to Gerry Allen), Washington vs. Chicago, September 15, 1968
Jim Plunkett (to Cliff Branch), L.A. Raiders vs. Washington, October 2, 1983
Ron Jaworski (to Mike Quick), Philadelphia vs. Atlanta, November 10, 1985

Highest Average Gain, Career:
8.63 Otto Graham, Cleveland, 1950-55 (1,565-13,499)

Highest Average Gain, Season:
11.17 Tommy O'Connell, Cleveland, 1957 (110-1,229)

Highest Average Gain, Rookie Season:
9.41 Greg Cook, Cincinnati, 1969 (197-1,854)

Highest Average Gain, Game:
18.58 Sammy Baugh, Washington vs. Boston, October 31, 1948 (24-446)

Most Touchdown Passes, Career:
342 Fran Tarkenton, Minnesota, 1961-66, 1972-78; N.Y. Giants 1967-1971

Most Touchdown Passes, Season:
48 Dan Marino, Miami, 1984

Most Touchdown Passes, Rookie Season:
22 Charlie Conerly, N.Y. Giants, 1948

Most Touchdown Passes, Game:
7 Sid Luckman, Chicago Bears vs. N.Y. Giants, November 14, 1943
Adrian Burk, Philadelphia vs. Washington, October 17, 1954
George Blanda, Houston vs. N.Y. Titans, November 19, 1961
Y.A. Tittle, N.Y. Giants vs. Washington, October 28, 1962
Joe Kapp, Minnesota vs. Baltimore, September 28, 1969

Most Consecutive Games, Touchdown Passes:
47 Johnny Unitas, Baltimore, 1956-1960

Most Consecutive Passes, None Intercepted:
294 Bart Starr, Green Bay, 1964-65

Most Attempts, No Interceptions, Game:
57 Joe Montana, San Francisco vs. Atlanta, October 6, 1985

Lowest Percentage Interceptions, Career:
2.70 Joe Montana, San Francisco, 1979-1988 (3,673-99)

Lowest Percentage Interceptions, Season:
0.66 Joe Ferguson, Buffalo, 1976 (151-1)

Lowest Percentage Interceptions, Rookie Season:
2.03 Dan Marino, Miami, 1983 (296-6)

The Best of the Best

Paddy Driscoll did well with the oversized balls of the 1920s.

Arnie Herber helped make the forward pass commonplace.

Ace Parker was a triple-threat, two-way back.

Player-coach Jimmy Conzelman led Providence to the 1928 title.

Versatile Dutch Clark was a three-time NFL scoring leader.

It's a Long Way to Canton, Ohio, Even If You're in the Passing Lane

Quarterbacks in the Pro Football Hall of Fame

Player	Ht., Wt.	College	Team
Sammy Baugh	6-2, 180	Texas Christian	Washington 1937-1952
George Blanda	6-2, 215	Kentucky	Chicago Bears 1949-1958, Baltimore 1950, Houston 1960-66, Oakland 1967-1975
Terry Bradshaw	6-3, 215	Louisiana Tech	Pittsburgh 1970-1983
Earl (Dutch) Clark	6-0, 185	Colorado College	Portsmouth 1931-32, Detroit 1934-38
Jimmy Conzelman	6-0, 180	Washington (St. Louis)	Decatur 1920, Rock Island 1921-22, Milwaukee 1923-24, Detroit 1925-26, Providence 1927-29
Len Dawson	6-0, 190	Purdue	Pittsburgh 1957-59, Cleveland 1960-61, Dallas Texans 1962, Kansas City 1963-1975
John (Paddy) Driscoll	5-11, 160	Northwestern	Chicago Cardinals 1920-25, Decatur 1920, Chicago Bears 1926-29
Otto Graham	6-1, 195	Northwestern	Cleveland (AAFC) 1946-49, Cleveland 1950-55
Arnie Herber	6-1, 200	Regis	Green Bay 1930-1940, N.Y. Giants 1944-45
Sonny Jurgensen	6-0, 203	Duke	Philadelphia 1957-1963, Washington 1964-1974
Bobby Layne	6-2, 190	Texas	Chicago Bears 1948, N.Y. Bulldogs 1949, Detroit 1950-58, Pittsburgh 1958-1962
Sid Luckman	6-0, 195	Columbia	Chicago Bears 1939-1950
Joe Namath	6-2, 200	Alabama	N.Y. Jets 1965-1976, L.A. Rams 1977
Clarence (Ace) Parker	5-11, 168	Duke	Brooklyn 1937-1941, Boston 1945, N.Y. Yankees (AAFC) 1946
Bart Starr	6-1, 200	Alabama	Green Bay 1956-1971
Roger Staubach	6-3, 202	Navy	Dallas 1969-1979
Fran Tarkenton	6-0, 185	Georgia	Minnesota 1961-66, 1972-78, N.Y. Giants 1967-1971
Y.A. Tittle	6-0, 200	LSU	Baltimore (AAFC) 1948-49, Baltimore 1950, San Francisco 1951-1960, N.Y. Giants 1961-64
Johnny Unitas	6-1, 195	Louisville	Baltimore 1956-1972, San Diego 1973
Norm Van Brocklin	6-1, 190	Oregon	L.A. Rams 1949-1957, Philadelphia 1958-1960
Bob Waterfield	6-2, 200	UCLA	Cleveland 1945, L.A. Rams 1946-1952

Records and Statistics

*Still active entering the 1989 season.

Top 20 Passers—Yards

Name	Years	Att.	Comp.	Pct.	Yards	TD	Int.
Fran Tarkenton	1961-78	6,467	3,686	57.0	47,003	342	266
Dan Fouts	1973-87	5,604	3,297	58.8	43,040	254	242
Johnny Unitas	1955-73	5,186	2,830	54.6	40,239	290	253
Jim Hart	1966-84	5,076	2,593	51.1	34,665	209	247
John Hadl	1962-77	4,637	2,363	50.4	33,503	244	268
Y.A. Tittle	1948-64	4,395	2,427	55.2	33,070	242	248
Ken Anderson	1971-86	4,475	2,654	59.3	32,838	197	160
Sonny Jurgensen	1957-74	4,262	2,433	57.1	32,224	255	189
John Brodie	1957-73	4,491	2,469	55.0	31,548	214	224
Norm Snead	1961-76	4,353	2,276	52.2	30,797	196	257
Roman Gabriel	1962-77	4,498	2,366	52.6	29,444	201	149
Joe Ferguson	1973-88*	4,421	2,323	52.5	29,263	193	201
Len Dawson	1957-75	3,741	2,136	57.1	28,711	239	183
Terry Bradshaw	1970-83	3,901	2,105	54.0	27,989	212	210
Kenny Stabler	1970-84	3,793	2,270	59.8	27,938	194	222
Craig Morton	1965-82	3,786	2,053	54.2	27,908	183	187
Ron Jaworski	1974-88*	4,056	2,151	53.0	27,805	177	159
Joe Namath	1965-77	3,762	1,886	50.1	27,663	173	220
Joe Montana	1979-88*	3,673	2,322	63.2	27,533	190	99
George Blanda	1949-58 1960-75	4,007	1,911	47.7	26,920	236	277

Watching Their Figures: Behind Every Great Passer Lies a Great Statistic

Fran Tarkenton

Dan Fouts

Team Career Passing Leaders

Name	Years	Att.	Comp.	Pct.	Yards	TD	Int.
Atlanta							
Steve Bartkowski	1975-85	3,329	1,870	56.2	23,468	154	141
Bob Berry	1968-72	1,049	598	57.0	8,489	57	56
Randy Johnson	1966-70	904	435	48.1	5,538	34	65
Dave Archer	1984-87	647	331	51.2	4,275	18	29
Buffalo							
Joe Ferguson	1973-84	4,166	2,188	52.5	27,590	181	190
Jack Kemp	1962-69	2,235	1,040	46.5	15,128	77	132
Jim Kelly	1986-88*	1,353	804	59.5	9,771	56	45
Dennis Shaw	1970-73	916	485	52.9	6,286	35	67
Chicago							
Sid Luckman	1939-50	1,744	904	51.8	14,686	137	132
Jim McMahon	1982-88*	1,513	874	57.8	11,203	67	55
Billy Wade	1961-66	1,407	767	54.5	9,958	68	66
Ed Brown	1954-61	1,246	607	48.7	9,698	63	88
Cincinnati							
Ken Anderson	1971-86	4,475	2,654	59.3	32,838	197	160
Boomer Esiason	1984-88*	1,830	1,038	56.7	14,825	99	65
Virgil Carter	1970-73	582	328	56.4	3,850	22	20
Turk Schonert	1981-85 1988*	348	216	62.1	2,756	7	12
Cleveland							
Brian Sipe	1974-83	3,439	1,944	56.5	23,713	154	149
Otto Graham	1946-55	2,626	1,464	55.8	23,584	174	135
Frank Ryan	1962-68	1,755	907	51.7	13,361	134	88
Bernie Kosar	1984-88*	1,427	831	58.2	10,355	57	33

Mike Livingston

Name	Years	Att.	Comp.	Pct.	Yards	TD	Int.
Dallas							
Roger Staubach	1969-79	2,958	1,685	57.0	22,700	153	109
Danny White	1976-88*	2,950	1,761	59.7	21,959	155	132
Don Meredith	1960-68	2,308	1,170	50.7	17,199	135	111
Craig Morton	1965-74	1,308	683	52.2	10,279	80	73
Denver							
John Elway	1983-88*	2,654	1,442	54.3	18,144	102	96
Craig Morton	1977-82	1,594	907	56.9	11,895	74	62
Frank Tripucka	1960-63	1,277	662	51.8	7,676	51	85
Charley Johnson	1972-75	970	517	53.3	7,238	52	52
Detroit							
Bobby Layne	1950-58	2,193	1,074	49.0	15,710	118	142
Greg Landry	1968-78	1,747	957	54.8	12,457	80	81
Gary Danielson	1976-84	1,684	952	56.5	11,885	69	71
Eric Hipple	1980-88*	1,528	823	53.9	8,697	55	67
Green Bay							
Bart Starr	1956-71	3,149	1,808	57.4	24,718	152	138
Lynn Dickey	1976-77 1979-85	2,831	1,592	56.2	21,369	133	151
Tobin Rote	1950-56	1,854	826	44.6	11,535	89	119
Randy Wright	1984-88*	1,119	602	53.8	7,106	31	57

Gary Danielson

Randy Wright

Houston							
George Blanda	1960-66	2,784	1,347	48.4	19,149	165	189
Dan Pastorini	1971-79	2,767	1,426	51.5	16,846	96	139
Warren Moon	1984-88*	1,977	1,059	53.6	14,669	78	85
Ken Stabler	1980-81	739	458	62.0	5,190	27	46
Indianapolis							
Johnny Unitas	1956-72	5,110	2,796	54.7	39,768	287	246
Bert Jones	1973-81	2,464	1,382	56.1	17,663	122	97
Mike Pagel	1982-85	1,155	587	50.8	7,474	39	47
Earl Morrall	1968-71	676	363	53.7	5,666	47	40
Kansas City							
Len Dawson	1962-75	3,696	2,115	57.2	28,507	237	178
Bill Kenney	1979-88*	2,430	1,330	54.7	17,277	105	86
Mike Livingston	1968-79	1,751	912	52.1	11,295	56	83
Steve Fuller	1979-82	817	465	56.9	5,333	22	32
Los Angeles Raiders							
Ken Stabler	1970-79	2,481	1,486	59.9	19,078	150	143
Daryle Lamonica	1967-74	2,248	1,138	50.6	16,655	148	115
Jim Plunkett	1978-86	1,697	960	56.6	12,665	80	81
Marc Wilson	1980-87	1,666	871	52.3	11,760	77	86
Los Angeles Rams							
Roman Gabriel	1962-72	3,313	1,705	51.5	22,223	154	112
Norm Van Brocklin	1949-57	1,897	1,011	53.3	16,114	118	127
Bob Waterfield	1945-52	1,618	814	50.3	11,893	99	128
Vince Ferragamo	1977-80 1982-84	1,288	730	56.7	9,376	70	71

Wade Wilson

Miami							
Bob Griese	1967-80	3,429	1,926	56.2	25,092	192	172
Dan Marino	1983-88*	3,100	1,866	60.2	23,856	196	103
David Woodley	1980-83	961	508	52.9	5,928	34	42
Don Strock	1974-87	688	388	56.4	4,613	39	37
Minnesota							
Fran Tarkenton	1961-66 1972-78	4,569	2,635	57.6	33,098	239	194
Tommy Kramer	1977-88*	3,512	1,934	55.1	23,869	152	150
Wade Wilson	1981-88*	1,035	581	56.1	7,612	45	45
Joe Kapp	1967-69	689	351	50.9	4,811	37	47
New England							
Steve Grogan	1975-88*	3,240	1,696	52.3	24,574	169	191
Babe Parilli	1961-67	2,413	1,140	47.2	16,747	132	138
Tony Eason	1983-88*	1,395	819	58.7	9,971	57	44
Jim Plunkett	1971-75	1,503	729	48.5	9,932	62	87

Tommy Thompson

Jim Zorn

New Orleans

Archie Manning	1971-82	3,335	1,849	55.4	21,734	115	156
Billy Kilmer	1967-70	1,116	592	53.0	7,490	47	62
Dave Wilson	1981 1983-88*	1,038	561	54.9	6,987	36	55
Bobby Hebert	1985-88*	1,032	588	57.0	6,981	42	36

New York Giants

Phil Simms	1979-81 1983-88*	3,253	1,752	53.9	23,174	142	123
Charlie Conerly	1948-61	2,833	1,418	50.1	19,488	173	167
Fran Tarkenton	1967-71	1,898	1,051	55.4	13,905	103	72
Y.A. Tittle	1961-64	1,308	731	55.9	10,439	96	68

New York Jets

Joe Namath	1965-76	3,655	1,836	50.2	27,057	170	215
Richard Todd	1976-83	2,623	1,433	54.6	18,241	110	138
Ken O'Brien	1983-88*	1,990	1,183	59.4	14,243	84	50
Al Dorow	1960-61	834	398	47.7	5,399	45	56

Philadelphia

Ron Jaworski	1977-86	3,918	2,088	53.3	26,963	175	151
Norm Snead	1964-70	2,236	1,154	51.6	15,672	111	124
Tommy Thompson	1941-42 1945-50	1,396	723	51.8	10,255	90	100
Sonny Jurgensen	1957-63	1,107	602	54.4	9,639	76	73

Vinny Testaverde

Dave Wilson

Phoenix

Jim Hart	1966-83	5,096	2,590	50.8	34,639	209	247
Neil Lomax	1981-88*	3,153	1,818	57.7	22,771	136	90
Charley Johnson	1961-69	2,047	1,030	50.3	12,928	108	110
Paul Christman	1945-49	1,014	453	44.7	6,751	51	69

Pittsburgh

Terry Bradshaw	1970-83	3,901	2,105	54.0	27,989	212	210
Bobby Layne	1958-62	1,156	569	49.2	8,983	67	81
Jim Finks	1949-55	1,382	661	47.8	8,854	55	88
Mark Malone	1980-87	1,374	690	50.2	8,582	54	68

San Diego

Dan Fouts	1973-87	5,604	3,297	59.0	43,040	254	242
John Hadl	1962-72	3,640	1,824	50.1	26,938	201	211
Jack Kemp	1960-62	815	389	47.7	5,996	49	37
Tobin Rote	1963-64	449	245	54.6	3,648	29	32

San Francisco

John Brodie	1957-73	4,491	2,469	55.0	31,548	214	224
Joe Montana	1979-88*	3,673	2,322	63.2	27,533	190	99
Y.A. Tittle	1951-60	2,194	1,226	55.9	16,016	108	134
Steve DeBerg	1977-80	1,201	670	55.8	7,220	37	60

Seattle

Jim Zorn	1976-84	2,992	1,593	53.2	20,122	107	133
Dave Krieg	1980-88*	2,344	1,358	57.9	17,549	148	96
Kelly Stouffer	1988*	173	98	56.6	1,106	4	6
Steve Myer	1976-79	160	83	51.9	851	6	14

Tampa Bay

Doug Williams	1978-82	1,890	895	47.4	12,648	73	73
Steve DeBerg	1984-87	1,250	714	57.1	8,543	57	55
Vinny Testaverde	1987-88*	631	293	46.4	4,321	18	41
Jack Thompson	1983-84	475	274	57.5	3,243	20	26

Washington

Joe Theismann	1974-85	3,602	2,044	56.7	25,206	160	138
Sonny Jurgensen	1964-74	3,155	1,831	58.0	22,585	179	116
Sammy Baugh	1937-52	3,016	1,709	56.5	22,085	187	203
Billy Kilmer	1971-78	1,791	953	53.2	12,352	103	75

Acknowledgments and Credits

No book ever is the work of only one or two individuals, regardless of what the front cover says. *Great Ones* is no exception.

Thanks are due to the entire staff at NFL Properties, Creative Services, but especially to John Wiebusch, Chuck Garrity, Sr., Bill Barron, Jere Wright, Dick Falk, Tina Dahl, Phil Barber, Jim Perry, Brian Davids, Paul Spinelli, Sharon Kuthe, Mark Sherengo, Rick Wadholm, Marilyn Cauley, and Jane Alexander.

Four members of the NFL family also deserve special mention—Dan Edwards of the Pittsburgh Steelers, Jim Gallagher of the Philadelphia Eagles, Joe Horrigan of the Pro Football Hall of Fame, and Dave Port of the NFL office.

Finally, I want to thank Dr. Elizabeth Cruwys for considerable assistance while I was working on *Great Ones*. Without her help, this book might not have reached fruition.

Beau Riffenburgh
Cambridge, England

Photography, Illustration, and Memorabilia Credits

Multiple images on a page are identified counter-clockwise from top right.

ABC-TV 78c
Tim Alexander 182b
Bob & Sylvia Allen 189c
Bill Amatucci 1, 8, 178b, 182d
Fred Anderson, 146b
Charles Aqua Viva 24, 139d, 139f, 146d
George Bartell 118a
Morris Berman 56c
John Biever 67b, 98, 106a, 168a, 169c, 176c
Vernon Biever 91a, 122c, 129a, 129e, 147k, 178a
David Boss 16b, 16d, 17a, 40-41, 42b, 72a, 75b, 78b, 84d, 87a, 87b, 90c, 105b, 114d, 121c, 123a, 124e, 128a, 137d, 145e, 145g, 146c, 147f, 147g, 147h, 147l, 173b, 174c, 182c, 183b, 185b, 185c, 189a, 190c
Clifton Boutelle 25, 130d, 181
Chance Brockway 124c
Peter Brouillet 114b, 127c, 131e, 190d
Rob Brown 51, 53, 100a
Jack Cakebread 83a
Larry Carroll 102
Jim Chaffin 134c, 191d
Merv Corning 3, 18, 33, 43, 48-49, 56a, 79, 118b, 165a
Scott Cunningham 17d, 97b, 120c, 114a, 128d, 169b
Jonathan Daniel 130b
F. Bruce Dean 93a
Dennis Desprois 141c
Brian Drake 105c, 112c, 113a
Edmonton Eskimoes 135b
Miguel Elliot 130a, 155a
Malcolm Emmons 46, 47b, 68, 80b, 84c, 85c, 89a, 92, 128e, 128f, 131a, 142c, 167b, 172a, 180d
Stan Evenson 89c
Nate Fine 60a, 63a, 124b, 173a, 144c
Paul Fine 185d
James F. Flores 83b, 83d, 85d, 86, 87b
Bart Forbes 9, 114c, 117a, 163d
George Gellatly 119b
Richard Gentile 91b
Michael Gershman Collection 119a, 145c
George Gojkovich 101c, 103b, 121b, 131d, 142d
Ignacio Gomez 120a
Green Bay Packers 122b
Pete J. Groh 5, 43c, 107b, 131b, 146e
David Grove 184
John Hamagami 122a
Rod Hanna 7, 139c, 179a
H. Lee Hansen 133b
Ken Hardin 60-61
Jon Hayt 66-67
Chris Hopkins 147i
Houston Oilers 139a, 147j
Walter Iooss, Jr. 80-81, 84a
Paul Jasienski 103a, 182a
Dave Jennings 134a

Allan Kaye 113b
Lon Keller 34
Jack Kirby 63b
Al Kooistra 106b
Ross Lewis 90d
Los Angeles Rams 147a, 183a
Louisiana Tech 141b
Amos Love 109a, 191b
Richard Mackson 104-105
Ed Mahan 147b, 164a
Tak Makita 129c, 163c
Fred Matthes 127b
John McDonough 2, 52, 116a, 189b
Al Messerschmidt 4, 176, 69a, 99a, 100b, 105a, 107a, 108, 109c, 109d, 112d, 123d, 125a, 128b, 142b, 142c, 161, 174d, 176a
Michigan State University 162a
Peter Read Miller 50, 55, 71, 89e, 95c, 101a, 112b, 134b, 147e, 168b, 175
Vic Milton 190b
Minnesota Vikings 180c
Bill Mount 85a, 109b
New England Patriots 180a
NFL Photos 49a, 49b, 49c, 49d, 58d, 69b, 77b, 83c, 95d, 105b, 132b, 133d, 137f, 147c, 178c, 178d
New York Jets 139b
Darryl Norenberg 72b, 90a, 93b, 145h, 163b
Philadelphia Eagles 124d, 144a, 145d, 167c, 191a
Photo Canada-Wide 135a
Pittsburgh Steelers 39b, 74, 137e
Pro Football Hall of Fame 13, 19a, 19b, 20a, 20b, 21, 30a, 30b, 31, 58c, 133a, 133b, 145b, 160, 162b, 170, 177a, 188all
Dick Raphael 38, 47a, 84b, 120b, 143a, 143b
Kevin W. Reece 70
Russ Reed 37, 58b, 127d, 128d, 128g, 136a, 138c, 147d
Chuck Ren 64, 88, 94a, 101b, 116c
Robert Riger 39a, 76
Frank Rippon 56b, 75a, 90b, 123b, 127e, 129b, 131c, 132a, 137c, 141a, 187
Fred Roe 10, 58a, 78a, 117b
Art Rogers 22
Bob Rosato 111, 164c
George Rose 110, 123c, 125b
Ron Ross 146a
Dan Rubin 36, 77a, 137a, 177b, 180b, 186
Manny Rubio 6, 116b, 122d, 164b, 169a, 172b
San Francisco 49ers 84e, 145a
Alan Schwartz 112a
Carl Skalak, Jr. 62, 173c
Bill Smith 65, 165b
Robert L. Smith 145i
Herb Snitzer 124a
Chuck Solomon 104a, 129f
Jay Spencer 174b
Paul Spinelli 143d
Sports Illustrated 32, 35, 137b
R.H. Stagg 59, 82, 99c, 168c
Stanford University 127a, 142a
Vic Stein 145f, 166
Dave Stock 97a
Street and Smith Books 126
Damian Strohmeyer 125c
Texas Christian University 140a
Tony Tomsic 16c, 23, 40a, 80a, 85b, 87c, 89d, 95a, 95b, 121a, 156b, 163a, 167a, 171, 176b

Corky Trewin 17c, 127f, 150b
Greg Trott 130c, 151, 154a, 158
Jim Turner 96a, 128c
University of California-Davis 143c
United States Naval Academy 140b
Ron Vesely 174a, 176d
Washington Redskins 16a, 144b
Herb Weitman 26, 44a, 57, 73a, 89b, 128g, 135c, 148, 157a, 159a, 180b
Lou Witt 42q, 99b, 130e, 136b, 138a, 138b, 139e, 185a
Hank Young 73b, 179b, 179c, 190a
Michael Zagaris 27, 94b, 149a, 149b, 150a, 152, 153, 154b, 155b, 157b, 159b, 176e
John G. Zimmerman 44-45